AN OUTLINE OF A
BIBLE-SCHOOL CURRICULUM

An Outline
of a
Bible-School Curriculum

By

George William Pease

Professor of Pedagogy in the
HARTFORD SCHOOL OF RELIGIOUS PEDAGOGY

WILDSIDE PRESS

WILDSIDE PRESS

Composed and Printed By
The University of Chicago Press
Chicago, Illinois, U. S. A.

PREFACE

THAT the Bible school has been an important factor in the moral and religious training of our children and young people is a fact freely admitted by the more discerning students of our national life. In spite of its neglect by professional educators, a neglect which is not easily accounted for, and the peculiarly difficult conditions under which it has had to do its work, much has been done for the formation of Christian character in the thousands who have come under its influence. That the work of the Bible school, judged from a teaching standpoint, has not been of a high character must be admitted even by its most ardent supporters; but that it has been one of the great moral influences in our land all must concede.

Within the last few years there has been a deepening interest in the Bible school, and in other institutions and agencies for moral and religious training, which has finally resulted in the formation of the *Religious Education Association*, whose object is "to promote religious and moral education." From this association much is hoped for, and the time seems not far distant when the problems connected with moral and religious education shall be clearly defined, and many of them satisfactorily solved.

It is with one of these problems, that of a pedagogical curriculum for the Bible school, that this book deals, and the attempt is made to indicate the principles which should govern in the preparation of such a curriculum, and to outline courses of study for the various grades in the Bible school which shall be in harmony with those principles. A general outline of the curriculum here presented was published in the August, 1900, number of the *Biblical World,* together with a fuller development of the topics and lessons for Primary Grade C. In two later issues of the same periodical, November and December, 1903, two articles were published, giving in full the outline of work for the Kindergarten Grades A and B, together with suggestive lesson plans for each grade, and reference and supplemental literature for teacher and pupil. My thanks are due to the editors and publishers of the *Biblical World* for permission to use this material in practically an unchanged form. A number of students of the school, in connection with their work in pedagogy, have assisted in the selection and arrangement of material for a number of the lesson plans presented, and for such help my thanks are due to Miss Alice S. Browne, Miss Mary G. Cone, Mrs. Frank P. Lane, Miss Mary E. Merriam, Miss Martha J. Taylor, Mr. Robert Scott, and Rev. Adams D. Archibald.

Preface

The author hopes that what is here presented may be helpful to those earnest, intelligent superintendents who are alive to the radical defects of the present system, and who are willing to test by actual experiment whatever gives promise of better results; and, further, that it may be suggestive to other students and workers in this important educational field.

GEORGE W. PEASE.

HARTFORD SCHOOL OF RELIGIOUS PEDAGOGY.

TABLE OF CONTENTS

INTRODUCTION

THE MODERN BIBLE SCHOOL

	PAGE
§ 1. Its Place and Plan	3
§ 2. The Course of Study	11
§ 3. The Trained Teacher	20
§ 4. A Suggested Plan of Organization	24

PART I

THE CHILDHOOD PERIOD AND THE PRIMARY DEPARTMENT

CHAPTER I. THE KINDERGARTEN CHILD 31
CHAPTER II. A COURSE OF STUDY FOR THE KINDERGARTEN GRADES 48
 § 1. Outline of the Course for Grade A 48
 § 2. Suggestive Lesson Plans for Grade A . . . 50
 § 3. Books Relating to the Work of Grade A . . 62
  A. Reference Reading for the Teacher . . 62
  B. Supplemental Reading for the Pupil . . 62
  C. Song Material for Grades A and B . . 63
 § 4. Outline of the Course for Grade B 64
 § 5. Suggestive Lesson Plans for Grade B . . . 66
 § 6. Books Relating to the Work of Grade B . . . 76
  A. Reference Reading for the Teacher . . 76
  B. Supplemental Reading for the Pupil . . 77
CHAPTER III. THE PRIMARY CHILD 78
CHAPTER IV. A COURSE OF STUDY FOR THE PRIMARY GRADES 92
 § 1. Outline of the Course for Grade C 92
 § 2. Suggestive Lesson Plans for Grade C . . . 94
 § 3. Books Relating to the Work of Grade C . . . 110
  A. Reference Reading for the Teacher . . 110
  B. Supplemental Reading for the Pupil . . 110
 § 4. Outline of the Course for Grade D 111

x   BIBLE-SCHOOL CURRICULUM

	PAGE
§ 5. Suggestive Lesson Plans for Grade D . . .	115
§ 6. Books Relating to the Work of Grade D . .	123
A. Reference Reading for the Teacher . .	123
B. Supplemental Reading for the Pupil . .	124
§ 7. Outline of the Course for Grade E	124
§ 8. Suggestive Lesson Plans for Grade E . . .	127
§ 9. Books Relating to the Work of Grade E . . .	138
A. Reference Reading for the Teacher . .	138
B. Supplemental Reading for the Pupil . .	138

PART II

THE BOYHOOD-GIRLHOOD PERIOD AND THE JUNIOR DEPARTMENT

CHAPTER V.   SOME CHARACTERISTICS AND NEEDS OF THE PERIOD   141

CHAPTER VI. A COURSE OF STUDY FOR THE JUNIOR DEPARTMENT   154

§ 1. Outline of the Course for Grade A . . .	154
§ 2. Suggestive Lesson Plans for Grade A . . .	156
§ 3. Books Relating to the Work of Grade A . .	169
A. Reference Reading for the Teacher . .	169
B. Supplemental Reading for the Pupil . .	169
§ 4. Outline of the Course for Grade B	170
§ 5. Suggestive Lesson Plans for Grade B . . .	172
§ 6. Books Relating to the Work of Grade B . .	185
A. Reference Reading for the Teacher . .	185
B. Supplemental Reading for the Pupil . .	186
§ 7. Outline of the Course for Grade C	186
§ 8. Suggestive Lesson Plans for Grade C . . .	188
§ 9. Books Relating to the Work of Grade C . .	201
A. Reference Reading for the Teacher . .	201
B. Supplemental Reading for the Pupil . .	202
§ 10. Outline of the Course for Grade D	202
§ 11. Suggestive Lesson Plans for Grade D . . .	204
§ 12. Books Relating to the Work of Grade D . .	214
A. Reference Reading for the Teacher . .	214
B. Supplemental Reading for the Pupil . .	215

TABLE OF CONTENTS   xi

PART III

THE YOUTH PERIOD AND THE INTERMEDIATE DEPARTMENT

CHAPTER VII. SOME CHARACTERISTICS AND NEEDS OF   PAGE
    THE PERIOD 219
CHAPTER VIII. A COURSE OF STUDY FOR THE INTER-
    MEDIATE DEPARTMENT 232
      § 1. Outline of the Course for Grade A 232
      § 2. Suggestive Lesson Plans for Grade A . . . 234
      § 3. Books Relating to the Work of Grade A . . 244
          A. Reference Reading for the Teacher . . 244
          B. Reading and Reference Books for the
            Pupil 245
      § 4. Outline of the Course for Grade B 245
      § 5. Suggestive Lesson Plans for Grade B . . . 248
      § 6. Books Relating to the Work of Grade B . . 277
          A. Reference Reading for the Teacher . . 277
          B. Reading and Reference Books for the
            Pupil 278
      § 7. Outline of the Course for Grade C 278
      § 8. Suggestive Lesson Plans for Grade C . . . 280
      § 9. Books Relating to the Work of Grade C . . 289
          A. Reference Reading for the Teacher . . 289
          B. Reading and Reference Books for the
            Pupil 290
      § 10. Outline of the Course for Grade D 290
      § 11. Suggestive Lesson Plans for Grade D . . . 292
      § 12. Books Relating to the Work of Grade D . . 300
          A. Reference Reading for the Teacher . . 300
          B. Reading and Reference Books for the
            Pupil 301

PART IV

THE EARLY MANHOOD AND WOMANHOOD PERIOD AND THE SENIOR DEPARTMENT

CHAPTER IX. SOME CHARACTERISTICS AND NEEDS OF THE
    PERIOD 305

xii   BIBLE-SCHOOL CURRICULUM

CHAPTER X. A COURSE OF STUDY FOR THE SENIOR DE- PAGE
PARTMENT 318
  § 1. Outline of the Course for Grade A 318
  § 2. Suggestive Lesson Plans for Grade A . . . 320
  § 3. Books Relating to the Work of Grade A . . 337
    A. Reference Reading for the Teacher . . 337
    B. Reading and Reference Books for the Pupil 339
  § 4. Outline of the Course for Grade B . . . 339
  § 5. Suggestive Lesson Plans for Grade B . . . 342
  § 6. Books Relating to the Work of Grade B . . 352
    A. Reference Reading for the Teacher . . 352
    B. Reading and Reference Books for the Pupil 354
  § 7. Outline of the Course for Grade C . . . 355
  § 8. Suggestive Lesson Plans for Grade C . . . 357
  § 9. Books Relating to the Works of Grade C . . 374
    A. Reference Reading for the Teacher . . 374
    B. Reading and Reference Books for the Pupil 375
  § 10. Outline of the Course for Grade D 376
  § 11. Suggestive Lesson Plans for Grade D . . . 378
  § 12. Books Relating to the Work of Grade D . . 386
    A. Reference Reading for the Teacher . . 386
    B. Reading and Reference Books for the Pupil 386

PART V
THE MANHOOD AND WOMANHOOD PERIOD AND THE ADULT
DEPARTMENT
CHAPTER XI. SUGGESTED COURSES OF STUDY WITH SELECTED REFERENCE BOOKS 389

SUMMARY AND CONCLUSION
CHAPTER XII. GENERAL SUMMARY OF THE COURSE . . 401
CHAPTER XIII. CONCLUDING SUGGESTIONS 411
CHAPTER XIV. A SHORT LIST OF HELPFUL BOOKS FOR THE TEACHER 416

INTRODUCTION

INTRODUCTION
THE MODERN BIBLE SCHOOL
§ 1. ITS PLACE AND PLAN

THE term "education" has been variously defined by thinkers from the earliest times to the present, and educational systems based upon these definitions have been formulated and put into operation. Some of these definitions, even those of modern educators, have little value for us because of the exceedingly narrow views of life which they connote; while others, expressing only vague generalities, are equally useless as guides to any system of educational practice. One of the most illuminating statements of the meaning and aim of education is that given by President Butler, of Columbia University. In answer to the question, "What does the term 'education' mean?" he says:

It must mean a gradual adjustment to the spiritual possessions of the race. Those possessions may be variously classified, but they certainly are at least fivefold. The child is entitled to his scientific inheritance, to his literary inheritance, to his æsthetic inheritance, to his institutional inheritance, and to his religious inheritance. Without them he cannot become a truly educated or cultivated man.[1]

He points out further[2] that education should not

---
[1] *The Meaning of Education*, p. 17.
[2] *Teachers College Record*, September, 1900, p. 16.

only aim to place the child in possession of this race-culture, but also to develop in him a certain efficiency, a capacity to control or modify his environment, and to adapt himself to new conditions of life; and finally to develop in him power — power for service in behalf of the advancement of others. This conception of the meaning of "education" is the more satisfying because it gives a place to the religious inheritance which is every child's birthright, and emphasizes power for service as one of the three essential elements in all true education.

Our public-school system as at present organized, from the kindergarten to the college, enables the child to come into gradual possession of four-fifths of his spiritual inheritance; namely, his scientific inheritance, his literary inheritance, his æsthetic inheritance, and his institutional inheritance; but makes no provision for securing to him his religious inheritance, which many consider as of equal, if not greater, importance. Dr. Butler says on this latter point:

> The religious element may not be permitted to pass wholly out of education, unless we are to cripple it and render it hopelessly incomplete.[3]

President Hopkins, of Williams College, in his recent inaugural address said:

> We refuse then to call that education liberal which fails

[3] *Op. cit.*, pp. 30, 31.

to provide for the part of man which is noblest and highest, which refuses to recognize the universal aspiration and longing of humanity after goodness and beauty, after spiritual truth, after perfection, after God. A Christian training, if consistent, must account sinfulness as well as ignorance a factor in its problems, and must believe in the spirit of God as a power available for its work. It must recognize the personality of Jesus Christ a fact and force as unquestioned as heat, light, or electricity, and no more to be ignored or driven out than gravitation. Under the unreligious training men dwindle as they go. In the name, therefore, of the spiritual nature, we protest against any organized educational system "for the extirpation of the religious faculty through disuse."

This religious instruction is all the more necessary because of its close relation to the development of that power for service which is so essential to a complete life. The scientific, literary, æsthetic, and institutional treasures of the past may make the fortunate possessor a cultured or a learned man; the capacity to control or to modify environment, to bend all things to one's will, may make the successful man; but there is need of those high ideals, those deep feelings, those strong impulses to Godlike action, which result from absorbing the religious treasures of humanity, to develop in us that power for service and to enable us to actualize the complete image of God in which we were created.

But this work of religious instruction cannot be undertaken by our public schools, for it has been decided by the highest courts in several of our states that the present laws of the land do not admit of such instruction being given. There is needed, then, to make our educational system complete, an effective agency for securing to the child his religious inheritance, and for developing his religious instinct into clear religious insight and unwavering faith. The church in its Bible school seems to furnish this agency. Not the Bible school utterly lacking in system which we find in so many places; not even the so-called graded Bible school of the present, with its loose classification, its uniform-lesson system, and its untrained teachers; but the Bible school organized and conducted in accordance with those sound educational principles which have made our modern public schools so successful. But if this ideal is ever to be realized, the church must no longer regard its Bible school as "the nursery," nor as one of its missionary enterprises, but must consider it as a most important educational institution, and must adequately provide for it as such.

The Bible school of the future which shall perform the distinctively educational functions of the church will be a carefully graded school. By this term "graded," now loosely applied to any school having more than one department, I mean a school in which four principles will be recognized and applied.

1. The pupils will be carefully classified with reference to general mental ability, the grade a pupil has reached in the public school being one of the criteria for determining his place in the Bible school. Although it will never be possible to classify in our Bible schools as thoroughly as we classify in our public schools, still, so far as possible, mental capacity should be the determining factor, and age, size, and social position should be only secondary considerations. In such a school there will be a number of departments corresponding to the developmental periods of the pupils, each of these departments being divided into grades, in each of which the pupils remain one year; and the various grades will include a number of classes dependent upon the size of the school. In this way minds of the same general capacity, with the same general interests and needs, will be grouped together, and the work of the teacher from an educational standpoint will be made much more effective.

2. The lesson system will be one in which there is unity, but not uniformity. The matter will be carefully selected with reference to the mental powers, the fundamental interests, and the spiritual needs of the pupils in the different departments, and the lesson work of the various grades and departments will be so related that the lesson system, covering a period of seventeen

years, from four to twenty-one years inclusive, will be a unit, progressively revealing the character and works of God to the expanding soul of the child. Modern pedagogy has thrown aside the method of Procrustes, and is now seeking a clear knowledge of the nature and needs of the child that the truth may be selected and fitted to him; and when our Bible schools become *real* schools, working in harmony with recognized principles of teaching, this Procrustean method, now so common in them, will also disappear.

3. The method of lesson presentation will be adapted to the intellectual development of the pupils. This will win and hold the attention of the pupils, enable them to assimilate the matter presented, and thus lay the foundation of an *intelligent* Christian life. One of the reasons why more of our young people are not in our Bible schools today is that the subject-matter is not presented in a way to secure their active mental co-operation; their interests are not aroused, the imagination is disregarded, the judgment is not called into play, little appeal is made to the reasoning powers. The religious inheritance is a part of our spiritual inheritance, in which all are deeply interested; for man is above all else a religious being; and the treasures of this inheritance, if carefully selected and presented at the right stage and in the proper way, will surely call forth

the highest intellectual activity, arouse the strongest feelings of interest, and inspire to the noblest type of action. In the primary classes of our schools the results are somewhat better, for more attention has been given to this department, and the teaching has been more closely adapted to the child nature; but even here there is much room for improvement, which will be brought about only by a more thorough study of the child and the best methods of presenting truth to him.

4. There will be regular advancement or promotion from grade to grade through the various departments of the school. Such advancement will not only be an incentive to do satisfactory work in order to obtain the certificate indicating work done, but will bring the pupils from time to time under the inspiring influence of new teachers, who have become efficient by confining their study and work to that department for which their natural tastes and abilities seem to fit them. It is undoubtedly very delightful, from a purely sentimental point of view, to have a class from the kindergarten grade to the adult department, and to watch the pupil's growth in the Christian life; but the wisdom of the plan may be seriously doubted when looked at from the educational standpoint. If it is best for the boy or girl, in passing from the kindergarten through the primary, grammar, high school, and college to the

university, to be instructed by different teachers, each an expert in one department or subject, it certainly seems wise that this same boy or girl, while passing through the various grades of the Bible school, should come into personal touch with different types of Christian character, and be taught by those who are by nature, training, and experience efficient instructors in particular departments, that the life may be well rounded and all its possibilities brought to light. Until we have this advancement of pupils with change of teachers our Bible schools will be lacking in educational efficiency.

In thus indicating the principles involved in a graded Bible school, classification of minds, selection of instruction matter, adaptation of method and promotion of pupils, it must not be understood that they have not been recognized by students of Bible-school work in the past, and to a certain extent applied to existing schools; but if the church school of the future is to fill the place here indicated for it, these four principles must be much more generally recognized and more extensively applied.

Such a school, with its carefully organized departments and grades, its curriculum prepared by educational experts in accordance with the accepted principles of education, its methods closely adapted to the varying capacities of its members, with its pupils advancing annually from grade to grade, and taught in each grade by teachers trained for the special work of that grade — such a school is today an educational necessity. When the church is fully aroused to its duty and opportunity in this direction, and adequately equips and properly maintains its educational department, then the Bible school will become the complement of the public school, and together they will send forth into the work of the world the man of culture, the man of efficiency, the man of power.

§ 2. THE COURSE OF STUDY

One of the greatest present needs of the Bible school is a course of study constructed upon sound educational principles, which shall put the pupil in possession of the elements of his religious inheritance as he passes through the various departments of the school from the primary to the adult department; which shall win him to an acceptance of the cardinal doctrines of the Christian faith, and make of him a loyal disciple of the world's Savior, Jesus the Christ. The preparation of such a curriculum is a difficult task, and will require much time and experimentation; but it is a task which must be undertaken by educators in behalf of the church. Speaking of the duty of students of pedagogy to the work of religious instruction, Dr. A. Caswell Ellis says:

The provisional arrangement growing out of the abuses of religion and the other necessities of the time, by which religious training has been divorced from the schools and considered beyond the pale of pedagogical science, must soon give place to the inevitable demand of nature. However useful such a separation has been in bridging over periods of retrogression and bigotry in both religion and pedagogy, permanently to keep religious and secular education separated is doing violence to our souls and trying to tear apart what is by nature one. The old faculty psychology is gone, a brighter era of religious toleration seems near, and now pedagogy must accept and own her whole field and face its problem of religious education squarely. To yield it longer to the theologians or to special providence is a criminal shirking of duty.[4]

Whether or not we agree with the writer's views concerning the relation of religious and secular education, we shall certainly agree with him in the emphasis which he has laid upon the obligation of pedagogical science to religious training, which obligation must be clearly seen and definitely accepted by educators at the present time.

The church, on the other hand, must not hesitate to call to her aid the skill and learning of Christian educators, for

This work is one that demands more of expert and highly trained intelligence than at present can be found within the ministry of the church. As in the creation of her cathedrals she calls to her aid those who have been trained as architects and builders, and in her worship those whom God has inspired with the gifts of music and song; so in

[4] *Pedagogical Seminary*, Vol. V, p. 195.

the education of her children the church may well command the service of those whose lives have been consecrated to the ministry of education, and whose minds have been inspired with that gift of God's Spirit by which they are called to rightly divide the words of knowledge and truth. Indeed, it is by so doing that the church will prove herself faithful to that most sacred trust of guiding the youth into the truth and knowledge of God.[6]

In the preparation of a course of study for the Bible school which shall measure up to our pedagogical standards three factors must be constantly kept in mind: (1) the pupil, (2) the subject-matter, and (3) the ideal or ends sought.

1. *The pupil.*— In these modern times it is a pedagogical truism to say that the material of religious instruction should be selected with reference to the powers, interests, and needs of the pupil. The child passes through distinct stages of development from birth to adulthood, each stage being characterized by the dominance of certain mental powers and interests, and presenting certain moral and religious needs which must be supplied, or else the later life will lack in strength, in breadth, and in power. The planner of a lesson system, then, must know the nature of the pupils who will be found in the various departments of a school, and select his lesson material with reference to their mental powers, to insure the possi-

[6] REV. PASCAL HARROWER in *Principles of Religious Education*, pp. 126, 127.

bility of a proper understanding of the lesson; with reference to their interests, to insure attention to and assimilation of the truths presented; and with reference to their moral and religious needs, that each stage may be lived out completely as a preparation for the next one.

2. *The subject-matter.*— As the pupil passes through the various stages of development, his interests widen and his needs become more complex. The curriculum, then, must be comprehensive, to touch him on all sides; must meet his widening horizon, must be rich in content, to supply fully every need, and not confined to any one aspect of divine revelation; else the life may become one-sided or narrow. For this reason we should not limit our choice of lesson material to biblical matter, as is done in most, if not all, of our present lesson systems (although this is the most important source), but should also select suitable material from the wonderful revelation of God in physical nature (phenomena of life and action) and in human nature (history and biography), especially from those portions of the latter which reveal most clearly the meaning and progress of God's kingdom on earth. But in thus selecting material from these various sources care must be taken that the whole is not made a mere patchwork. The complete course of study must be progressive and interrelated. It is the assimi-

lated truth that has a value in character-building, and this assimilation of the new presentation is the function of the related old mental content. The entirely new — *i. e.*, that which is entirely unrelated to any part of our mental content — is unassimilable, and hence what is presented from week to week and month to month must be progressively presented to be readily assimilated. One of the greatest defects of our present system is the lack of this progression and interrelation. Fragments are taught with scarcely an attempt to tie them together. This results in loss to both the teacher's energy and the pupil's time. But even more important than this interrelation of the parts of a course of study is the relation of the various elements of such a course — geography, biography, history, poetry, prophecy, etc. — to vital truth in such a way as to give a setting and support to that truth. Unless we have such a relationship, our efforts will result simply in informing the intellect and not in developing a Christian character.

3. *The ideal or ends sought.*— In the preparation of a Bible-school curriculum we must have more than a knowledge of the powers, interests, and needs of the developmental periods; more than a knowledge of the sources of revelation to serve as guides in the selection and arrangement of material. It is necessary that we have a clear

view of the ends sought in religious training. These ends are four in number:

a) To give a knowledge of religious principles. Man is a religious being. Brinton in his *Religions of Primitive Peoples* says:

> The religiosity of man is a part of his psychical being. In the nature and laws of the human mind, in its intellect, sympathies, emotions, and passions, lie the well-springs of all religions, modern or ancient, Christian or heathen. To these we must refer; by these we must explain whatever errors, falsehoods, bigotry, or cruelty have stained man's creeds or cults; to them we must credit whatever of truth, beauty, piety, and love have glorified and hallowed his long search for the perfect and the eternal. .... The fact is that there has not been a single tribe, no matter how rude, known in history or visited by travelers, which has been shown to be destitute of religion under some form.[6]

The religious conceptions and forms of worship of these primitive peoples are untrue, extremely crude, and even grotesque; but as we rise in the scale of civilization we find a corresponding refinement in religious ideas and modes of expression. This religious instinct, or "religiosity" of nature as Brinton calls it, is a part of the child's inheritance from the race, and his early theological conceptions closely parallel in many respects those of primitive peoples. As this part of his nature develops, he needs help in forming right concep-

[6] Quoted by BUTLER in an article in *Educational Review*, December, 1899.

tions of God and His relations to man, and intelligent guidance to those vital principles, those living truths, which shall set him free and enable him to actualize completely his potential manhood. The matter of instruction, then, must be selected partly with reference to such right conceptions and vital truths.

b) To develop a keenness of ethical vision. It will not suffice that the great principles which should govern conduct are known; there must be a direct connection between these known principles and the particular occasions calling for their application. In other words, a mere knowledge of governing principles will be of no value unless the pupil has that ethical insight which shall enable him to see clearly the application of those principles to actual concrete cases as they arise in his own experience. In the story of the temptation of Jesus in the wilderness we are impressed with this fact that Jesus not only knew the principles contained in the three verses which he quoted, but that he also had that keen insight which showed him that the three temptations were specific occasions for the application of those principles or truths. This ethical sense must be developed in the child by presenting to him concrete cases involving ethical problems, and guiding him to their solution; *i. e.*, the child must be led to do his own moralizing. The matter of instruction, then, must be selected partly with reference to the ethical problems which it is desirable to present to the pupil.

c) To win the affectional nature to high ideals. It is possible for one to have knowledge of principles of right conduct, and insight into the application of those principles to daily life, and yet not to live in accordance with such. If living is to follow knowing, the feelings, the springs of action, must be enlisted on the side of the truth. Interest is the feeling side of voluntary attention; we are interested in what we attend to; we attend to what interests us. Ideas associated with strong feelings tend to discharge themselves in action. Therefore, if we would have righteous action follow righteous knowledge, we must associate in the pupil's mind strong feeling with the new ideas presented. The ideals which are presented, then, must be such as shall arouse the feelings, that the pupil may not only be attracted to these ideals as such, but also that he may be impelled to actualize them in his daily life. The ideals which appeal to the developing individual in the various stages of development are different for each period. The matter of instruction, then, must be selected partly with reference to the appeal which it will make to the feelings, and the method of presentation must be such as to win the affections to the truth.

d) There is yet another end in all religious

training—the development of power. Power comes only through action, through service. Our Bible schools are weak in this respect, that they do not offer many opportunities for the development of power through service. This weakness is due partly to the system of organization, partly to the lack of co-operation between the school and the home, and partly to the unpedagogical selection of instructional material. The testimony of Josephus to the Mosaic plan is pertinent here. He says:

> For there are two ways of coming at any sort of learning and a moral conduct of life; the one is by instruction in words, the other by practical exercises. Now, other lawgivers have separated these two ways in their opinions, and, choosing one of those ways of instruction, or that which best pleased every one of them, neglected the other. . . . . But for our legislator [Moses] he very carefully joined these two methods of instruction together; for he neither left these practical exercises to go on without verbal instruction, nor did he permit the hearing of the law to proceed without the exercises for practice.[7]

Although the great need here is the co-operating home, the school must do what it can to bring about this development of power. One condition is in its power to fulfil: it can provide in its course of study a selection of such truths as have an active side, that can be put into immediate practice in the home and social life of the pupils. In the

[7] *Contra Apion*, Book II, secs. 17, 18.

preparation of the Bible-school curriculum this end must be borne in mind, and the matter selected partly with reference to it.

In indicating the above as the aims of religious training, it is not intended to assert that these are to govern the selection of every lesson of the curriculum, for the subject-matter of any course of study has a logic of its own which must be observed; but only that they are to be kept in mind in selecting the material for the various grades and departments, and followed as general guiding principles, where not in conflict with other and possibly more fundamental ones.

§ 3. THE TRAINED TEACHER

The other great need of the Bible school of the present day is the trained teacher. Many years ago Socrates, in a conversation with Callias, the son of Hipponicus, asked him this searching and memorable question: "Callias, if your two sons were foals or calves, there would be no difficulty in finding someone to put over them; we should hire a trainer of horses, or a farmer probably, who would improve and perfect them in their proper virtue and excellence; but, as they are human beings, whom are you thinking of placing over them?" This question would be an exceedingly pertinent one to put to the church today: Whom are you thinking of placing over the millions of human beings who gather from week to week for religious instruction? The simply consecrated teacher of the past will not do; he must give way, and the consecrated and *trained* teacher must take his place. This will be readily admitted if it is conceded that the Bible school should occupy the place indicated for it in the former section (see § 1), for the trained teacher is necessary to the realization of the ideal there presented. When to consecration in the teacher we add education and special pedagogical training, we may look for a much more adequate return for the effort expended in our thousands of Bible schools. The teachers who will be selected by the church in the future for the work of teaching in the Bible school will have had a liberal education, supplemented by a two- or three-year training in the church teacher-training or normal class, holding its weekly sessions of one and one-half hours for nine months in the year. The course pursued by such a class would include a study of the general structure of the Bible, its form, contents, gradual development, and principal teachings; a study of the child in his various stages of growth from early childhood to adult life, emphasis being placed upon the mental powers, interests, characteristics, and religious needs of each period; a study of the principles and methods of teaching, with practice work in the preparation and presentation of lessons; and a study of the Bible school, its history, organization, and administration, that the teacher may work more intelligently and in full harmony with the ideals of the school's officers. The service rendered by these teachers will be a voluntary offering to the church, although the superintendent of the school, together with the department superintendents or supervisors, giving their whole time to the work, will be salaried.

The desirability and practicability of having trained teachers in the Bible school were set forth in a series of short articles forming a symposium on the subject, "Should Professional and Salaried Teachers Be Employed in the Sunday School?" published in the *Biblical World*. To this series the author contributed, and the short paper is here quoted in full:

The question of professional salaried instruction in the Bible school divides itself into three parts: (1) Is it desirable? (2) If desirable, to what extent? and (3) How may such instruction be secured to our schools?

1. Is professional salaried instruction desirable in the Bible school? The answer to this is a most emphatic yes. The character of the teaching in our public schools has undergone a marked change since the days of Horace Mann, through the influence and work of normal schools and teachers' colleges. As a result our boys and girls are well taught during the week by trained and experienced teachers, in thoroughly graded schools with carefully planned courses of study. But in the Bible school they

INTRODUCTION

find very different conditions prevailing; imperfect classification, poor teaching by incompetent though consecrated teachers, and a course of study planned in ignorance of, or without regard to, accepted pedagogical principles. The result of this is seen in the majority of schools which have been established for any length of time — the boys and girls and the young people are drifting away. It is only by adding to the consecration of the teacher that other essential to the largest success, viz., professional training, that the school may hope to retain its hold upon its members from the primary to the adult departments. Another, and perhaps more cogent, reason why such professional instruction is desirable is the importance of the work of the Bible-school teacher. However much we may lament the fact, the Bible school is today practically the only institution for definite religious instruction. The home has largely given up its privileges to the church school, the public school is debarred from exercising such privilege, and "the Sunday school is in this way brought into a position of great responsibility and importance, for it is, in fact, a necessary part of the whole educational machinery of our time." If the trained teacher is needed for the development of the intellectual side of the scholar's nature, surely some training is needed for those who would undertake the important and delicate task of developing the spiritual powers of a soul.

2. To what extent is professional salaried instruction desirable? Granting the desirability of some professional training for all Bible-school teachers, is it necessary in order to obtain teachers with such an equipment that they be paid a definite salary? Such a plan, even if thought desirable, which I very seriously question, is altogether impracticable; but to have the superintendent of the school a professionally equipped man (or woman?), giving his

entire time to the educational interests of the church and receiving an adequate salary, is practicable in the great majority of cases. In the larger schools the heads of the various departments might also be trained and salaried workers. An important part of the work of such superintendents and assistants would be the training of the class teachers, the instruction being given in normal classes organized as a department of the school, with courses of study carefully planned along biblical, psychological, pedagogical, and sociological lines. In this way the schools would soon have a body of trained teachers, working under skilled leadership, the results of which would be quickly apparent.

3. How may such instruction be secured to our schools? By stirring the church to a realization of its obligations in the matter. The church must properly evaluate the different elements of its organization; the child must be considered of more value than the choir, the teacher of more importance than the sexton, and class-room accommodations of greater moment than church adornment. With an enlightened intellect and an awakened conscience the means for providing professional salaried instruction, as indicated above, will be forthcoming.[8]

§ 4. A SUGGESTED PLAN OF ORGANIZATION

There have been many plans of organizing the Bible school suggested and put into operation. The historic division into Infant department and Main school is going out of use except in the very small country schools. A large proportion of the schools of the present are organized with three

[8] *Biblical World,* December, 1900, pp. 420, 421.

departments — the Primary, the Intermediate, and the Senior or Adult department. Many of our better schools, especially the larger ones in the cities, recognizing the importance of careful classification of the pupils, are organizing their schools with a larger number of grades and departments.

Leaving out of consideration the Home, Normal, and Library departments, there would seem to be a need, in the average school, for five departments where class instruction is given. The first department, the Primary, would receive the children from four to nine years of age. This department would be subdivided into two sections: (1) the Kindergarten section, with two grades, A and B; and (2) the Primary section proper, with three grades, C, D, and E. In each of these grades the pupils remain one year.

At about nine years of age there are well-marked changes in the development of the child. The senses at this time reach practical perfection; certain mental powers, such as verbal memory, the power of inference, etc., begin to develop more rapidly; the interests change, especially the literary interests. This appears to be the time to change the pupils to a higher department where they can be taught and disciplined in a way to appeal to their more developed mental condition. This next higher department, the Junior, would receive the children at nine and hold them until they were thirteen years of age. The department would be divided into four grades — A, B, C, and D — the pupils remaining in each grade one year.

At about thirteen years of age there are well-marked changes incident to puberty. This is the time of the new birth, physically and psychically. The thoughts and desires of the boys and girls entering this period are very different from those of the preceding one and call for very different treatment by the teacher. The reasoning and imaginative powers are developing strongly; the interests are many-sided, but wavering; the moral nature is beginning to assert itself; the desires, emotions, and impulses are strong, but erratic; the moods are fluctuating; and in short, the whole period beginning at this age is one of restlessness and change. These conditions call for the separation of the boys and girls from the younger and the older members of the school into a separate department, the Intermediate, which would hold its members from thirteen to seventeen years of age. This department also would have four grades — A, B, C, and D — the pupils remaining in each one year.

By seventeen years of age the restlessness and turmoil of the preceding period have largely disappeared, and the young men and women are in a condition, both physically and mentally, to look out upon the world and try to understand it and their relation to it. At this time, then, the young men and women should meet by themselves in classes under competent teachers, and should have the matter and method of instruction adapted to their enlarged mental vision. For these young people from seventeen to twenty-one years of age the Senior department should be organized, with four grades — A, B, C, and D — each grade covering a year's work.

All over twenty-one years of age would become members of the Adult department, where they would find classes, teachers, and courses of instruction suited to their stage of life.

The following chart shows the proposed classification of pupils:

Department	Ages	Grades
Primary..........	4–9	Kindergarten Sec., 2—A, B Primary Sec., 3—C, D, and E
Junior............	9–13	4—A to D
Intermediate......	13–17	4—A to D
Senior...........	17–21	4—A to D
Adult............	21 up	Various classes suited to the membership

The above plan is the one followed in this book. It will be seen that it calls for a course of study extending through seventeen years, beginning with the child at four years of age. In the pages following an attempt is made to indicate suitable material for religious instruction in each of the seventeen grades, with reasons for such selection.

PART I

THE CHILDHOOD PERIOD AND THE PRIMARY DEPARTMENT

CHAPTER I

THE KINDERGARTEN CHILD

THE little child, God's most wonderful creation, is born into this world in a condition of utter helplessness. He is weak, ignorant, neither good nor bad; but there lie within that small body wonderful possibilities — the possibility of strength and activity, of unlimited knowledge, of a pure and noble moral character, which shall fit him for a life of service among men and of communion and companionship with the Divine.

As he starts out in this life he is ignorant of everything, of himself as well as of the world about him. He finds himself in a world of chaos, he being a part of that chaos. He begins his education by learning something of himself, of the parts of his own body and their relation to each other and to the whole; and this is a long process, taking many months. It is several years, as Sully shows,[1] before he knows his own body as an object separate from all other objects, and with all of its parts connected and vitally related. In illustration of this Sully quotes a number of stories, among others one from the Worcester Collection,[2] of a child of three and a half years

[1] *Studies of Childhood*, pp. 110-15.
[2] *Ibid.*, p. 111.

who on finding his feet stained by some new stockings observed: "Oh, mamma! these ain't my feet, these ain't the feet I had this morning."

But it is with the rapid development of the senses that he begins his acquaintance with the outer world, and upon their perfection his future progress very largely depends. During the childhood period this activity of sense-perception is the chief characteristic of his intellectual life. But this power very slowly develops, full and correct observation coming only in later years. Though only slowly coming to anything like perfection, the observing powers of the young child are very active, and through them he is gaining a great mass of mental pictures of the world which surrounds him, and these images he is constantly using as an aid in the interpretation of that wonderful world in which he finds himself placed. When he thus begins to interpret, his progress is rapid.

Some characteristics of the period.—A marked characteristic of this early part of the childhood period is the strength of the animistic impulse — the impulse to invest inanimate objects with all of the attributes of personality. Young children have a lively imagination, which "in an active constructive form takes part in the very making of what we call sense-experience."[3]

[3] *Ibid.*, p. 29.

Their powerful imagination and strong feelings master them so that they do not distinguish clearly between the real and the imaginary, and until they are four or five often do not know that their dreams are not realities. The line between feeling, will, and intellect is hardly distinguishable, as was shown by their utter inability to see in their dolls anything but what they felt or desired about them. This confusion begins to clear up after five or six, but the stronger impulse to attribute to everything else the child's own feelings, or animism, is still present at seven, and falls away only slowly till adolescence.[4]

Although movement and sound help to suggest life to the child, such is not necessary for the play of the animistic impulse; for, as Sully says:

The most unpromising things come in for this warm vitalizing touch of the child's fancy. He will make something like a personality out of a letter..... A little boy well on in his fourth year, when tracing a letter L happened to slip so that the horizontal limb formed an angle thus, ⌐. He instantly saw the resemblance to the sedentary human form and said: "Oh, he's sitting down." Similarly when he made an F turn the wrong way and then put the correct form to the left thus, F ꟻ he exclaimed: "They're talking together."[5]

Another characteristic of the period is the extreme suggestibility of the child. Small, in his extended study of the subject, comes to these conclusions: "that in healthy children suggestibility is (1) a universal condition; (2) high in

[4] ELLIS, *Pedagogical Seminary*, Vol. V, p. 172.
[5] *Op. cit.*, p. 30.

degree; (3) largely within the control of anyone who knows the working of the child-mind."[6] He emphasizes the need of a closer companionship with children on the part of the teacher and parent. The teacher may strongly influence the child in the formation of his tastes, aspirations, and ideals; but to do this he must have a personal interest in and attachment for his pupils, for "although a bright teacher may interest pupils in a study, large sympathies, personal interest in the pupil, and ability to appreciate the good in him are necessary to awaken purpose and develop strong character."[7]

Somewhat closely related to this suggestibility of the child is the imitative instinct. The power of imitation and the power of imagination form two of the most potent factors in child-development. Imitation plays a large part in moral and religious education. Dr. J. R. Street, in concluding a "Study in Moral Education," says: "Moral action, in early period of life, and even in early manhood and womanhood, is a matter of imitation and suggestion rather than of intellect."[8] Compayre, speaking of the imitative instinct in the child, ascribes its power to three causes — ignorance, weakness of personality, and sympathy. He says:

[6] *Pedagogical Seminary*, Vol. IV, pp. 176 ff.
[7] *Op. cit.*, p. 218.
[8] *Op. cit.*, Vol. V, p. 39.

The power of the imitative instinct in the child is due to several causes; and first of all to his ignorance. Having as yet at his disposal but a small amount of knowledge and a very slender stock of ideas, the child is at the mercy of the perceptions which incite him on all sides. His supple thought, free from prepossessions, responds to the call of exterior images, and follows without resistance the current into which it is urged by the impressions which strike it. On the other hand, the child is weak; he is lacking in personality. He needs to act, but his will does not yet exist. Powerless to act from his own initiative, he acts in accordance with what he sees others do. His weakness is the principal cause of his imitative disposition. Sympathy is still another source of the imitative instinct. We all have a secret tendency to put ourselves in agreement, in our sentiments and actions, with the men who surround us, and particularly with those whom we love. To love anyone is to desire to resemble him. The child who feels an ardent affection for his companions is naturally inclined to imitate them. The more causes of sympathy there are, such as resemblances in condition or age, the more powerfully will the imitative instinct manifest itself.[9]

Miss Frear's "Study of Imitation"[10] indicates that there is a strong tendency in the child to imitate adult activities, and that there is a steady growth of the impulse to imitate the idea involved in the action rather than the action itself. When we consider the strength of this imitative instinct in the child, and the almost hypnotic state of suggestibility in which we find him dur-

[9] *Lectures on Pedagogy*, PAYNE translation, pp. 220, 221.
[10] *Pedagogical Seminary*, Vol. IV, pp. 382–86.

ing the early part of childhood, the importance of his environment and of the suggestions which come to him from the teacher in class or parent in the home cannot be overestimated.

During the childhood period the imagination is extremely active. Children differ widely in imaginative power, however, some seeming to be "matter of fact" children with little of the "power of fancy," while others are dreamers, living almost continuously in the "land of make-believe." W. H. Burnham says:

> Popular speech divides the world into two classes — the imaginative and the unimaginative. But all children, unless they be idiots, probably have productive or creative imagination in some measure; and among them the differences in degree are more important than is usually supposed.[11]

Sully's studies lead him to the conclusion that a large majority of boys and girls alike are for a time fancy-bound. Burnham says further, with reference to the individual differences in children in productive imagination:

> With some children it may be necessary to check imagination. With others the effort should be to develop it. And it is well to remember that most children have sufficient imagination to vivify what is dull, prosaic, and dead to us. What you tell a child of wolves and bears, of tramps and robbers, of the dark forest and all-devouring sea, of giants, ogres, angels, devils, and future punishment, is

[11] *Op. cit.*, Vol. II, p. 212.

not apperceived in the dull prosaic way in which you tell it; but it grows appalling in that vivid ideal world in which it finds lodgment. The whole subject of religious education especially should be studied in relation to the child's productive imagination.[12]

In speaking of the influence of imagination upon the moral life Sully says:

In the moral life again we shall see how easily the realizing force of young imagination may expose it to deception by others, and to self-deception too, with results that closely simulate the guise of a knowing falsehood. On the other hand, a careful following out of the various lines of imaginative activity may show how moral education, by vividly suggesting to the child's imagination a worthy part, a praiseworthy action, may work powerfully on the unformed and flexible structure of his young will, moving it dutyward.[13]

The imagination in children needs the support of sense-perception. It matters not what the object is, nor how little it resembles the final fancied product, it is yet "a sensible object, and as such gives support and substance to the realizing impulse." For this reason the teacher should not hesitate to use objects, pictures, rough drawings, or any form of illustrative material which will aid the child to visualize the scene as it is presented to him verbally in the story, for "the toy, the picture, being, however roughly, a likeness or show,

[12] *Op. cit.*, p. 223.
[13] *Op. cit.*, p. 28.

brings the idea before the child's eye in a way which the word-symbol cannot do."[14]

Before leaving this part of the subject, two other characteristics of the period should be noted — the child's selfishness and his fears. All the impulses of the young child are centered in self and the satisfaction of its wants. This selfishness manifests itself in many ways: in anger, when his wants or wishes are interfered with by others; in envy, when he wishes things which he sees others possess; in jealousy, when he desires for himself the attentions paid to others. "There seems to be little doubt that these [anger, envy, jealousy] are among the commonest and most pronounced characteristics of the first years."[15] But to counterbalance somewhat this selfishness, we find in the child the germs of altruism. Selfishness tends to isolation, but children are naturally sociable, and do not like to be alone. Manifestations of selfishness are thus somewhat checked by the desire for companionship. Generosity and the desire to please are natural impulses with most children, and both of these tend to counteract to a limited extent the effect of selfishness. While we cannot expect to make unselfishness a dominant characteristic in very young children, still our course of instruction should be planned so as to

[14] *Ibid.*, p. 55.
[15] *Op. cit.*, p. 234.

provide for a natural development of whatever germs of altruism may be present. Although the adolescent period is the period for the most marked change from selfishness to altruism, there is a general improvement in this respect during the second half of the childhood period.

Young children are naturally fearful. This fear in very early childhood "is most often a vague haunting terror of the dark, of awful shapes, of something I know not what."[16] In a study on fears, reported by Miss Calkins,[17] it was shown that with children under six fears due to real objects were much more numerous than imaginary fears, but that the number of these latter fears increases very rapidly as the child grows older. In this study the source of nearly one-half the fears is given as environment, they being accidentally acquired or directly taught the child by parents or older children; and about one-fourth are inborn or inherited from the past. Some few children under six seem to be without fear, but practically all children over that age have fears of some kind. There are a number of causes for this fearfulness exhibited by children, among which might be mentioned their weakness, their ignorance, their nervous condition, their sense of utter helplessness, and their vivid imagination,

---

[16] Miss Holbrook, *Studies in Education*, Vol. I, p. 19.
[17] *Pedagogical Seminary*, Vol. III, pp. 319 ff.

although this latter is a more fertile source of fears in the next stage, from six to twelve years of age.

Some interests of the period.— One of the earliest and strongest interests of the young child is that of the origin of things, the interest in the causal idea. The child's first form of question is, What? It is the result of ignorance on his part, and is an attempt to gain knowledge about those things which have come under his eye. But this form of question soon changes to, Why? or, How? which clearly indicates his search after the reason or cause of things. The child is confronted daily by many new and puzzling things, which he must try to understand, *i. e.,* to bring into some relation to his mental content; and thus, as Sully says,

The fundamental significance of the "Why?" in a child's vocabulary is the necessity of connecting the new with the old, of illuminating what is strange and dark by light reflected from what is already a matter of knowledge.[18]

In a study by Miss Davis on "Children's Interest in the Causal Idea,"[19] she finds that the "fields in which interest in the causal idea is shown are natural phenomena, motion, animals, and religious objects." Religious objects were not the first to interest the children, but "before reaching

[18] *Op. cit.,* p. 78.
[19] *Child Study Monthly,* September, 1896, pp. 226 ff.

the age of seven nearly all . . . . show interest in the causal idea pertaining to God, heaven, death, etc." The field in which children find earliest and best opportunity for the development of interest in the causal idea is that of nature. The studies of Barnes[20] and Shaw[21] show that practically the only interest which young children have for objects is in their use and action; "only later in life do they become actively interested in the qualities of objects and then only gradually."

When we come to the theological interests and ideas of children, "we find an odd patchwork of thought, the patchwork being due to the heterogeneous sources of the child's information, his own observations of the visible world on the one hand, and the ideas supplied him by what is called religious instruction on the other."

A study by Professor Earl Barnes[22] on the theological ideas of California children shows that "the world of spirits is for the most part attractive; there is very little dark and forbidding imagery; terror is unknown; the ideas are generally vague." The children's attitude toward theology is interesting and important.

The young children under six . . . . accept what they have been told without question or comment. They, how-

[20] "A Study of Children's Interests," *Studies in Education*, pp. 203 ff.
[21] *Child Study Monthly*, July-August, 1896, pp. 152 ff.
[22] *Pedagogical Seminary*, Vol. II, pp. 442 ff.

ever, recast their theology into forms that appeal to their experiences and their modes of thought. The spirit-world is simply a beautiful playground where children have what they want; God is a more serious form of papa; the angels are playfellows; and Satan is simply a "boogie," while hell is a dark closet.

Two of Professor Barnes's conclusions have reference to the period we are discussing. They are as follows:[23] (1) If young children are to be taught a theology, it must have an anthropomorphic and realistic form. We may teach that God is a spirit, but the child's mind at once invests him with a human form and human attributes. If we do not furnish exalted and worthy imagery, the child fills out the form with random pictures, *Punch* and *Judy* impressions, and images from grocery labels. (2) Since pictures furnish so much of the imagery, children should be surrounded with worthy pictures, such as Raphael's "Sistine Madonna." Dr. Hall's study, "The Contents of Children's Minds on Entering School,"[24] also shows that the children's ideas of theological matters are extremely anthropomorphic, they translating all the adult terms into terms of their own experience. Sully, in speaking of the theological interests and ideas of children, concludes with these words:

[23] *Op. cit.*, p. 448.
[24] *Op. cit.*, Vol. I, pp. 139 ff.

I have tried to show that children seek to bring meaning, and a consistent meaning, into the jumble of communications about the unseen world to which they are apt to be treated. I agree with Miss Shinn that children about three and four are not disposed to theologize, and are for the most part simply confused by the accounts of God which they receive. Many of the less bright of these small minds may remain untroubled by the incongruities lurking in the mixture of ideas, half mythological or poetical, half theological, which is thus introduced. Such children are no worse than many adults, who have a wonderful power of entertaining contradictory ideas by keeping them safely apart in separate chambers of their brain. The intelligent, thoughtful child, on the other hand, tries at least to reconcile and to combine in an intelligible whole. His mind has not, like that of so many adults, become habituated to the water-tight compartment arrangement, in which there is no possibility of a leakage of ideas from one group into another. Hence his puzzlings, his questionings, his brave attempts to reduce the chaos to order. I think it is about time to ask whether parents are doing wisely in thus adding to the perplexing problems of early days.[25]

The dominant literary interest of young children is in fairy-tales and folk-lore stories and in stories of this type. With the majority of children this interest lasts until "ten years of age, when it rapidly declines, almost to extinction by the thirteenth year, with a possible rejuvenation later from another standpoint."[26]

The mental powers during the period.— The

[25] *Op. cit.,* p. 132.
[26] ELLIS, *Pedagogical Seminary,* Vol. V, p. 174.

perceptive powers are the earliest to develop. Young children are interested in perceptions — what they see, hear, feel, taste, etc. — rather than in conceptions concerning the qualities, relations, classification, meaning, etc., of all these images of the senses. In attempting to understand thoughts presented to them, they translate everything, so far as possible, into terms of sense-experience, and their ability to understand these thoughts when presented is largely dependent upon the development of their perceptive powers and the extent of their sense-ideas.

The memory is active, but it is a memory for things and concrete facts. Imagination, as has already been said, is also strongly active, but it is crude and undeveloped, needing the support of the perceptive powers.

The thought-powers are comparatively undeveloped. Professor Earl Barnes says that one of the marked characteristics of the young untrained mind is that

It thinks in bits, pieces, fragments. Lacking continuity, it is easily played upon by suggestion, and goes off along lines of associated ideas. If one could have a map of the ground over which the mind of an ordinary ten-year-old child travels during the forenoon in school, it would be at many points of the course miles away from the route laid down by the curriculum and traveled over by the teacher.[27]

This is perhaps even more true of the very young

---

[27] *Studies in Education*, Vol. I, p. 264.

child in the Bible school session. During this period, then, the teacher, while not neglecting to lead the child-mind to a definite understanding of definite truths, should endeavor to teach as much as possible by suggestion on the one hand, and by example on the other.

As conscience plays but a small rôle in connection with moral action until about nine years of age, and little then until thirteen years of age, the teacher should not appeal to it nor rely upon it as an important factor in her work.

Some conclusions with reference to a course of study for the child from four to six years of age.— The foregoing presentation of some of the characteristics, powers, and interests of the young child, together with the fact that the earliest ideas which he gets of God ordinarily center in His creative activity, the child envisaging God as a great being, somewhat of an enlarged father, who is the great world-worker, capable of doing all things, seem to call for the presentation to the child during the first two years of Bible-school instruction (*i. e.*, from four to six years of age) of the creative aspect of God's nature. This is the simplest and most easily grasped aspect of God's nature, which in itself would indicate its adaptability to the child. Caird says in his *Fundamental Ideas of Christianity*[28] that

[28] Vol. I, pp. 56, 57.

The conceptions of natural theology, the idea of God as the Creator, Preserver, Moral Governor, of the world, and of the attributes of power, wisdom, goodness, and so on, with which he is invested, do not seem foreign to our intelligence, for they are based on human analogies, and even where they transcend all finite parallels they can be represented to our minds as only an indefinite extension of human qualities. Ordinary thought, in other words, finds no impossibility in representing to itself a personality who is simply a magnified man.

The child should be brought into touch with nature at first hand where possible, God as seen in his works being the guiding thought for the teacher in the presentation of the lesson material. Nature should be presented directly as the handiwork of God, without any of the sentimentalism so often associated with nature-study. "In the beginning God created the heavens and the earth." "The heavens declare the glory of God and the firmament sheweth his handiwork." As then, so now, the world of things is first, and "in the beginning" of the child's religious development the "heavens and the earth" are the elements which first appeal to him, and through which he can get his first glimpse of the Creator, of the "glory of God." If through the use of this nature material we can impress the child with somewhat of a sense of God's power, wisdom, love, and rule, he will just as surely react with reverence, trust, love, and obedience as will his brain react light when the optic nerve is stimulated, or sound when the auditory nerve is excited.

An outline of a suggested course of study is given in the next chapter. In Grade A the child is shown the love of God in providing for all the needs of all his creatures, and in Grade B he is shown that all things are co-operating with God in this work of providence. The purpose of the two-year course will have been accomplished if the children receive the idea that God is a God of power, wisdom, and love, and if a desire is created in them to co-operate with God, to become "workers together with him."

CHAPTER II

A COURSE OF STUDY FOR THE KINDERGARTEN GRADES

GENERAL SUBJECT: GOD THE WORKMAN — THE CREATOR — AND HIS WORKS

§ 1. OUTLINE OF THE COURSE FOR GRADE A

GRADE SUBJECT: GOD THE CREATOR PROVIDING ALL THINGS FOR ALL HIS CREATURES

Topic 1 — Creating.

The creation story:
1. The great round ball on which we live.
2. The coming of plants, trees, and flowers.
3. The coming of fishes, birds, and animals.
4. The coming of man.
5. *Review.*

Topic 2 — Providing food for all.

6. For the trees and plants.
7. For the animals of field and forest.
8. For the birds of the air.
9. Food for us.
10. Food for us.
11. Our beautiful land of plenty.
12. *Review.*

Topic 3 — Providing drink for all.

13. The story of the rain clouds.
14. The story of the spring.
15. The story of the well.
16. The story of the mountain stream.
17. *Review.*

Kindergarten Course of Study

Topic 4—Providing clothing for all.
  18. Feather clothing — for the birds.
  19. Fur clothing — for the rabbit.
  20. Hair clothing — for the dog.
  21. Children's winter clothing — wool.
  22. Children's summer clothing — cotton.
  23. *Review.*
  24. Thanksgiving for these things — food, drink, clothing.

Topic 5—Providing shelter for all.
  25. Homes in the earth — fox or rabbit.
  26. Homes in the water — beaver or muskrat.
  27. Homes in the trees — birds.
  28. Homes for us.
  29. Homes for us.
  30. *Review.*

Topic 6—Providing rest for all.
  31. The winter rest of the earth.
  32. The winter rest of the trees.
  33. The winter rest of the animals.
  34. *Review.*
  35. The nightly rest of birds and animals.
  36. The nightly rest of the workman.
  37. The nightly rest of children.
  38. *Review.*
  39. The beginning of the sabbath rest.
  40. Jesus teaching about the sabbath rest.
  41. Our sabbath rest.
  42. *Review.*

Topic 7—Providing pleasure for all.
  43. Pleasure through light.
  44. Pleasure through color.
  45. Pleasure through music.

46. Pleasure through activity.
47. *Review.*
48. Thanksgiving for these things — shelter, rest, pleasure.

Special Lessons.
49. Preparation for the Christmas lesson.
50. The Christmas lesson (in its proper place).
51. Preparation for the Easter lesson.
52. The Easter lesson (in its proper place).

---

§ 2. SUGGESTIVE LESSON PLANS FOR GRADE A
(LESSONS 6-8)

LESSON 6

GOD PROVIDING FOOD FOR TREES AND PLANTS

Lesson Material.

For story: Gould, *Mother Nature's Children,* pp. 81–88; also see the story outline below, "God Providing Food for the Trees and Plants."

For study: Ps. 104: 10, 13, 14, 16, 24; Dana, *Plants and Their Children;* Allen, *The Story of the Plants,* in Appleton's "Library of Useful Stories;" Buckley, *Fairy Land of Science,* Lecture VII; Chase, *Plant Babies and Their Cradles,* and *Buds, Stems and Roots.*

Illustrative Material and Suggestions.

Objects: Growing plants and grasses with well-defined roots. A maple or oak which has just started.

Pictures: The following Mumford pictures: "Forest Trees," "Liberty Roses," and "Easter Lily."

Literature: Use the following verses, "Waiting to Grow," by Amanda Turner in *Kindergarten Magazine:*

Think what a host of queer little seeds,
Soon to make flowers and mosses and weeds,
Are under the leaves and the ice and the snow,
Waiting, waiting to grow.

Think of the roots getting ready to sprout,
Reaching their slender, brown fingers about,
Under the leaves and the ice and the snow,
Waiting, waiting to grow.

Nothing's so small, or hidden so well,
That God cannot find it and presently tell
His sun where to shine, and his rain where to go,
Helping, helping them grow.

Memory verse printed on slips of paper for distribution.

Observation: Ask the children to plant some grass seed in a small box of good soil, keep the box where it can get the sunshine, water it well, and when the little seeds *begin* to grow, tell them to pull up some of the blades and see the little rootlets. Or they can put a bulb in a glass part full of water and watch the roots form and grow.

Lesson Treatment.

Connecting links: Review very briefly the lessons about the Creation Story. We have learned about the creating of the world, the trees and the flowers, the fish of the sea, the animals of the field, the birds of the air, and finally of man himself. For the next few Sundays we are to learn about how God in his love and wisdom provides abundant food for all of his creatures upon this "big round ball on which we live."

Preparation: Question the children about what they need to make them grow tall and strong. Sunshine, and pure air, and exercise. Yes, all of these and plenty of — good food. Nothing can grow without food. Today our story will tell us how God provides food for the trees and plants, and what they do to get this food.

Presentation: Present the story matter in the following detail:
1. The food in the earth.
   a) The food stored away in the rocks and hills.
   b) The crumbling rocks make soil.
   c) The seeds are planted in this soil.
   d) The rain prepares the food for the plants.
2. The food in the air.
   a) Some food the plants need is not in the soil.
   b) This food is stored away in the air.
   c) The winds blow the air about so all can get this food.
3. The plant seeking food from the earth.
   a) The sun and rain awaken the plant to life.
   b) It begins to send out tiny roots.
   c) These go in all directions seeking the food in the earth.
   d) These rootlets are little mouths which drink in the liquid food they find in the earth.
4. The plant seeking food from the air.
   a) The seed sends out roots into the earth; it also sends out stems and leaves into the air.
   b) These leaves act like lungs and breathe in food which they find in the air.
   c) The wind constantly changes the air and brings more food.

Suggestions for developing the story and using the illustrative material: Begin the story by referring to the previous topic, the Story of Creation. God knew that all living things would need food, so when he made the world he stored away an abundance of food for

KINDERGARTEN COURSE OF STUDY 53

every living thing. In telling about the rocks crumbling and making soil, speak of the combined action of water and frost; perhaps some of the children have had some experiences with pitchers of water or milk which have been broken by being frozen. The rain preparing the food — dissolving the mineral food substances — may be made clear by dissolving a little sugar in water. When the story of the plant seeking food in the earth and air is told, show to the children the roots and leaves of the plants which have been prepared, calling attention to the great number of these roots and leaves and to the way in which they go out in all directions in their search for food in the earth and air. Show the pictures, and give the class the thought that the strength and size of the trees, and the beauty and fragrance of the flowers, are made possible because God has provided an abundance of the right kind of food for them. Ask the children a few simple questions, the answers to which shall express the main elements of the story, and encourage the children to talk freely about what they have learned. Then repeat to the class the verses "Waiting to Grow;" and finally give the memory verse and have the class repeat it, but do not try to have it committed to memory at this time.

Desired Results.

An impression of the wisdom of God: he knows just what the trees and plants need; and of the love of God: he provides abundantly for all their needs. An impression of the thoughtfulness of God for all of his creatures: he never forgets their needs, not even those of the trees and the plants. The associating in the child's mind of God with all natural phenomena.

Memory Verse.

"Your heavenly Father feedeth them" (Matt. 6:26).

Home Work.

Pasting into the album the pictures, together with the slips containing the memory verse and the verses "Waiting to Grow." Review of the lesson story by the parents. Reading to the child the verses "Waiting to Grow." Helping the child to commit to memory the memory verse. Observation work as suggested.

LESSON 7

GOD PROVIDING FOOD FOR THE ANIMALS OF FIELD AND FOREST

Lesson Material.

> For story: A portion of the story "Ready for Winter," found in Palmer's *One Year of Sunday School Lessons for Young Children*, pp. 159-63; also see the story outline below, "God Providing Food for the Animals of Field and Forest."
>
> For study: Pss. 104:10-22; 147:7-9; Gen. 1:11, 12, 30; Gould, *Mother Nature's Children*, pp. 185-92; Burroughs, *Squirrels and Other Fur Bearers;* Miller, *Little Folks in Feather and Fur.*

Illustrative Material and Suggestions.

> Objects: Grass, corn, grain, and various kinds of nuts.
> Pictures: The following Mumford pictures: "The Cow," No. 487; "The Horse," No. 494; "Brittany," No. 342; and "The Fox Squirrel," No. 179; also "Piper and Nutcrackers," Landseer; "Little Freehold," Carter.
> Blackboard: At the left of the board sketch a bit of growing grass, some grain, a few stalks of corn, and

the outline of a barn; at the right, an oak tree with acorns on the ground beneath, and a tree stump with an opening into the hollow within.

Literature: Use the following verses from Gaynor's *Songs of the Child World:*

Child:
"O busy squirrel with shining eyes,
  And bushy tail so round,
Why do you gather all the nuts
  Which fall upon the ground?"

Squirrel:
"I must prepare for winter's cold,
  My harvest I must reap;
For when Jack Frost the forest claims,
  Within my hole I keep."

Also the following verses from Smith's *Songs for Little Children:*

We plow the fields and scatter
  The good seed o'er the land,
But it is fed and water'd
  By God's almighty hand.

He sends the snow in winter,
  The warmth to swell the grain,
The breezes and the sunshine,
  And sweet refreshing rain.

Memory verse printed on slips of paper for distribution.

Observation: Ask the children, during the week, to find out about the kinds of food which other animals use. What does the dog eat? The cat? etc.

Lesson Treatment.

Connecting links: Review briefly the last lesson. Question the children about their observation work. We have learned about how God provides abundantly for the trees and plants, and today we are to learn how he cares for the animals of the fields and forests.

Preparation: Question the children about the horse. What does he do for us? And what does he need to make him strong to work? Question about the cow. What does the cow do for us? And what must she have that she may do this? Have you ever seen the squirrels in the trees, or the chipmunks running along the fence? They must have had good food and plenty of it, else they would not be so lively. Today our story will tell us about the food which God provides for the animals, and how they are cared for all the year around.

Presentation: Present the story matter in the following detail:

1. Food for the horses and cattle.
    a) Summer food — grass of the fields.
        (1) The sun awakens the seeds to life.
        (2) The rain helps them to grow.
        (3) They keep on growing until winter.
    b) Winter food — hay, corn, grain.
        (1) The farmer sows the seed.
        (2) God sends his sunshine and rain.
        (3) At harvest time all is stored away in the great barns.
2. Food for the squirrels and their friends.
    a) Daily gathering of summer food.
        (1) Many kinds of nuts from the forest.
        (2) Corn and grain from the fields.
        (3) Grass seed from the meadow.
    b) The storing of food for winter.
        (1) The autumn the squirrels' busy time.
        (2) They prepare their storerooms for the food.

(3) They gather the food from forest and field and carry it home in their "cheek pockets."
(4) They store away an abundance of nuts and grain.
(5) When winter comes they have plenty to eat.

Suggestions for developing the story and using the illustrative material: As the first part of the story is told, sketch the blackboard scenes in their order — the grass, grain, corn, and barn. Show the pictures of the horse and the cows. In the second part of the story sketch the other parts of the blackboard scenes, and use the three pictures of the squirrels. In both parts the blackboard work must develop with the story. Let the children examine the pictures and encourage them to talk about them. Ask the class a few simple questions, the answers to which shall express the main elements of the story. In connection with these questions use the objects which have been prepared. Then repeat to the class the selected verses; and finally ask the children to repeat the memory verse learned last Sunday, which is also the memory verse for today's lesson.

Desired Results.

A deepening of the impression of the wisdom and love of God in providing an abundance of the right kind of food for the animals of field and forest. Also a deepening of the impression of the thoughtfulness of God in remembering his creatures at all times, in winter as well as in summer. The awakening of a feeling of gratitude to God for his goodness (this developed in Lessons 9-11).

Memory Verse.

"Your heavenly Father feedeth them" (Matt. 6:26).

58 BIBLE-SCHOOL CURRICULUM

Home Work.

Pasting into the album the pictures "Brittany" and "The Fox Squirrel," together with the slips containing the memory verse and the verses about the squirrels and the plowman. Review of the lesson story by the parents. Reading to the child the selected verses. Helping the child to commit thoroughly to memory the memory verse. Observation work as suggested.

LESSON 8

GOD PROVIDING FOOD FOR THE BIRDS OF THE AIR

Lesson Material.

For story: Gould, *Mother Nature's Children*, pp. 57-64; also see the story outline below, "God Providing Food for the Birds of the Air."

For study: Merriam, *Birds through an Opera-Glass;* Burroughs, *Birds and Bees;* Buckley, *Winners in Life's Race,* chaps. vi-vii; Longfellow, "The Birds of Killingworth."

Illustrative Material and Suggestions.

Pictures: The following Mumford pictures: "The Robin," No. 16; "The Humming Bird," No. 212; "The Woodpecker," No. 521; "Sea-Gulls," No. 185; and "The Crow," No. 26.

Literature: Use the following verses: "Lisa and the Birds," adapted from the Norwegian by Emilie Poulsson, from *In the Child's World,* pp. 13, 14:

> "Tell me," said little Lisa,
>   The pretty child so sweet,
> "Where do you tiny birdies
>   Find all you need to eat?"

The little birds in answer
  Sang cheerily: "We know!
For us a dainty table
  Is spread where'er we go;
The good brown earth, so kindly,
  Has scarce a single plant
Which will not feast the birdies
  When seeds or fruits they want."

Then said the loving Lisa:
  "When winter cold is here
And everything is frozen,
  Oh, you will starve, I fear!"
Again the birds chirped gaily:
  "O little maiden kind,
We fly to lands of sunshine,
  Where summer joys we find.
And for the birds who stay here,
  Ev'n when cold winter comes,
Some child as sweet as you, dear,
  Will surely scatter crumbs."

Memory verse printed on slips of paper for distribution.

Observation: Ask the children, during the week, to watch the birds, and to find out all they can about the different kinds of food the birds eat.

Lesson Treatment.

Connecting links: Briefly review the last lesson. Question the children about their observation work. We have learned about how God provides food for the plants and trees, and for the animals of the fields and forests, and today we are to learn about how he cares for the birds of the air.

Preparation: Question the children about the birds. What kinds have they seen? Where have they seen them? What have they been doing? Have they ever seen them searching for food? Where? What do they find? Today our story will tell us about how God cares for the many kinds of birds, providing plenty of just the right kind of food for each one.

Presentation: Present the story matter in the following detail:

1. Food from the sea.
    a) The abundance of fish in the sea.
    b) The sea-gulls and other birds find their food there.
        (1) They live near the sea.
        (2) They have strong wings.
        (3) They are expert fishers.
2. Food from the earth.
    a) The robins find worms in the earth.
    b) The woodpeckers find insects in the tree trunks.
    c) The humming-birds find honey in flowers.
        (1) The honey hidden away in the bottom of the flower.
        (2) The humming-bird has a long, slender bill to reach the honey.
        (3) In addition to this he has a long, slender tongue.
    d) Many birds find abundance of food in the seeds of plants.
    e) Corn, grain, and all kinds of fruit also provide the birds with food.
3. Food from the air.
    a) The air is full of insect life.
    b) The swift-flying swallows find their food here.

Suggestions for developing the story and using the illustrative material: As each part of the story is given, show the picture of the bird told about. Encourage the children to question freely, and to tell the class if they have noticed anything about the birds feeding. The sparrow, robin, and other birds feeding is such a common sight that even little children have probably noticed it. Ask the class a few simple questions, the answers to which shall express the main elements of the story. Repeat to the class the verses about "Lisa and the Birds," and then question the children as to what they have learned about the food provided for the trees and plants, for the animals, and for the birds. Who provides all this food? Have the class repeat the memory verse several times to make sure that the thought of the verse has been associated with the lessons already given.

Desired Results.

God's wisdom and love in providing an abundance of the right kind of food for all of his creatures now clearly seen. The impression of the thoughtfulness of God in remembering all of his creatures all the time now a matter of knowledge and belief. The strengthening of the awakened feeling of gratitude to God for all of his goodness.

Memory Verse.

"Your heavenly Father feedeth them" (Matt. 6:26).

Home Work.

Pasting into the album the selected picture (let the children select from the number suggested above), together with the slips containing the memory verse and the verses about "Lisa and the Birds." Review of the lesson story by the parents. Reading to the child the verses "Lisa and the Birds." A further drill upon the memory verse. Observation work as suggested.

BIBLE-SCHOOL CURRICULUM

§ 3. BOOKS RELATING TO THE WORK OF GRADE A

A. REFERENCE READING FOR THE TEACHER

Allen, *The Story of the Plants* (D. Appleton & Co., New York).

Beard, *Curious Homes and Their Tenants* (D. Appleton & Co., New York).

Buckley, *Fairy Land of Science, Life and Her Children,* and *Winners in Life's Race* (D. Appleton & Co., New York).

Burroughs, *Squirrels and Other Fur-Bearers,* and *Birds and Bees* (Houghton, Mifflin & Co., Boston).

Dana, *Plants and Their Children* (American Book Co., New York).

Gould, *Mother Nature's Children* (Ginn & Co., Boston).

Kelly, *Leaves from Mother Nature's Story Book* (Educational Publishing Co., Boston).

Merriam, *Birds through an Opera-Glass* (Houghton, Mifflin & Co., Boston).

Miller, *Little Folks in Feather and Fur* (E. P. Dutton & Co., New York).

Seeley, *The Story of the Earth* (D. Appleton & Co., New York).

Shaler, *Outlines of the Earth's History* (D. Appleton & Co., New York).

Warren, *From September to June with Nature* (D. C. Heath & Co., Boston).

Wilkinson, *The Story of the Cotton Plant* (D. Appleton & Co., New York).

The magazine *Birds and All Nature* (A. W. Mumford, Chicago).

B. SUPPLEMENTAL READING FOR THE PUPIL

(Containing story material to be read to the pupils by the parents)

Andrews, *Stories Mother Nature Told Her Children* (Ginn & Co., Boston).

Bass, *Stories of Plant Life* (D. C. Heath & Co., Boston).

Booth, *Sleepy Time Stories* (G. P. Putnam's Sons, New York).
Griel, *Glimpses of Nature for Little Folks* (D. C. Heath & Co., Boston).
Lindsay, *Mother Stories* (Milton Bradley Co., Springfield, Mass.).
McCullough, *Little Stories for Little People* (American Book Co., New York).
Winnington, *The Outlook Story Book for Little People* (The Outlook Co., New York).

C. SONG MATERIAL FOR GRADES A AND B

Gaynor, *Songs of the Child World* (The John Church Co., New York).
Hailmann, *Songs, Games and Rhymes* (Milton Bradley Co., Springfield, Mass.).
Hill, *Song Stories for the Kindergarten* (Clayton F. Summy Co., Chicago).
Jenks and Rust, *Song Echoes from Child Land* (Oliver Ditson Co., Boston).
Knowlton, *Nature Songs for Children* (Milton Bradley Co., Springfield, Mass.).
Mills and Merriam, *Nature Songs and Stories* (The Terry Engraving Co., Columbus, O.).
Smith, *Songs for Little Children,* Parts I and II (Milton Bradley Co., Springfield, Mass.).
Walker and Jenks, *Songs and Games for Little Ones* (Oliver Ditson Co., Boston).

NOTE.— In this and the following lists of books for teachers, only a few of general interest are suggested. Most of these, however, give condensed bibliographies of the subject of which they treat, thus enabling the teacher to study a subject as thoroughly as desired.

§ 4. OUTLINE OF THE COURSE FOR GRADE B

GRADE SUBJECT: ALL NATURE WORKING TOGETHER WITH GOD THE CREATOR

Topic 1 — The sun.
　The story of a sunbeam:
　　1. Giving light.
　　2. Giving warmth.
　　3. Giving life.
　　4. *Review.*

Topic 2 — The rain.
　The story of the rain:
　　5. Refreshing the flowers.
　　6. Refreshing the animals.
　　7. Cooling the air.
　　8. *Review.*

Topic 3 — The wind.
　The story of the wind:
　　9. Scattering the seed.
　　10. Carrying the rain clouds.
　　11. Changing the air.
　　12. Helping man.
　　13. *Review.*

Topic 4 — The seasons.
　14. The story of the spring — waking time.
　15. The story of the summer — growing time.
　16. The story of the autumn — harvest time.
　17. The story of the winter — resting time.
　18. *Review.*

Topic 5 — The insects.

The story of the ants:
19. Their home life.
20. Their daily work.

The story of the bees:
21. Their home life.
22. Their daily work.
23. *Review.*

Topic 6 — The birds.
24. The story of the bird's nest.
25. The story of the birdlings.
26. The story of the watchful father.
27. The story of the first lessons.
28. *Review.*

Topic 7 — The animals.
29. The story of the beavers — building houses.
30. The story of the squirrels — laying up food.
31. The story of the deer — warning of danger.
32. The story of the horse — protecting the weak.
33. *Review.*

Topic 8 — The work of man.

The story of some grains of wheat:
34. In the great wheat field.
35. In the flour mill.

The story of some drops of water:
36. In the rain clouds.
37. Supplying our homes.
38. *Review.*

The story of the forest tree:
39. In the great forest.
40. In the saw-mill.

The story of a piece of coal:
41. In the dark mine.
42. In the factory and home.
43. *Review.*
44. The story of a bit of wool.
45. The story of a bit of cotton.
46. The story of the flowers.
47. The story of a picture.
48. The story of a song.
49. The story of a book.
50. *Review.*

Special Lessons.
51. The Christmas lesson (in its proper place).
52. The Easter lesson (in its proper place).

§ 5. SUGGESTIVE LESSON PLANS FOR GRADE B
(LESSONS 9–11)

LESSON 9
THE WIND SCATTERING THE SEED

Lesson Material.
For story: "How the West Wind Helped Dandelion," from Poulsson's *In the Child's World*, pp. 65 ff.
For study: Gould, *Mother Nature's Children*, pp. 121-28; Morley, *Little Wanderers;* Weed, *Seed Travellers;* Beal, *Seed Dispersal.*

Illustrative Material and Suggestions.
Objects: Dandelion, maple, milkweed, and thistle seeds.
Picture: "Spring," Knaus.
Blackboard: As the story is developed, sketch the picture of the dandelions with the wind blowing away the seeds.

Literature: Use the following verse, adapted from the "Weather Vane" by Laura E. Richards, given in Blow's *Songs and Music of Froebel's Mother Play*.

"Pretty seeds, what makes you fly,
   Now here, now there, now low, now high?"
      "'Tis the wind lifts me!
         'Tis the wind drifts me!
   Tosses me in merry play,
   Here and there and every way."

Memory verse printed on slips of paper for distribution.
Observation: Ask the children to watch, during the week, for seeds that the wind can scatter about, thus helping God to make the world beautiful.

Lesson Treatment.

Connecting links: Review the lessons about the Rain Helping. Also review the memory verse and the other verses which may have been learned in connection with the lessons. For the next few Sundays we are to learn about another helper which God has and which we have, and about some of the ways in which this helper helps.

Preparation:

General for the section:
Question the children about the wind. It cannot be seen, but we know it is here because we feel it. Who sends the wind? What does it do? Our stories for the next few Sundays will tell us of different ways in which the wind works or helps.

Special for the lesson:
Question the children about garden seeds. If one wants flowers, what must be planted? Who plants the seeds? Where? But we find flowers and plants in the fields and in the woods, not alone in the gar-

dens. Do they come from seeds? Do these seeds have to be planted? Yes, and we shall see in our story today how this is done.

Presentation: Present the story matter in the following detail:

1. Dandelion and her friends.
    a) Field friends — sun, rain, wind, birds, wild flowers.
    b) Garden friends — cultivated flowers, morning glory, sweet pea, etc.
2. Dandelion at work, making seeds.
3. Dandelion and the two children.
    a) Max and Nannie gathering seeds.
    b) They slight Dandelion in the gathering.
    c) Dandelion's questions.
4. Dandelion and the friendly wind.
    a) Dandelion's wish.
    b) Dandelion's wish answered by the wind.
    c) Dandelion's happiness.

Suggestions for developing the story and using the illustrative material: Try to have the children see the four pictures as suggested by the story outline. As the dandelion and her field friends and garden friends are described, sketch on the board the garden with the dandelion prominent. When the description of dandelion at work making seeds is given, draw the seed balls; and when the work of the west wind is spoken of, make seeds flying from the balls in the direction of the wind. At the close of the story show the different seeds, and point out to the children how well adapted the seeds are to being carried about by the wind. Show the picture, and encourage the children to talk about it. Ask the children a few simple questions, the answers to which shall express the main elements of the story. Then repeat to the class the verse about the "Seeds and the Wind," and finally give the memory verse and have the children repeat it, but do not try to have it committed to memory at this time.

Desired Results.

The impression of the wind as another one of God's helpers helping him in his plans by scattering the seeds everywhere to make the world beautiful. A deepening of the impression that everything is doing something to help, and a strengthening of the desire on the part of the child to be a helper in whatever way he can.

Memory Verse.

"He causeth his wind to blow" (Ps. 147: 18a).

Home Work.

Pasting into the album the selected picture, "Spring," together with the slips containing the memory verse and the verse about the "Seeds and the Wind." Review of the lesson story by the parents. Reading to the child the verse about the "Seeds and the Wind." Helping the child to commit to memory the memory verse. Observation work as suggested.

LESSON 10

THE WIND CARRYING THE RAIN CLOUDS

Lesson Material.

For story: A portion of the story (adapted) "Do What You Can," from Poulsson's *In the Child's World*, p. 235; see the story outline below, "How the Wind Helped the Farmer."

For study: 1 Kings 18: 41–46; Gray, *Nature's Miracles*, Vol. I, pp. 60–87; Buckley, *Fairy Land of Science*, Lectures III, IV; Eytinge, "Story of the Morning-Glory Seed," in the *Boston Collection of Kindergarten Stories*.

Illustrative Material and Suggestions.

Pictures: "June Clouds," Hunt; "Landscape with Mill," Ruisdael.

Blackboard: A sketch of the field, the growing corn, the gathering clouds, and finally the welcome rain. A very few lines with the crayons will suggest the various parts of the picture; the simpler the sketch the better.

Literature: Use the following verse adapted from Robert Louis Stevenson's "Wind Song":

> O wind a-blowing all day long!
> O wind that sings so loud a song!
> I saw you toss the kites on high,
> And blow the clouds about the sky,
> And all around I heard you pass
> Like ladies' skirts across the grass.
> O wind a-blowing all day long!
> O wind that sings so loud a song!

Memory verse printed on slips of paper for distribution.

Observation: Ask the children to watch, during the week, for the wind blowing the clouds about. Perhaps they may see the wind blow the rain clouds across the sky, bringing rain to them.

Lesson Treatment.

Connecting links: Briefly review the last lesson. Last Sunday we saw one way in which the wind helps. Today we shall learn about another way in which this helper works.

Preparation: Question the children about plant growth. After the seeds are planted, what is needed to make them grow? Plenty of good air? And sunshine? Yes, and something else. The rain. Yes, and our story today will tell us **how** the wind helps to bring the rain.

Presentation: Present the story matter in the following detail:
1. The farmer and his cornfield.
    a) The farmer prepares his field.
    b) He sows the corn.
    c) He cares for the field — harrowing and weeding it.
2. The need of rain.
    a) No rain falls upon the field.
    b) The corn begins to wither.
    c) The farmer fears he will lose his crop.
    d) He goes out every day to watch for rain.
3. The gathering of the rain clouds.
    a) Great rain clouds are seen in the distance.
    b) The farmer anxiously watches the clouds.
    c) His great disappointment — no rain comes.
4. The wind and how it helped.
    a) The wind sees the farmer's trouble.
    b) It blows the rain clouds over the corn-field.
    c) Abundance of rain falls.
    d) The joy and thanksgiving of the farmer.

Suggestions for developing the story and using the illustrative material: Try to have the children see the four pictures as suggested by the story outline. As the story is developed, sketch the various scenes. In the first scene the flat side of the crayon may be used to draw the field; one or two stalks of corn will be enough to suggest the entire field to the children. As the second part of the story is told, sketch the sun in the upper left-hand corner of the board. For drawing the rain clouds use the flat side of the crayon and begin at the right of the board. As the last part of the story is told, erase the sun and fill in the sky with more of the heavy clouds. A few downward strokes of the crayon from the clouds will suggest the rain storm. At the close of the story show the two pictures, and let the children talk about them. Ask the children a few simple questions, the answers to which shall express the main elements of the story. Then repeat to the class the verse about the wind; and finally have the children repeat the memory verse, and ask them what they have already learned about this wind that God causes to blow.

Desired Results.

A deepening of the impression of the wind as one of God's helpers, helping him in his plans by blowing the rain clouds about that the seeds which have been planted everywhere, in the fields and in the gardens and in the meadows, may have the rain which is needed to make them grow. A deepening of the impression that everything is doing something to help, and a strengthening of the desire on the part of the child to be a helper in whatever way he can. The wind helps in various ways; the children may help in various ways.

Memory Verse.

"He causeth his wind to blow" (Ps. 147: 18a).

Home Work.

Pasting of the selected picture, "June Clouds" or "Landscape with Mill," into the album, together with the slips containing the memory verse and the verse from Stevenson's "Wind Song." Review of the lesson story by the parents. Reading to the child the verse about the "Wind." Helping the child to commit thoroughly to memory the memory verse. Observation work as suggested.

KINDERGARTEN COURSE OF STUDY 73

LESSON 11
THE WIND CHANGING THE AIR

Lesson Material.

For story: See the story outline below, "How the Wind Brought Gladness to Many."

For study: McRoy, "The Story of a Breeze," in Poulsson's *In the Child's World*, pp. 390-92; Bryant, "The Evening Wind;" Gray, *Nature's Miracles,* Vol. I, pp. 60-87; Buckley, *Fairy Land of Science,* Lectures III, IV.

Illustrative Material and Suggestions.

Pictures: Use pictures of any large city, such as the Perry, Nos. 2001, 2002, 2003, and 2004.

Literature: Use the following verses, "What the Winds Bring," by E. C. Stedman, found in the *Boston Collection of Kindergarten Stories:*

"Which is the Wind that brings the cold?"
"The North Wind, Freddie, and all the snow;
And the Sheep will scamper into the fold
    When the North begins to blow."

"Which is the Wind that brings the heat?"
"The South Wind, Katy; and Corn will grow,
And Peaches redden for you to eat,
    When the South begins to blow."

"Which is the Wind that brings the rain?"
"The East Wind, Arty; and farmers know
That Cows come shivering up the lane
    When the East begins to blow."

"Which is the Wind that brings the flowers?"
"The West Wind, Bessie; and soft and low
The Birdies sing in Summer hours
    When the West begins to blow."

Memory verse printed on slips of paper for distribution.

Observation: Ask the children to watch, during the week, for the wind blowing the smoke from the chimneys. Also ask them to note changes in the air due to the warm and the cold winds that blow at different times.

Lesson Treatment.

Connecting links: Review the last two lessons. Have the review include the memory verse and the results of the children's observation work. We have learned about two ways in which the wind helps, and today we shall learn about a third way.

Preparation: Question the children about their summer experiences. Was the weather ever warm? And were they sometimes very hot and tired? Were they always well? If sick, how did they feel on a very hot day? Was the air always clear and pure? Why not? (Smoke, gas, dust, etc.) And have they often wished that the air might be made pure and refreshing and cool? Our story today will tell us how this is done, and of the helper who does it.

Presentation: Present the story matter in the following detail:

1. The wind clearing the air.
    a) Smoke, gas, and dust make the air impure.
    b) The need of pure air.
    c) The wind makes the air pure by blowing away the smoke, gas, and dust.
    d) All the people are glad as they breathe the pure air.
2. The wind cooling the air.
    a) The hot days in the city streets.
    b) The suffering it brings to all — men and animals.

  c) The north wind blows and cools the air.
  d) All feel the cool breeze and are glad.
 3. The wind refreshing the workers.
  a) The great shops and factories of the city.
  b) The many hot and tired workers.
  c) The cool wind blows through the open windows.
  d) The workers are cheered and strengthened.
 4. The wind refreshing the sick.
  a) The great city hospitals.
  b) The many sick ones.
  c) The discomfort and pain caused by hot days.
  d) The wind changes and cools the air.
  e) The sick ones are refreshed and helped.

Suggestions for developing the story and using the illustrative material: As the blackboard is not to be used, the teacher will have to make the story a word-picture, presenting the four scenes as vividly as possible. Show the pictures of the city streets and buildings as the story is told, and let the children talk freely about the different scenes after they have been pictured to them. Ask the children a few simple questions, the answers to which shall express the main elements of the story. Then repeat to the class the verses about the "Winds," and have the children repeat the memory verse. At the lesson's close ask about the three ways they have found this wind that God causes to blow, helping him in his plans.

Desired Results.

The deepening of the impression of the wind as another one of God's helpers, helping him in his plans by changing and cooling the air, thus bringing health and gladness to all of God's creatures. A further deepening of the impression that all the natural forces are God's helpers, working with him, and a strengthening of the awakened desire on the part of the child to be a helper like them. If the wind can help in so many ways, surely a little child can find many ways in which to help.

Memory Verse.

"He causeth his wind to blow" (Ps. 147: 18a).

Home Work.

Pasting of the selected picture into the album, together with the slips containing the memory verse and the verses about the "Winds." Review of the lesson story by the parents. Reading to the child the verses about "What the Winds Bring." Review and drill on the memory verse. Observation work as suggested.

---

§ 6. BOOKS RELATING TO THE WORK OF GRADE B

A. REFERENCE READING FOR THE TEACHER

Andrews, *The Story of My Four Friends* (Ginn & Co., Boston).

Baskett, *The Story of the Birds* (D. Appleton & Co., New York).

Bradish, *Stories of Country Life* (American Book Co., New York).

Buckley, *The Fairy Land of Science,* and *Winners in Life's Race* (D. Appleton & Co., New York).

Burroughs, *Birds and Bees,* and *Sharp Eyes and Other Papers* (Houghton, Mifflin & Co., Boston).

Chase and Clow, *Stories of Industry,* Parts I and II (Educational Publishing Co., Boston).

Edgar, *The Story of a Grain of Wheat* (D. Appleton & Co., New York).

Gould, *Mother Nature's Children* (Ginn & Co., Boston).

Kelly, *Leaves from Nature's Story Book* (Educational Publishing Co., Boston).

Lindsay, *The Story of Animal Life* (D. Appleton & Co., New York).

Martin, *The Story of a Piece of Coal* (D. Appleton & Co., New York).
Merriam, *Birds of Village and Field* (Houghton, Mifflin & Co., Boston).
Miller, *A First Book of Birds* (Houghton, Mifflin & Co., Boston).
Rawlings, *The Story of Books* (D. Appleton & Co., New York).
Vincent, *The Animal World* (D. Appleton & Co., New York).
Weed, *The Insect World* (D. Appleton & Co., New York).
Wilkinson, *The Story of the Cotton Plant* (D. Appleton & Co., New York).
The magazine *Birds and All Nature* (A. W. Mumford, Chicago).

B. SUPPLEMENTAL READING FOR THE PUPIL

(Containing story material to be read to the pupils by the parents)

Bass, *Stories of Animal Life* (D. C. Heath & Co., Boston).
Bartlett, *Animals at Home* (American Book Co., New York).
Chase, *Stories from Birdland,* and *Stories from Animal Land* (Educational Publishing Co., Boston).
Eddy, *Friends and Helpers* (Ginn & Co., Boston).
Pierson, *Among the Farmyard People, Among the Meadow People, Among the Pond People, Among the Forest People, Among the Night People* (E. P. Dutton & Co., New York).
Poulsson, *In the Child's World* (Milton Bradley Co., Springfield, Mass.).

CHAPTER III

THE PRIMARY CHILD

THE primary child — *i. e.*, the child from six to nine years of age — is in many respects like the kindergarten child, but in some respects he is quite different. The senses continue their development, reaching practical perfection toward the close of the period. It is also a time of rapid muscular and neural development, and of the development to functional activity of the brain cells. In general, we may say that the characteristics noted in the first half of the childhood period are all present in this half, some more developed and some weaker; and, in addition, some other characteristics become more prominent.

Some characteristics of the period.— The animistic tendency, although still strong, is gradually weakening, and during the next period may be practically disregarded. The child is still very suggestible, but, owing to the strengthening of his will and the increase of his stock of ideas, he is not so open to suggestions from his environment, but acts more from his own initiative. The imitative instinct is still active. There seems to be a slight increase in the tendency to imitate adult activities. There is also a strengthening of the tendency to imitate the idea rather than the actual thing, due to the growth of the understanding and the imagination, and to combine dramatic speech with dramatic action in imitative playing.[1] The power of the imagination still holds the child in its grasp. The field for its activity has widened, and the material at hand for its use has greatly increased in amount. The imagination, although still crude, is developing rapidly into a higher form of the productive or creative type. The growth of the intellectual and feeling sides of the child's nature strongly influences the direction of his imagination, which is so intimately bound up with this life of feeling that it will assume as many directions as this life assumes.

Hence the familiar fact that in some children imagination broods by preference on gloomy and terrifying objects, religious and other, whereas in others it selects what is bright and gladsome; that while in some cases it has more of the poetic quality, in others it leans rather to the scientific or to the practical type.[2]

Because of this intimate relationship a study of the children's imaginings will give the teacher many a clue to their spontaneous interests. Burnham, speaking of this relation of imagination to interest, says:

[1] MISS CAROLINE FREAR, *Pedagogical Seminary*, Vol. IV, pp. 382 ff.

[2] SULLY, *op. cit.*, p. 27.

Here in a child's imaginings is a vast fund of spontaneous interest. How to utilize it; how to check imagination when extreme without wasting this spontaneous interest; how to develop imagination when deficient — in a word, how to adapt education to individual differences in productive imagination — such are the teacher's problems. These questions have not been satisfactorily answered, and only by the patient study of many children and of the effects of various methods of education can a satisfactory answer be obtained. But modern education has recognized one fact: God has made men different. It is the merest platitude of everyday philosophy that there is infinite variety in the talents and in the deficiencies of human beings. Teachers must study the individual differences in their pupils.[8]

There is certainly as great need of emphasizing the importance of a study of individual differences in children in connection with their religious training, for too many of our Bible-school teachers of the present time treat their classes as units rather than as an aggregate of units, each individual differing in some respects from all other members of the class. In normal children there is a growth in unselfishness during these years. Miss Frear's study of "Imitation" shows a marked development of the social instinct which, as previously noted, tends to counteract the expression of selfishness. She says in this connection:

[8] *Pedagogical Seminary*, Vol. II, p. 224.

The tendency for a child to play with an adult is marked during the first year, after which for two or three years he is satisfied to play by himself. Then this tendency decreases, and with the development of the social instinct the tendency to play with other children increases rapidly and steadily.⁴

The growth of the spirit of sympathy and helpfulness also tends to bring under control the selfish spirit. The fears of children tend to increase during the years from six to ten; the increase being of fears having their source in the imagination, which at this time is rapidly developing. These fears may then to a certain extent be controlled by restraining or guiding the imagination, and also by a watchful care of the environment of the children and of the stories they read and hear; for these are two of the most fertile sources of the fears of this latter part of childhood.

A serious charge brought against children is that of lying. This term seems too harsh a term to apply to the untruths and little deceptions of young children, for

a lie connotes, or should connote, an assertion made with full consciousness of its untruth and in order to mislead. It may well be doubted whether little children have so clear an apprehension of what we understand by truth and falsity as to be liars in this full sense. Much of what seems

⁴ *Ibid.*, Vol. IV, p. 384.

shocking to the adult unable to place himself at the level of childish intelligence and feeling will probably prove to be something far less serious.[5]

Sully mentions five of the most common causes of untruthfulness, or so-called lying, as follows:[6] (1) The desire to secrete things or hold back information considered private. This leads only to very mild forms of deception, but may lead in its more serious aspects to serious results. (2) The power of the childish imagination. This is one of the most fertile sources of children's lies so-called. The child is scarcely able to distinguish between a memory-image derived from the senses and one which is due entirely to the imagination. (3) Susceptibility of the child to suggestion. Older people's wishes and expectations strongly influence the child-mind, and may lead to misstatements. Sometimes imagination and suggestion combine to produce startling results. (4) The wish to please and the fear of giving offense. (5) Our methods of moral discipline. Fear of restraint or punishment will lead many children to tell untruths. At times questions asked in connection with moral discipline may also result in falsehoods.

Lies due to other causes are reported by

[5] SULLY, op. cit., p. 252.
[6] Ibid., pp. 252–61.

President G. Stanley Hall.[7] Among these are the following: (1) The lie heroic. This is justified in the mind of the one telling the lie as a means to a noble end. Here belong false confessions where strong children assume penalties of weaker ones. (2) Personal likes and dislikes; truth for friends and lies for enemies. The child in this respect is like the savage. (3) Selfishness; manifested in games, plays, in school work, or in any case where there is a likelihood of advantage being gained or lost.

The facility with which a whole street or school may be corrupted in this respect, often without suspicion on the part of adults, by a single bold, bad, but popular child; the immunity from detection which school offers so much more than home, for even habitual liars of this class; as well as the degree of moral degradation to which they may lead, all point to selfish falsehoods — especially when their prevalence is taken into account — as on the whole the most dangerous, corrupting, and hard to correct of any of our species. Excessive emulations, penalties, opportunities, and temptations should of course be reduced, but it should be clearly seen that all these lies are at bottom forms of self-indulgence, and should in the great majority of cases be treated as such, rather than dealt with directly as lies.[8]

In coming to conclusions concerning the importance of the subject, we must remember that a lie told usually brings in with it a train

[7] *Pedagogical Seminary*, Vol. I, pp. 211-18.
[8] HALL, *ibid.*, p. 213.

of lies for support of the first one; that the impulse to stick to an untruth is very strong, and is increased by the fear of discovery and punishment; that the habit of lying is easily formed; and that lying is apt to be contagious, perhaps due to the power of suggestion and the imitative instinct.

Another common characteristic of childhood is the teasing and bullying propensity. This manifests itself in various ways — fighting, assertion of authority, tormenting for various ends, like exciting fear, anger, shame, temper, etc. The study of the subject by Frederic L. Burk [9] shows that the characteristic is not marked during the early half of the period, but increases very rapidly from six to ten years of age, in most cases growing weaker after this. All the manifestations mentioned seem to be rooted in and to develop from a sense of power. If these impulses or this sense of power can be associated with the right ethical ideas as to use and direction, they may have a large educative effect upon the child, and be of great value in his moral and religious development.

The attitude of children toward law is difficult to determine, as there are so many factors to be taken into acount. Two distinct views are held: one, that children are essentially disobedi-

[9] *Ibid.*, Vol., IV, pp. 336 ff.

ent; and the other, that they are by nature law-abiding.[10] The truth would seem to be in both claims; children rebel against restraint of any kind, but at the same time have an instinctive respect for custom or rule. A study by Miss Darrah[11] shows clearly that children regard the law embodied in personal commands as of great importance, but have little regard for general laws and their penalties. This study also shows that there is a steady growth in the children's regard for general law from the age of eight years upward. The studies of Barnes,[12] Miss Schallenberger,[13] and Miss Frear[14] agree in general with these results.

Many children, perhaps the majority, are superstitious. There are a few superstitions, such as the belief in pin-luck, that seem to be generally known and practiced by all children; many others are individual affairs. From a study of the subject Miss Vostrovsky concludes that

the superstitions of seven-, eight-, and nine-year-old children are more simple and general in character than the superstitions of older children. . . . . Superstitions spread,

---

[10] For illustrations of both attitudes see SULLY, *op. cit.*, pp. 267–97.

[11] *Studies in Education*, Vol. I, pp. 254 ff.

[12] *Ibid.*, Vol. I, pp. 366.

[13] *Pedagogical Seminary*, Vol. III, pp. 87 ff.

[14] *Studies in Education*, Vol. I, p. 332.

like other traditions, mainly through personal communications. . . . . Total disbelief in superstitions increases with age.[15]

She concludes her study with these words:

> One thing more of importance to pedagogy that comes out strikingly in the study is the seeming ignorance of our school children concerning natural causation. This seems hardly excusable in this so-called scientific age. If there ever was need of children's realizing and understanding, as far as they can understand, that nothing in the world happens arbitrarily or through mere chance, there is certainly a need of it now. They should begin to know, even in the primary grades, that the world is governed by law.

The Bible-school teacher can be of service here by impressing upon the child, not only that the world is governed by law, but that law is but an expression of God's will. This aspect of God's nature, however, would be more fully dwelt upon in the next period, the boyhood-girlhood period, from nine to thirteen years of age.

Some interests of the period.— The interest in the causal idea is still strong, the causal idea pertaining to religious objects, such as God, heaven, death, etc., attracting more attention than in the preceding years. It is not a time, however, of great religious interest, which does not come until adolescence. What was said in the preceding chapter concerning the theological ideas and interests of the very young child would also

[15] *Ibid.*, pp. 123 ff.

describe this period, except that there is a tendency to question some of the statements made by parent and teacher, although these questions are few in number and vague in meaning.

The literary interest in fairy and folk-lore stories continues, but toward the close of the period gives way to an interest in narrative history,[16] although a strong interest in history is not felt until the boyhood-girlhood period. Professor Wissler's study[17] indicates an interest in animal stories, but the greatest interest is in stories of daily life, stories in which the human element is prominent. In answer to the question as to why they liked certain stories, nearly 40 per cent. of the children examined answered, because they were true to life. Dr. Dawson, in his study of "Children's Interest in the Bible,"[18] finds the same thing to be true, that "the larger percentage of children of all ages are attracted more strongly to the personal elements of the Bible than to any other." In selecting material for instructional purposes, then, we might use Bible stories which are of the folk-lore type for the first year, and some of the narrative-history stories, preferably the stories of the life of Jesus, in the last year.

One other fact should be noted: that children

[16] MRS. BARNES, *Studies in Education*, Vol. I, p. 89.
[17] *Pedagogical Seminary*, Vol. V, pp. 523 ff.
[18] *Ibid.*, Vol. VII, pp. 151 ff.

during this period begin to show an interest in stories which have a definite moral content, but the moral purpose must not be obtrusive, for "the moral lesson without the formal statement in conclusion, but bearing upon it the marks of a moral purpose, received less attention than the simple story whose moral force was felt and appreciated." [19]

The mental powers during the period.— The perceptive powers are still the dominant ones, and in all lesson work an appeal must be made to the senses.

Memory, especially toward the close of the period, is rapidly growing stronger, and considerable memory work may be given; but it must be kept in mind that verbal memory does not reach its maximum strength until the age of thirteen or fourteen, and care should be taken at this time not to strain the memory by requiring the committal from week to week of a large number of Bible verses. Imagination is stronger, but still needs an objective basis for its activity.

The reasoning powers are not sufficiently developed to be appealed to to any great extent. The teaching must continue to be largely suggestive and by analogies, and the method must lead the children by very clear and easy steps to the lesson truths.

[19] WISSLER, *loc. cit.*, p. 535.

Conscience is more active in normal children with normal environment, but as yet it is not an important factor in the work.

Some conclusions with reference to a course of study for the child from six to nine years of age.—During these years God as a Worker, as a Provider of all needful things, is the general aspect of God's nature which would continue to appeal to the child; but as at this time the interest in the home and the home activities, privileges, and duties is stronger, and the home means more to the child, God may be presented as a Father working and providing for his children. We must be careful, however, in this connection to present only those truths after which the child is beginning to reach out, or which he sees as expressions of parent love in the home. Such topics as God's care, help, protection, guidance, and the like are within the child's comprehension, and, if rightly presented, will help him to a simple but helpful conception of God as a Father, although all his mental imagery will be anthropomorphic in form. Following this, he might have presented to him some of the homely but important ethical truths, and their application to his life indicated; and some of the simpler, more fundamental truths concerning God and the relation of the child to him. The material for this part of the course would be selected from the Old Testament rather than from the New, for the content and form of these Old Testament stories seem much better adapted to the interests and powers of this stage of childhood. Before leaving the primary department for the next higher one, he should become acquainted with the life of Jesus, this life of lives, however, being presented in its humanity rather than in its divinity, leaving this latter aspect to be emphasized in the period of adolescence. In presenting to the child such a course of instruction as is here suggested the teacher must beware of generalizations and abstractions. The true and the good must be given concretely, the story matter being presented as a unit, and the child led by slow, easy steps to a clear perception of definite aspects of such truths as are within his comprehension and which seem to be called for by his condition. The child-mind develops slowly, and because his thought-powers are comparatively weak he grasps the content of an idea only after repeated presentations of that idea in concrete form. After he has in his childish way glimpsed a great truth, he must not be left to himself to apply it, but the teacher must suggest possible applications of that truth, thus guiding as well as stimulating him to the helpful actualization of the thought in character.

An outline of a suggested course of study is given in the next chapter. In Grade C the father-love of God is presented, this love being shown in providing for the needs of the child other than his physical ones; in Grade D the wise Father indicates certain laws which are to be kept, these laws being for the child's own good; and in Grade E there is a simple presentation of the life of Jesus as the children's friend and helper. The children who take this course of three years, following that of the kindergarten grades, will have their view of God's goodness, wisdom, love, and power broadened, their sense of gratitude to the heavenly Father deepened, and their desire to know and to follow the laws of God strengthened.

CHAPTER IV
A COURSE OF STUDY FOR THE PRIMARY GRADES

GENERAL SUBJECT: GOD THE LOVING FATHER AND HIS CHILDREN

§ 1. OUTLINE OF THE COURSE FOR GRADE C

GRADE SUBJECT: GOD THE LOVING FATHER PROVIDING FOR HIS CHILDREN'S NEEDS.

Topic 1—Providing care.
1. Caring for all nature.
2. Caring for Elijah.
3. Caring for Moses.
4. Caring for Ishmael and Hagar.
5. Caring for many. (The story of the children of Israel in the wilderness.)
6. Caring for us.
7. Our helping God to care for all things.
8. *Review.*

Topic 2—Providing help.
9. The unseen helpers. (Story of Elisha at Dothan.)
10. Helping Peter.
11. Helping Naaman.
12. Helping Elijah.
13. Helping many. (Story of the crossing of the Red Sea.)
14. Helping us.
15. Our helping God to help all.
16. *Review.*

Topic 3—Providing protection.
17. Promising protection. (Story of Jacob at Bethel.)
18. Protecting Joseph.

Primary Course of Study

19. Protecting David.
20. Protecting Daniel.
21. Protecting many. (Story of the cloud of fire.)
22. Protecting us.
23. Our helping God to protect all.
24. *Review.*
25. Psalm 23. Teaching and memory work.

Topic 4—Providing a home.
26. Elijah taken home.
27. Moses taken home.
28. The home beautiful.
29. Who shall live there?
30. A home for all.
31. Jesus going before.
32. A home for us.
33. *Review.*

Topic 5—Providing a guide-book.
34. Abram the first guide.
35. Moses the guide of many people.
36. The prophets the guides of kings.
37. The beginning of the guide-book. (The formation of the Old Testament.)
38. Jesus the guide of all.
39. The completion of the guide-book. (The formation of the New Testament.)
40. A guide for us.
41. *Review.*

Topic 6—Providing a helper.
42. The coming of the helper.
43. The early life of the helper.
44. Helping his own people.
45. Helping a strange people.
46. Helping his disciples.

47. A helper for all today.
48. Our helper.
49. *Review.*
50. The Lord's Prayer. Teaching and memory work.

Special Lessons.
51. The Christmas lesson (in its proper place).
52. The Easter lesson (in its proper place).

---

§ 2. SUGGESTIVE LESSON PLANS FOR GRADE C
(LESSONS 1–8)
LESSON 1
CARING FOR ALL NATURE

Lesson Material.

For story: Gen. 1:1–31; 2:1–3; Ps. 104:10–24; Gen. 8:22; 9:12–17.
For study: Gen. 1:1–31; 2:4–25.

Illustrative Material and Suggestions.

Pictures: "By the River Side" and "The Shepherdess," Le Rolle; "The Gleaners," "The Sower," and "The Rainbow," Millet; "Forests," "The Song Sparrow," and "The Gray Squirrel" (Nature Study Publishing Co.); "Sources of the Jordan at Dan."

Blackboard: Draw a circle for the "great round ball on which we live," and print the memory verse around it.

Connecting Links.

Review (by questions so far as possible) enough of the work of the preceding grades to revive the memories of God's power, wisdom, and love in caring for the birds, the flowers, the animals, etc. In these other classes

(Grades A and B) you have learned about the power, wisdom, and love of God as seen in nature, as you have studied the birds, the animals, the flowers, the trees, etc. Now we are to learn more about God through the beautiful stories which we have about him in the book called the Bible. Today we have the story of a wonderful promise God made to man — a promise about his care for all the world.

Preparation.

Question as to the child's love for growing plants, for birds, animals, etc. His love shown by the care given them. When a new pet is given do we promise to care for it? Do we always keep the promise? Ought we to keep it? We have a beautiful story today of a promise God made to man long, long ago, which he has kept perfectly all these long years. And he has given us something to help us remember the promise.

Presentation.

Present the story matter in the following detail:
1. God the Creator.
    a) Making the heavens and the earth.
    b) Everything pronounced good.
    c) Resting and blessing the seventh day.
2. God caring for all things.
    a) Providing springs to supply water.
    b) Providing grass for the cattle.
    c) Providing homes for the birds and animals.
    d) Providing food for all.
3. God's wonderful promise of care.
    a) The promise — seedtime and harvest to continue.
    b) The promise made for all, men and animals.
    c) The rainbow a memory sign for us.
    d) God's goodness in thus promising.
    e) God's faithfulness in keeping the promise.

Desired Results. (Impressions.)

Reviving of the impressions gained in the two preceding grades, A and B, concerning God's power, wisdom, and goodness. A crystallizing of these impressions into the one — God's care for all things. A strengthening of the child's trust in God's promises. The rainbow now a phenomenon with meaning.

Memory Verse.

"The earth is full of the loving kindness of the Lord" (Ps. 33: 5*b*).

Home Work.

Review of the lesson. Parents help the child to retell the story in his own words. In lesson-book paste picture — Millet's "The Rainbow" — and draw a circle for the "great round ball on which we live," with the memory verse printed around it.

Lesson 2

CARING FOR ELIJAH

Lesson Material.

For story: 1 Kings 17: 1-16; James 5: 17, 18.

For study: Heb. 11: 32-34; 1 Kings 18: 2*b*-6; 19: 1-8; Gen. 41: 29-31, 46-49, 53-57; "Men of the Bible" series, *Elijah*, pp. 19-39; Geikie's *Hours with the Bible*, Vol. III, pp. 47-50.

Illustrative Material and Suggestions.

Pictures: "Elijah Fed by Ravens," Allston; Pictures of ravens.

Blackboard: Sketch scene at Cherith — mountains, trees, brook, etc. Sketch scene at Zarephath — walls and gate of the city, path leading to the gate, etc.

Connecting Links.

We have seen how God cares for the birds, animals, flowers, and all nature. We have a story today showing how God cared for one of his servants, a man named Elijah.

Preparation.

Recall the pictures of the birds bringing food to their young. God teaches them to do this. He also provides the food for them. He also provides food for man. Sunshine and rain needed to supply man with food. Results if the rain stops — a *famine*. Our story today is about a time when the rain stopped, a time of famine, and how God cared for one of his servants during that time.

Presentation.

Present the story in the following detail:
1. Elijah the messenger of God.
    a) General appearance — dress, looks, etc.
    b) Sudden appearance before King Ahab.
    c) The message from God to the king.
    d) Why the famine was to be sent.
2. The famine. (Describe.)
3. God's care for Elijah during the famine.
    a) At the brook Cherith; Elijah obeys God and camps at the brook Cherith; the brook furnishes water; the ravens, sent by God, bring food; Elijah's trust and God's care.
    b) At the city Zarephath: Elijah obeys God and journeys to Zarephath; the poor widow and her trouble; Elijah's request and the woman's answer; the promise of God through Elijah his messenger; the promise kept; Elijah and the poor widow cared for; Elijah's trust and God's care.

Desired Results. (Impressions.)

Reviving and deepening of the impression of God's control of all things: his power to do all things; uses the ravens to do his will. God loved Elijah; Elijah trusted God; God cared for Elijah. God's love the same today as in the time of Elijah. We must trust as Elijah did.

Memory Verse.

"The Lord is good" (Ps. 34:8).

Home Work.

Review of the lesson. Parents help the child to retell the story in his own words. In lesson-book paste picture — Allston's "Elijah Fed by Ravens" — and print memory verse beneath.

LESSON 3

CARING FOR MOSES

Lesson Material.

For story: Exod. 1:22—2:10; Acts 7:17-21; Heb. 11:23.

For study: Exod. 1:8-20; Matt. 2:13-15, 19-21; 2 Kings 11:1-3; Ps. 33:10-22; "Men of the Bible" series, *Moses*, pp. 1-20.

Illustrative Material and Suggestions.

Pictures: "Moses Exposed on the Nile," Doré; "Moses Hidden by His Mother," Düsseldorf; "Moses Found by Pharaoh's Daughter," Shopin; "The Finding of Moses," Delaroche; "Moses Exposed on the Nile," Perrault; "Moses Saved from the Nile," Raphaellino. (Select from the above.)

Blackboard: Print the memory verse in plain, neat letters, and uncover when needed.

Objects: Papyrus plant, woven reeds, bitumen. (From Bancroft's *Biblical Object Charts*.)

Connecting Links.

Review the last lesson. We have seen that God cares for men — for his messengers. But God also cares for others. Our story today is about how God cared for a little baby boy.

Preparation.

Recall home life and scenes. The baby in the home. The mother and father, the brother and sister, love for the baby. The parents watch over the baby, care for it, and protect it from all harm. Our story today is about a little baby boy and the wonderful way in which he was kept from harm.

Presentation.

Present the story matter in the following detail:

1. The Hebrews in Egypt.
    a) Their great numbers.
    b) Their heavy burdens — at work for the king.
    c) The king's wickedness in oppressing them.
2. The wicked command of the king.
    a) Intended to prevent the increase of the Hebrews.
    b) The spies sent to watch the Hebrews.
3. The birth of the baby.
    a) The parents' joy.
    b) Joy of the brother and sister, Aaron and Miriam.
    c) Sorrow in the thought of the king's wicked command.
4. The plan to save the baby.
    a) The making of the basket of bulrushes.
    b) The careful placing of the baby in the basket.
    c) Setting the basket afloat on the Nile.
    d) The mother's *trust in God* and prayer to him.
    e) The watch of Miriam the sister.

5. The baby saved and cared for.
   a) The princess with her attendants comes to bathe in the river.
   b) The baby is discovered and saved.
   c) The mother called and given the baby to nurse.
   d) The return home.
6. The thankfulness of all in the home for God's wonderful care.

Desired Results. (Impressions.)

Strengthening of the impression already gained of God's control of all things; not limited to the use of one class of agents; here uses people to do his will. God's love leads him to care for those in need. The parents of Moses trusted in God just as Elijah did; they did all they could to help; and God cared for their beautiful boy baby Moses. We must trust in God's care and do all we can to help him in caring for all.

Memory Verse.

"The Lord is good" (Ps. 34:8).

Home Work.

Review of the lesson. Parents help the child to retell the story in his own words. Give a tracing outline of the little basket-boat for the child to copy, and on the same card print again the memory verse. Paste this card in the lesson-book with Delaroche's picture, "The Finding of Moses."

Lesson 4

CARING FOR ISHMAEL AND HAGAR

Lesson Material.

For story: Gen. 21:8-20.

For study: Gen. 16:1-16; 1 Kings 19:1-8; "Men of the Bible" series, *Abraham*, pp. 88-95.

PRIMARY COURSE OF STUDY 101

Illustrative Material and Suggestions.
  Pictures: "Hagar and Ishmael in the Wilderness," Murat; "Abraham Sends Hagar Away," Vernet; "Hagar and Ishmael in the Desert," Coply; "Hagar and Ishmael," Liska. (Select from above.)
  Blackboard: Print the memory verse in plain, neat letters, and uncover when needed.
  Sand-table: Present the desert scene: tents of Abraham in the distance; some small shrubs; concealed well.

Connecting Links.
  Briefly review the last two lessons, comparing the ways in which God cared for Elijah and for Moses the little baby boy. Our lesson today tells of God's care for an older boy and his mother who were lost in a desert.

Preparation.
  Describe a desert. Compare with some known barren land. Speak of the heat and the scarcity of water. Recall times when the pupils have taken long journeys on hot days — have become very thirsty. Show need of water to sustain life. Our story today is of a boy and his mother traveling in the desert, and of how God cared for them.

Presentation.
  Present the story matter in the following detail:
   1. The great chief Abraham.
      a) His home and household — describe.
      b) His two sons, Ishmael and Isaac.
      c) Abraham and Hagar plan for Hagar's journey.
   2. The departure for Egypt, Hagar's old home.
      a) Preparations — securing of food, drink, etc.
      b) The start early in the morning.
      c) The journey as far as the desert.

3. In the desert.
    a) The barren country; the heat; difficulties of travel.
    b) At last the drinking-water all used.
    c) Ishmael's cry.
    d) Hagar's prayer to God.
    e) God hears the cry and the prayer; answers by showing Hagar the well of water.
4. Hagar's and Ishmael's thankfulness to God for his care.

Desired Results. (Impressions.)

Deepening of the impression of God's knowledge of our needs, and of his love which impels him to care for those in need. Elijah trusted God and was cared for; the parents of Moses trusted God, and their baby was cared for; Hagar trusted God and prayed to him, and he cared for her boy and herself in the desert. He cared for them by guiding the mother. God hears prayer today and cares for those who trust him. We must trust him and pray for his care.

Memory Verse.

"The Lord is good" (Ps. 34:8).

Home Work.

Review of the lesson. Parents help the child to retell the story in his own words. Give a tracing outline of a stone well in a desert, and have the child print again the memory verse on the card. Paste this card in the lesson-book with Liska's picture of "Hagar and Ishmael."

LESSON 5
CARING FOR MANY

Lesson Material.

For story: Exod. 16:1-36; 17:1-6; Numb. 20:1-11; Josh. 5:12.

For study: Deut. 8:3; Numb. 11:4-9; Matt. 15:32; article "Manna" in *Bible Dictionary;* Geikie's *Hours with the Bible,* Vol. II, pp. 120-28.

Illustrative Material and Suggestions.

Pictures: "Moses Striking the Rock," Raphael; water-carriers; caravans in the desert.

Blackboard: Desert scene: mountains in the background; plains dotted with tents. Print the words of the memory verse of preceding lessons over the scene. At the close of the lesson add the words "to all" making the new memory verse, and underneath the picture print the words (recalled from the pupils) *Elijah, Moses, Ishmael, Many People.*

Connecting Links.

Review briefly the last lesson. We have seen how God in different ways cared for one of his servants, Elijah; for a little baby boy, Moses; and for a boy and his mother, Ishmael and Hagar, who were lost in the desert. But God can care for a great many just as easily as he can for one, and our story today tells of his care for a great many people.

Preparation.

Recall to mind what the class knows of a desert. (Review last lesson for this.) Question upon a journey some of the class may have taken. What was needed in traveling? Food and drink. Sometimes they can stop at stations and get food, but sometimes have to take supply with them. What would happen if the supply of food and drink gave out? Our story today is about how God cared for a great many people who were traveling in the desert when their supply of food and drink gave out.

Presentation.

Present the story matter in the following detail:

1. The Hebrews in Egypt.
    a) Their great numbers.
    b) The oppression by the wicked Egyptian king.
    c) God's plan for their deliverance.
    d) Moses appointed their leader and guide.
    e) He gives directions about the journey.
2. The preparations for the journey.
    a) They gather together all their possessions — flocks, herds, household goods, etc.
    b) They prepare large quantities of food and many skins of water.
    c) The final preparations — last meal — during the night ready for an early start.
3. The journey.
    a) The great numbers who started.
    b) The difficulties of the journey.
    c) God's care given — protection, guidance.
4. In the wilderness or desert.
    a) The bread gives out, and the people murmur against Moses.
    b) God's promise of food.
    c) The wonderful supply of manna.
    d) The manna given until they come to the end of their long journey.
    e) The water brought from the rock at Rephidim.

Desired Results. (Impressions.)

Widening and deepening of the impression of God's care and control to include all people. The largeness of God's love — not confined to a few nor to any one class of people. Our love in helpfulness must not be given to a few, but go out to all.

Memory Verse.

"The Lord is good to all" (Ps. 145:9).

Home Work.

Review of the lesson. Parents help the child to retell the story in his own words. Give a tracing outline of the blackboard scene, made as simple as possible, and print the new memory verse on this card. Picture for lesson-book, "Caravans in the Desert."

LESSON 6
CARING FOR US

Lesson Material.

For story: Matt. 6:25–32; 10:29–31; Pss. 34:10*b*; 107:1.

For study: Luke 12:22–30; Pss. 145:8–21; 107:35–38; Phil. 4:19.

Illustrative Material and Suggestions.

Pictures: "Swallows," "Sparrows," M. Laux; "Apple Blossoms," "Golden Rod," "Iris," "Ruby-Throated Humming-Bird," "Bluebird," and "Robin" (Nature Study Publishing Co.; select from above); "The Angelus," Millet.

Blackboard: Print the memory verse in attractive letters, and uncover when needed.

Connecting Links.

Briefly review the preceding lessons, recalling the ways in which God cared for the different ones. He cared not for a few, but for many; not for men alone, but for children — boys and girls — and women. Will God care for us as he did for those about whom we have been studying? Our lesson today will answer this question.

Preparation.

Speak of the parents' care for the different things in the house. To what do they give the most care? How strange it would be not to care for what we love best. Our story today tells us something more about God's love, of his care, and of what he has promised to do.

Presentation.

Present the story matter in the following detail:
1. God's care for the birds.
    a) The great number of birds of all kinds.
    b) They do not sow, nor reap, nor gather into barns.
    c) God knows their needs, continually thinks of them, supplies them with food.
2. God's care for the flowers.
    a) The great variety of flowers.
    b) They do not toil nor spin.
    c) They live but a little while.
    d) But are made very beautiful by God.
3. God's love for us.
    a) We are of more value than all the birds and flowers.
    b) God knows all about us.
    c) He never forgets us.
    d) He wants us to trust him.
    e) He promises to care for us in every way.
4. Our thankfulness to God for all his goodness. (Show the "Angelus.")
    a) For food, clothing, shelter.
    b) For parents, teachers.
    c) For companions, books, etc.

Desired Results. (Ideas.)

A clear idea of the goodness of God in caring for each one. A clear recognition of the fact that God promises to care for each one. An outgoing of the child's nature in a personal trust in God for all things, and thankfulness to him for his many blessings.

Memory Verse.

"He careth for you" (1 Pet. 5:7b).

Home Work.

Review of the lesson. Parents help the child to retell the story in his own words. Picture for lesson-book, Millet's "The Angelus." Print the memory verse beneath the picture.

LESSON 7
HELPING GOD CARE FOR ALL

Lesson Material.

For story: Prov. 12:10 a; Gen. 24:19, 20, 31, 32; Exod. 2:16, 17; 3:1; Ps. 23:2a; Luke 6:35, 36.

Illustrative Material and Suggestions.

Pictures: "The Pet Bird," von Bremen; "At the Watering Trough," Dagnan-Bouveret; "Feeding the Hens," Millet; "The Sheepfold," Pierce; "In the Meadow," Dupré.

Blackboard: Print the memory verse in attractive letters, and uncover when needed.

Connecting Links.

We have had many lessons, many stories, which show us that God cares for all things. But he does not do this work all alone; he has helpers. In our story today we shall learn something about his helpers.

Preparation.

Question concerning the children's interest in the things in their own homes. Do they take care of their own things? Do they help mother and father take care of their things? Why do they do this? (Because of love.) Do mother and father like to have them do this? Our story today is about God our heavenly Father, and what he wants his children to do for him.

Presentation.

Present the story matter in the following detail:
1. People who love God show their love.
   a) They remember his care for all things.
   b) They are kind to all.
   c) By so doing they are like God — they help him.
2. Helping in the care of animals.
   a) Rebekah and Laban caring for the camels.
   b) Moses caring for his flock.
   c) David caring for his flock.
3. Helping in the care of people.
   a) The poor widow helping God care for Elijah. (Review from Lesson 2.) She gave what she had; God used what she gave; God gave her much more.
   b) Miriam helping God care for Moses. (Review from Lesson 3.) Miriam watching baby Moses; she asks the princess if she shall call a nurse; she calls the baby's mother to be the nurse.
4. We must help in the care of all.
   a) God cares for all — is kind to all.
   b) We are his children.
   c) We must try to be like him.
   d) We must help care for all and be kind to all.

Desired Results. (Ideas linked with desire.)

Reviving in consciousness the thought of God's universal care, extending to all living things. He is our Father; we are his children. We ought to want to help our Father in his work. This is one way of showing to him our love and thankfulness.

Memory Verse.

"Love . . . . is kind" (1 Cor. 13:4a).

Home Work.

Review of the lesson. Parents help the child to retell the story in his own words. Give the child a card with the memory verse printed at the top, and have the child write on this card ways in which in the home he can help God care for all things. Picture for lesson-book, Dagnan-Bouveret's "At the Watering Trough."

Lesson 8

REVIEW

Plan.

Try to lead the child to express himself freely — in his own words, and in his own way and order — along the following lines:

1. The need of care for all.
2. Different ways in which God cared for people.
3. The love of God in caring for all.
4. What God has done for each child.
5. The love of God — personal — for each child.
6. Our thankfulness to God.
7. Our thankfulness and love shown by helping God; by trying to be like him; by being kind to all.
8. Ways in which they may have helped God.

In connection with the above plan of developing the review-thought use the pictures, blackboard sketches, and other illustrative aids when needed.

Desired Results.

Correcting any wrong impressions which may have been gained. Making permanent the right impressions and ideas gained, by a free expression of such on the part of the children. Strengthening of the *desire* to help in caring for all by suggestions from the class and the teacher.

NOTE.— With the pictures given the children for their lesson-books there should be given the memory verse lightly printed on cards or heavy paper, which the children can trace over after pasting the card in the book. Children who can print might do without the use of the tracing outline.

---

§ 3. BOOKS RELATING TO THE WORK OF GRADE C

A. REFERENCE READING FOR THE TEACHER

Baldwin, *Old Stories of the East* (American Book Co., New York).

Bennett and Adeney, *The Bible Story* (The Macmillan Co., New York).

Foster, *The Story of the Bible* (Charles Foster Publishing Co., Philadelphia).

Geikie, *Old Testament Characters* (James Pott & Co., New York).

Geikie, *A Short Life of Christ* (James Pott & Co., New York).

Guerber, *The Story of the Chosen People* (American Book Co., New York).

Ottley, *A History of the Hebrews* (The Macmillan Co., New York).

Smyth, *How We Got Our Bible* (James Pott & Co., New York).

B. SUPPLEMENTAL READING FOR THE PUPIL

Baldwin, *The Shepherd Pslam for Children* (F. H. Revell Co., Chicago).

Brown, *The Bible in Lesson and Story* (United Society of Christian Endeavor, Boston).

Endicott, *Stories of the Bible,* Vol. I (Educational Publishing Co., Boston).

Lawson, *The Lord's Prayer for Children* (F. H. Revell Co., Chicago).

Scudder, *Attractive Truths in Lesson and Story* (F. H. Revell Co., Chicago).

PRIMARY COURSE OF STUDY

§ 4. OUTLINE OF THE COURSE FOR GRADE D

GRADE SUBJECT: GOD THE LOVING FATHER PROVIDING WISE LAWS FOR HIS CHILDREN

Part 1. The Child and Himself.

Topic 1— The law of the body.

"Glorify God in your body" (1 Cor. 6: 20*b*).

1. The story of the house wonderful. (Wonders of our bodies.)
2. Daniel and his companions.
3. The wise king's advice.

Topic 2— The law of the mind.

"Whatsoever things are true . . . . pure . . . . think on these things" (Phil. 4: 8).

4. The story of Timothy — the boy who studied.
5. Mary learning of Jesus.
6. Following after wisdom.

Topic 3— The law of the soul (character).

"Be ye doers of the word and not hearers only" (Jas. 1: 22).

7. Moses's noble choice — to help his people.
8. Joshua's noble choice — to serve God.
9. The story of Samuel — the boy who lived true.
10. The rock and sand foundations. (Closing section of the Sermon on the Mount.)
11. *Review.*

Part 2. The Child and Others.

Topic 4— One law of the home: obedience to parents.

"Honor thy father and thy mother" (Exod. 20: 12).

12. Joseph obeying his father.
13. Jesus obeying his parents.
14. Honoring our parents.

Topic 5 — A second law of the home: brotherly kindness.
"Be ye kind one to another" (Eph. 4:32).
15. Esau's kindness to Jacob.
16. Joseph's kindness to his brothers.
17. Jonathan's kindness to David.
18. *Review.*

Topic 6 — The law of helpfulness.
"By love serve one another" (Gal. 5:13b).
19. Esther helping her people.
20. Elisha helping the Shunammite woman.
21. The story of the Good Samaritan.

Topic 7 — The law of truthfulness.
"Speak ye every man the truth to his neighbor" (Zech. 8:16b).
22. Samuel telling the truth to Eli.
23. Jonathan telling the truth to David
24. The prophet (Micaiah) telling the truth to the king.
25. *Review.*

Topic 8 — The law of unselfishness.
"Thou shalt love thy neighbor as thyself" (Matt. 22:39).
26. The story of the separation of Abram and Lot.
27. Judah and Benjamin before Joseph in Egypt.
28. The story of Ruth and Naomi.

Topic 9 — The law of kindness to all.
"Be kindly affectioned one to another with brotherly love" (Rom. 12:10a).
29. God's kindness to all.
30. David's kindness to Mephibosheth.
31. Barzillai's kindness to David.
32. *Review.*

PRIMARY COURSE OF STUDY 113

Part 3. The Child and God.

Topic 10 — The law of trust
"Trust in him at all times" (Ps. 62:8).

33. David trusting God.
34. Hezekiah trusting God.
35. Our trusting God.

Topic 11 — The law of obedience.
"Thou shalt obey the voice of the Lord thy God" (Deut. 27:10a).

36. Noah obeying God.
37. Moses obeying God.
38. Our obeying God.
39. *Review.*

Topic 12 — The law of God's day.
"Remember the sabbath day to keep it holy" (Exod. 20:8).

40. The creation and the blessing of the seventh day.
41. God teaching his people about the sabbath.
42. Our keeping the sabbath.

Topic 13 — The law of God's house.
"Enter into his gates with thanksgiving and into his courts with praise" (Ps. 100:4a).

43. The beautiful temple of the Lord.
44. Giving to the temple.
45. Loving God's house.

Topic 14 — The law of God's name.
"Thou shalt not take the name of the Lord thy God in vain" (Exod. 20:7a).

46. Loving and honoring the name of God.

Topic 15—The law of prayer.

"Watch and pray that ye enter not into temptation" (Matt. 26: 41a).

47. Jesus praying for himself.
48. Jesus praying for his disciples.
49. Our praying for help.
50. *Review.* Also teaching and memory work on the commandments:

COMMANDMENT	LESSONS
III	46
IV	40, 41, 42
V	12, 13, 14
IX	22, 23, 24

Special Lessons.

51. The Christmas lesson (in its proper place).
52. The Easter lesson (in its proper place).

---

§ 5. SUGGESTIVE LESSON PLANS FOR GRADE D
(Lessons 7-10)

Lesson 7
MOSES'S NOBLE CHOICE

Lesson Material.

For story: Exod. 1: 22 — 2: 11a; 3: 1-10; 4: 18, 20-23, 27-31.

For study: Acts 7: 18-36; Heb. 11: 24-26; Gen. 13: 8, 9; "Men of the Bible" series, *Moses*, pp. 51-60, 70-84; Geikie, *Hours with the Bible*, Vol. II, pp. 61-67, 75-77.

Illustrative Material and Suggestions.

Pictures: "Moses and the Burning Bush," Doré; "Moses and Aaron before Pharaoh," Doré.

Blackboard: Sketch at the left of the board a palace and at the right a bit of valley and mountain — flock of sheep in the foreground, several tents in background.

Connecting Links.

Review the last lesson briefly, and have the law of the mind repeated. We have learned what God wants us to do that we may have the purest and best minds; now we are to learn what he would have us do that our characters, our lives, may be strong and true.

Preparation.

Question the children about the times when they had to make a choice. Do they sometimes have to choose between being selfish or unselfish? Which is the better, nobler choice? Is it always easy to choose to be unselfish? Our story today is about a choice made by Moses, about whom we have already had several stories. We shall see what kind of a choice it was, and I think it will help us to understand a little better how it was that Moses became such a great and good man.

Presentation.

Present the story matter in the following detail:
1. Moses's early life. (Briefly review Lesson 3, Grade C.)
   a) The birth.
   b) Adoption by the king's daughter.
   c) Early training at the court.
2. Moses's noble choice.
   a) Sees his people's suffering.
   b) Wishes very much to help them.
   c) Finally chooses to give up his position to help them.
   d) Tries at first to help them in his own way.
   e) Then waits for God to show him the way.

3. Moses learns the way to help his people.
    a) Goes to the pasture lands of Midian.
    b) Becomes a shepherd and keeps Jethro's flocks.
    c) At last God speaks to him and tells him how he can help the people.
    d) Moses listens to God and obeys.
4. Moses's return to his people.
    a) Upon leaving, Jethro blesses him.
    b) God encourages him.
    c) Aaron meets him and goes with him to Egypt.
    d) He tells the people that he has come to help them.
    e) The people gladly receive him.

Desired Results.

The idea that doing unselfish acts helps to make strong, true characters or lives. Inspiring the child to unselfishness of action as a basis for such character. Not always easy to choose the best things — not always easy to do that which we choose. We must not only *know* about the unselfish things to do, but we must *do* these unselfish things. It is not enough to hear about unselfish acting and of the unselfish actions of others; we ourselves must do unselfish deeds if we are to grow into strong and true men and women. God was with Moses; so he will be with us to help us.

Memory Verse.

"Be ye doers of the word and not hearers only" (Jas. 1:22).

Home Work.

Review the lesson story. Picture for the "Book of God's Laws" — "Moses and Aaron before Pharaoh," Doré. Print the law, "*Be ye doers of the word and not hearers only.*" Paste beneath it the picture, and beneath the picture print the word *Moses*.

Lesson 8
Joshua's Noble Choice

Lesson Material.

For story: Josh. 1:1-9; 24:1, 14-18, 24-27.

For study: Gen. 18:19; Deut. 4:9-10; 6:4-9; Ruth 1:15-17; 1 Kings 18:17-39; John 6:66-69; "Men of the Bible" series, *Joshua,* pp. 196-201.

Illustrative Material and Suggestions.

Pictures: "Moses's Successor," von Schnorr; "Israelites Worshiping the Golden Calf," Raphael; "The Vale of Shechem" (from nature).

Blackboard: Print the memory verse in plain, attractive letters, and uncover when needed.

Word-picture: Present a word-picture of the scene: the valley between the two mountains; the great crowds; Joshua the leader; his earnest words; the sorrow of the people; their promise; the setting up of the witness stone.

Connecting Links.

Review the last lesson. We have learned that unselfish choices and actions help to make true, good lives. But there are other kinds of choices to be made, and today we are to learn about one of them.

Preparation.

Again question the children about the times when they had to make a choice. Are they sometimes tempted to do wrong? They have to choose then between doing right and doing wrong. Which is the better, nobler choice? Is it always easy to choose the right? Our story today is about a choice made by a great captain, Joshua. We shall see what he chose to do, and I think it will help us to understand why Joshua became such a great and good man.

Presentation.

Present the story matter in the following detail:
1. Joshua the new leader.
    a) Moses's death.
    b) Joshua chosen leader.
    c) God's command to Joshua to study and follow his law.
    d) God's promise to be with him in his new work.
2. The people's wickedness.
    a) Disobeyed God's commands.
    b) Worshiped idols.
    c) Forgot God's goodness to them.
3. Joshua's noble choice.
    a) He gathers all the people together.
    b) Recalls to mind all that God has done for them.
    c) Commands them to put away idols.
    d) Tells them of *his* choice — to serve God.
    e) The people follow his example and promise to serve God.
    f) The stone witness to the promise.

Desired Results.

The idea that choosing and doing right also helps to make strong, true characters or lives. Inspiring the child to chose the right under all circumstances as a further basis for such a character. Not always easy to choose the right; not always easy to do the right. This takes true courage. We must not only *know* what is right, but we must *do* what is right. It is not enough to hear about the right actions of others; we ourselves must do right deeds, if we are to grow into strong and true men and women. God was with Moses and helped him to be unselfish; he was with Joshua and helped him to do what was right; so he will be with us to help us make unselfish and right choices, and do unselfish and right acts.

Memory Verse.
"Be ye doers of the word and not hearers only" (Jas. 1:22).

Home Work.
Review the lesson story. Picture for the "Book of God's Laws"—"Moses's Successor," von Schnorr. Print the law: "*Be ye doers of the word and not hearers only.*" Paste beneath it the picture and beneath the picture print the word *Joshua*.

LESSON 9
THE STORY OF SAMUEL, THE BOY WHO LIVED TRUE

Lesson Material.
For story: 1 Sam. 1:20, 24–28; 2:18, 19, 26; 3:1–4, 11–21; 4:1a; 8:1–5, 21, 22; 11:14, 15; 12:1–5, 19–24.
For study: "Men of the Bible" series, *Samuel*; Geikie, *Hours with the Bible*, Vol. III, pp. 35–54; Gaskoin, *Children's Treasury of Bible Stories*, Part I, pp. 124–32.

Illustrative Material and Suggestions.
Pictures: "The Infant Samuel," Reynolds; "Samuel Presented to Eli," Opie; "Samuel Anointing Saul," von Schnorr.

Blackboard: Print the memory verse in plain, attractive letters. Beneath the memory verse print the words *Doers of the word,* and beneath these words the names *Moses* and *Joshua*. After the lesson has been taught add to this list the name *Samuel*.

Connecting Links.
Briefly review the last two lessons. These two lessons show us that unselfish and right actions help to make true, strong characters. Our story today is about a boy who tried to be unselfish and to do right acts at all times. We shall learn about what kind of a man he became.

Preparation.

Question the children as to the need of practice. What must they do in order to play well the piano, or to become a good ball-player? What would happen if we did not practice at all? But if we practiced for a day and not again for a week, what then? If we want to do anything easily and well, what then must we do? Our story today is about a boy who practiced doing right every day, and we shall see what kind of a man he became.

Presentation.

Present the story matter in the following detail:
1. Samuel the child.
   a) His birth.
   b) His godly home.
   c) Given to the Lord's service.
2. Samuel the boy.
   a) Life in the tabernacle with Eli.
   b) The vision at night.
   c) Samuel true to Eli — tells him all things.
3. Samuel the man.
   a) Becomes a great prophet.
   b) Becomes a judge or ruler of the people.
   c) Samuel true to the people — deals justly with them.
4. Samuel in his old age.
   a) The people ask for a king.
   b) Samuel chooses a king for them.
   c) Saul is made king at Gilgal.
   d) Samuel bids the people farewell. The gathering of the people; Samuel's last public words; the people witness to his true, unselfish, beautiful **life.**

Desired Results.

The impression of the idea that it is only by continually living the right kind of a life that our lives become strong and true. It is the daily living (practice) that tells. Samuel lived truly as a boy, as a youth, as a young man, as a man; and in his old age the people admired and loved him. God was with Moses and Joshua helping them to do right; he was with Samuel all through his life helping him to be true; so he will be with us if we try to be at all times doers of righteousness not hearers only.

Memory Verse.

"Be ye doers of the word and not hearers only" (Jas. 1:22).

Home Work.

Review the lesson story. Picture for the "Book of God's Laws"—"The Infant Samuel," Reynolds. Print the law: "*Be ye doers of the word and not hearers only.*" Paste beneath it the picture and beneath the picture the word *Samuel*.

LESSON 10
THE ROCK AND SAND FOUNDATIONS

Lesson Material.

For story: Matt. 7:24-29.

For study: Luke 6:13-49; Matt. 5:1—7:29; Farrar, *The Life of Christ*, pp. 133-44; Edersheim, *The Life and Times of Jesus the Messiah*, Vol. I, pp. 524-41; Miller, *The Master's Blesseds*.

Illustrative Material and Suggestions.

Pictures: "The Sermon on the Mount," Dubufe; "The Mount of Beatitudes" (from nature).

Blackboard: Repeat the blackboard work of Lesson 9. Above this print the words *God's law*, and beneath the three names print the word *wise* (at the lesson close).

Connecting Links.

Briefly review the last lessons. We have seen how Moses and Joshua and Samuel became true and noble men by daily right living. We have today a story told by Jesus many years ago, which will tell us something more about our memory verse.

Preparation.

Question the children as to what would happen to a house built upon a sand foundation, if a flood should come. What would happen to a house built upon a solid rock foundation? Our story today is one Jesus told a long time ago, about two men who built two houses. This story is called a parable, which is a story with a hidden meaning, and we shall try to find this hidden meaning.

Presentation.

Present the story matter in the following detail:
1. Jesus teaching the people.
    a) Place — mountain in Galilee.
    b) Great crowds listen to him.
    c) Jesus teaches about many things.
2. The story of two builders.
    a) One builds his house upon a sand foundation.
    b) One builds his house upon a rock foundation.
    c) The storm and its effects.
3. The meaning of the story.
    a) Some persons are like the foolish man — mere hearers of the words of truth Jesus taught. Right *actions* make strong, true lives; those who are only hearers of the word are weak; when tempted, they fall; they know the right, but have not formed the habit of doing right. Jesus says such people are like the foolish man in the story.

b) Some persons are like the wise man: they are both hearers and doers of the words of truth Jesus taught. Right *actions* make strong, true lives; those who are doers of the word become strong in right doing; when tempted, they resist and overcome the evil, for they have formed the habit of doing right. Jesus says such people are like the wise man in the story.

4. These are Jesus' own words to warn us all to be doers of the word and not hearers only.

Desired Results.

Final clear idea of the law of action as related to life. This law more deeply impressed because directly taught and illustrated by Jesus. We are wise if we follow the law; foolish, if we do not. Every action counts. Evil actions make evil characters or lives; right actions make noble characters or lives. Jesus wants us to be wise, not foolish.

Memory Verse.

"Be ye doers of the word and not hearers only" (Jas. 1:22).

Home Work.

Review the lesson story. Picture for the "Book of God's Laws" — "The Sermon on the Mount," Dubufe. Reproduce the blackboard work on a card, and paste this card in the book on the page opposite the picture.

§ 6. BOOKS RELATING TO THE WORK OF GRADE D

A. REFERENCE READING FOR THE TEACHER

Baldwin, *Old Stories of the East* (American Book Co., New York).

Baldwin, *The Story of the Mind* (D. Appleton & Co., New York).

Barnett, *The Making of the Body* (Longmans, Green & Co., New York).

Bennett and Adeney, *The Bible Story* (The Macmillan Co., New York).

Foster, *The Story of the Bible* (Charles Foster Publishing Co., Philadelphia).

Geikie, *Hours with the Bible* (James Pott & Co., New York).

Geikie, *Old Testament Characters* (James Pott & Co., New York).

Guerber, *The Story of the Chosen People* (American Book Co., New York).

Ottley, *A History of the Hebrews* (The Macmillan Co., New York).

Yonge, *Young Folks' Bible History* (D. Lothrop & Co., Boston).

B. SUPPLEMENTAL READING FOR THE PUPIL

Barnard, *The Door in the Book* (F. H. Revell Co., Chicago).

Brown, *The Bible in Lesson and Story* (United Society of Christian Endeavor, Boston).

Dawes, *Bible Stories for Children* (Thomas Y. Crowell & Co., New York).

Endicott, *Stories of the Bible*, Vol. II (Educational Publishing Co., Boston).

Scudder, *Attractive Truths in Lesson and Story* (F. H. Revell Co., Chicago).

§ 7. OUTLINE OF THE COURSE FOR GRADE E

GRADE SUBJECT: GOD THE LOVING FATHER PROVIDING GUIDANCE AND HELP FOR HIS CHILDREN THROUGH

Jesus the Friend of All.

Topic 1—The coming of the Friend.
1. The birth of Jesus.
2. The angels' song and shepherds' visit.
3. The naming and presentation in the temple.

4. The visit of the wise men.
5. The journey to Egypt and return.
6. *Review.*

Topic 2— The Friend preparing for his work.
7. Growing. Story of the childhood of Jesus.
8. Obeying his parents. Story of the visit to Jerusalem.
9. Obeying God. Story of the baptism.
10. Proving that he was ready. Story of the temptation.
11. Choosing his helpers. Story of the first disciples.
12. *Review.*

Topic 3— The Friend and the children.
13. Blessing the little children.
14. The story of the good shepherd.
15. The story of the vine and branches.

Topic 4— The Friend in the home.
16. Helping in the home. The miracle at Cana.
17. Bringing joy to the home. Raising Jairus's daughter.
18. Making the home better. The visit to Zaccheus.
19. *Review.* Topics 3 and 4.

Topic 5— The Friend helping the needy everywhere.
20. Feeding the five thousand.
21. Stilling the tempest.
22. Healing the blind and the deaf.
23. Healing the lame.
24. Healing many sick in Capernaum.
25. Healing the foreigner — the gentile woman.
26. *Review.*

Topic 6— The Friend teaching about many things.
27. Attentive hearing. Story of the sower.
28. Forgiveness. Story of the prodigal son.
29. Forgiveness. Healing the paralytic.

30. Forgiveness. Jesus teaching the disciples.
31. Service. Jesus and his disciples on the shores of the Sea of Galilee.
32. Service. Jesus washing his disciples' feet.
33. *Review.*
34. The Father's house. Jesus cleansing the temple.
35. The Father's day. Healing of the withered hand.
36. True giving. Story of the widow's two mites.
37. How to treat others. Story of the Golden Rule.
38. *Review.*

Topic 7—The Friend teaching about happiness.

39. Blessed are the poor in spirit. Illustrative story: the Pharisee and publican.
40. Blessed are they that mourn. Illustrative story: the penitent woman.
41. Blessed are the meek. Illustrative story: Jesus and his disciples passing through a Samaritan village.
42. Blessed are they which do hunger and thirst after righteousness. Illustrative story: Jesus in the home of Mary and Martha.
43. Blessed are the merciful. Illustrative story: the sheep fallen in a pit.
44. Blessed are the pure in heart. Illustrative story: the story of Nathanael.
45. Blessed are the peacemakers. Illustrative story: the sending forth of the Twelve.
46. Blessed are they which are persecuted. Illustrative story: the story of the missionary Paul.
47. *Review.* Memorizing of the Beatitudes.

Topic 8—The Friend returning to his heavenly home.

48. Jesus' death and resurrection.
49. Jesus' last meetings with his disciples.
50. The ascension of Jesus.

PRIMARY COURSE OF STUDY 127

Special Lessons.
51. The Christmas lesson (in its proper place).
52. The Easter lesson (in its proper place).

§ 8. SUGGESTIVE LESSON PLANS FOR GRADE E
(LESSONS 1–5)
LESSON 1
THE BIRTH OF JESUS

Lesson Material.
For story: Luke 1:26–35; 2:1–7; Matt. 1:18–25.
For study: Farrar, *The Life of Christ,* chap. i; Edersheim, *The Life and Times of Jesus the Messiah,* Vol. I, Book II, chap. vi; Phelps, *The Story of Jesus Christ,* pp. 1–22; Bennett and Adeney, *The Bible Story,* pp. 212–17.

Illustrative Material and Suggestions.
Pictures: "The Annunciation to Mary," Hofmann; "The Arrival at Bethlehem," Merson; "The Nativity," Hofmann; "Sistine Madonna," Raphael.
Blackboard: Print the memory verse in attractive lettering, and uncover when needed.

Connecting Links.
We have been studying for a year about some of the wise laws God, our heavenly Father, has given us to guide us in our actions. Our study for this new year is to be about Jesus, God's Son, who came from heaven to earth to be our friend, to teach us many things, and to help us do what God wishes us to do. And our first story is about the coming of this Friend and Helper.

Preparation.
Question the children about the coming of a little baby brother or sister into the home. Have they had such a

one come to their home? Were mother and father happy? Were the sisters and brothers glad? Yes, it is a glad time for all in the home when a little baby boy or girl is given them to love and care for. Our story today tells of the coming of our Friend and Helper into a very humble home in the little town of Bethlehem.

Presentation.

Present the story matter in the following detail:
1. The message to Mary.
    a) The angel visitor.
    b) The wonderful promise of a son.
    c) The child to be called Jesus.
    d) Promise of his future greatness.
2. The vision to Joseph.
    a) The angel of the Lord appears to him.
    b) He is told of the promised son.
    c) The child to be called Jesus — Savior.
3. The birth of the babe.
    a) The journey to Bethlehem.
    b) The arrival at Bethlehem.
    c) The babe is born and laid in a manger.

Desired Results.

An awakening of an interest in the coming of the Friend and Helper. A sense of God's goodness in sending his Son into the world to help us. A feeling of gratitude and love as a result of this manifestation of the Father's love. "We love him because he first loved us" (1 John 4: 19). A consciousness of the nearness of this Friend to all, and of his sympathy with all through his coming into the world as a little child.

Memory Verse.

"Behold, I bring you good tidings of great joy which shall be to all the people; for there is born to you this day in the city of David a Saviour, which is Christ the Lord" (Luke 2: 10, 11).

Home Work.

The home work suggested for the lessons of this year's course is the making of an *Illustrated Life of Jesus the Friend and Helper.* The picture which the child receives each Sunday should be pasted into an album, with the lesson title over it, and the memory verse printed or written beneath it. In addition to this, the lesson should be reviewed each Sunday by the parents, and the child helped to memorize the memory verse. Picture for Lesson Album "The Nativity," by Hofmann.

LESSON 2

THE ANGELS' SONG AND SHEPHERDS' VISIT

Lesson Material.

For story: Luke 2: 8–20.

For study: Edersheim, *The Life and Times of Jesus the Messiah,* Vol. I, Book II, chap. vi; Farrar, *The Life of Christ,* chap. i; Phelps, *The Story of Jesus Christ,* pp. 22–26; Bennett and Adeney, *The Bible Story,* pp. 212–17.

Illustrative Material and Suggestions.

Pictures: "The Arrival of the Shepherds," LeRolle; "The Angels and the Shepherds," Plockhörst.

Blackboard: Print the memory verse in attractive lettering, and uncover when needed.

Sand-table: Model the Bethlehem hills: Bethlehem in the distance; flocks of sheep in charge of shepherds in the foreground; describe journey of shepherds going to Bethlehem and returning to their flocks.

Connecting Links.

Briefly review the last lesson. We have had the beautiful story of the coming of the Friend and Helper; but his coming was known only to a few in the inn at Bethlehem. Our story today will tell of the wonderful way in which his coming was made known to others.

Preparation.

Recall the thought of the baby brother or sister coming into the home. Recall also the gladness of all in the home. Did those in the home keep this joy all to themselves? Whom did they tell? How was the glad news made known to those who lived near? To those who lived at a distance? Our story today tells of the wonderful way the glad news of the birth of the Friend and Helper was made known to some shepherds, and what they did when they heard the news.

Presentation.

Present the story matter in the following detail:
1. The good news made known.
   a) The watching shepherds.
   b) The angel of the Lord appears to them.
   c) The message of glad tidings.
   d) The sign — the babe lying in a manger.
   e) The wonderful song of praise.
2. The good news proved true.
   a) The shepherds leave their flocks and walk to Bethlehem.
   b) They find the babe lying in a manger.
   c) They tell the friends the wonderful story of the angels' visit.
   d) They return to their flocks, praising God.

Desired Results.

A deepening of the already awakened interest in the Friend and Helper, and of the feeling of love and gratitude to the Father. The angels were glad and sang praises to God; the shepherds were glad and praised God for his goodness; shall we not also be glad over the "good tidings of great joy which shall be to all the people," and praise and thank God? In this lesson the children should gain the thought that this Friend and Helper is to be the Friend and Helper of all — children as well as grown people, in this and in other countries. Thus this lesson might be the means of awakening a missionary interest.

Memory Verse.
"And the shepherds returned, glorifying and praising God for all the things that they had heard and seen" (Luke 2: 20).

Home Work.
Picture for the Lesson Album — either the "Arrival of the Shepherds," by LeRolle, or "The Angels and the Shepherds," by Plockhörst. Printing or writing of the lesson title over the picture, and of the memory verse beneath it. Review of the lesson by the parents. Memorizing of the memory verse.

LESSON 3
THE NAMING AND PRESENTATION IN THE TEMPLE

Lesson Material.
For story: Luke 2: 21–38a; 1: 30, 31; Matt. 1: 20, 21.
For study: Exod. 13: 2; 22: 29; 34: 20; Numb. 3: 13; Edersheim, *The Life and Times of Jesus the Messiah*, Vol. I, Book II, chap. vii; Bennett and Adeney, *The Bible Story*, pp. 218, 219; Farrar, *The Life of Christ*, chap. ii.

Illustrative Material and Suggestions.
Pictures: "The Presentation in the Temple," Champaigne.

Blackboard: Print the memory verse in attractive lettering, and uncover when needed.

Connecting Links.

Briefly review the last lesson. We have heard the story of the coming of the Friend and Helper, and of how the good news of his birth was told by the angels to the shepherds. We are to hear today about the naming of the Friend and Helper, and about how two more persons were made glad by his coming.

Preparation.

Question the children about the naming of a baby in the home. How many names are thought of? How hard it is to decide! Finally a name is chosen. Then have the children recall a baptism which they may have witnessed in church. Let them describe the scene. Who were present? What was done? What was the meaning of the ceremony? Our story today tells about what was done when a little child was born into a Jewish family living in the long-ago time in the country of Palestine.

Presentation.

Present the story matter in the following detail:
1. The naming of the child.
    a) The name revealed to Mary and Joseph in dreams.
    b) When eight days old the child was named *Jesus*.
    c) The meaning of the name.
2. The presentation in the temple.
    a) The journey to Jerusalem.
    b) Mary's presentation of Jesus.
    c) Simeon's thanksgiving.
        (1) He sees Jesus and takes him in his arms.
        (2) God tells him that this child is the promised Friend and Helper.
        (3) He praises God for his goodness.

Primary Course of Study

d) Anna's joy and thanksgiving.
e) The return of Jesus and his parents to Bethlehem.

Desired Results.

A further strengthening of the impressions, already received from the previous lessons, of God's goodness in sending this Friend and Helper. A fuller realization of the mission of this Jesus, a "Savior" of "all people," leading to a further development of the missionary interest. Simeon and Anna both spoke of Jesus as the Friend and Helper of all. We ought to let others know of this Jesus.

Memory Verse.

"Thou shalt call his name *Jesus;* for it is he that shall save his people from their sins" (Matt. 1: 21*b*).

Home Work.

Picture for the Lesson Album, "The Presentation in the Temple," by Champaigne. Printing or writing of the lesson title over the picture, and of the memory verse beneath it. Review of the lesson by the parents. Memorizing of the memory verse.

Lesson 4

THE VISIT OF THE WISE MEN

Lesson Material.

For story: Matt. 2: 1-12.
For study: Farrar, *The Life of Christ,* chap. iii; Edersheim, *The Life and Times of Jesus the Messiah,* Vol. I, Book II, chap. viii; Bennett and Adeney, *The Bible Story,* pp. 220-22; Phelps, *The Story of Jesus Christ,* 26-35.

Illustrative Material and Suggestions.

Objects: Specimens of gold coins, frankincense, and myrrh from any collection of oriental objects.

Pictures: "The Worship of the Magi," Hofmann; "The Magi on the Way to Bethlehem," Protaels.

Blackboard: Draw a number of small houses for Bethlehem; a road from a distant point at the right leading to Bethlehem; a caravan journeying along this road; star in the sky; change the position of the star as the caravan approaches the village. Print the memory verse in attractive lettering over the scene, and uncover when needed.

Connecting Links.

Briefly review the last lesson. After Jesus had been presented in the temple, Mary and Joseph went back quietly to Bethlehem. While there they had some strange visitors from a far country, who came to see their baby Jesus. Our story today will tell us about these visitors.

Preparation.

Question the children about any journey they may have taken. Where did you go? How did you go? What did you see? Was it a long journey? Did you make your plans for it a long time ahead? Our story today is about a very long journey some men took to see someone whom they had been waiting a long time to see.

Presentation.

Present the story matter in the following detail:

1. The wise men seek Jesus.
    a) They journey from the East to Jerusalem.
    b) They inquire of King Herod where Jesus should be born.
    c) Herod inquires of the Jewish leaders.
    d) Herod gives a message and a command to the wise men.

PRIMARY COURSE OF STUDY 135

2. The wise men find Jesus.
   a) They are led by the star to Bethlehem.
   b) They find Jesus and worship him.
   c) They present their gifts to him.
3. The wise men return to their home.
   a) They are warned by God in a dream.
   b) They return to their home by another way.

Desired Results.

A deepening of the sense of gratitude to God, with a suggestion as to how this gratitude may be manifested. The wise men from the East were glad to know of the coming of the Friend and Helper. They showed their joy by their gifts. Our gladness may be shown in a similar way. The thought that when we give to needy ones we give to Jesus. "Inasmuch as ye did it unto one of these my brethren, even these least, ye did it unto me" (Matt. 25: 40).

Memory Verse.

"Opening their treasures they offered unto him gifts, gold and frankincense and myrrh" (Matt. 2: 11b).

Home Work.

Picture for the Lesson Album, "The Worship of the Magi," by Hofmann. Printing or writing of the lesson title over the picture, and of the memory verse beneath it. Review of the lesson by the parents. Memorizing of the memory verse.

LESSON 5
THE JOURNEY TO EGYPT AND RETURN

Lesson Material.

For story: Matt. 2: 13–23; Luke 2: 40.

For study: *Expositor's Bible,* "Matthew;" Farrar, *The Life of Christ,* chap. iv; Phelps, *The Story of Jesus Christ,* pp. 35–40.

Illustrative Material and Suggestions.

Pictures: "The Flight into Egypt," Fürst.

Blackboard: Print the memory verse in attractive lettering, and uncover when needed.

Sand-table: Mold Bethlehem hills in distance (upper right-hand corner) with a road leading in a southwest direction toward Egypt. At the right, about the middle of the board, place several pyramids (made of cardboard). In the middle of the foreground place a tent under palms. In the distance to the left the Nile River and the Mediterranean Sea.

Connecting Links.

Briefly review the last lesson. After the magi had returned to their far-away home in the East without telling King Herod about the finding of Jesus, this wicked king sought to harm Jesus. Our story today will tell us how he was saved from harm.

Preparation.

Question the children about their parents' care for them. How watchful they are to guard them from harm! Why do they do this? Our story today tells about the wicked King Herod who planned to do harm to the baby boy Jesus. We shall see what was done to protect Jesus from this harm.

Presentation.

Present the story matter in the following detail:
1. Herod's wicked plans.
    a) He hears that a new king is born in Bethlehem.
    b) He plans to destroy this king.
    c) He sends his soldiers to Bethlehem to do this.
2. The journey of the Holy Family to Egypt.
    a) Joseph warned in a dream of Herod's wicked plan.

      b) He at once starts with Mary and Jesus for Egypt.
      c) They stay some time in Egypt.
  3. The return to Galilee.
      a) The wicked king Herod dies.
      b) Joseph told in a dream to return to his own country.
      c) Warned by God they pass by Jerusalem.
      d) They go to Nazareth and make their home there.

Desired Results.

A widening of the idea of God's goodness, shown now in caring for Jesus when harm threatened him. An impression of the watchfulness and love of God. From these five lessons the children should receive impressions of God's goodness and love in sending this Friend and Helper to us, and in caring for him in the way he did. They should gain the idea that this Jesus has come to be a helper to "all people" in all lands. These impressions and ideas ought to bring from the children a response of love and gratitude to God, and of desire to have this Jesus for their Friend and Helper.

Memory Verse.

"God is .... a very present help in trouble" (Ps. 46:1).

Home Work.

Picture for the Lesson Album, "The Flight into Egypt," by Fürst. Printing or writing of the lesson title over the picture, and of the memory verse beneath it. Review of the lesson by the parents. Memorizing of the memory verse.

§ 9. BOOKS RELATING TO THE WORK OF GRADE E

A. REFERENCE READING FOR THE TEACHER

Craigin, *The Story of Jesus* (Fords, Howard & Hulbert, New York).

Edersheim, *The Life and Times of Jesus the Messiah*, 2 vols. (Longmans, Green & Co., New York).

Farrar, *The Life of Christ* (various editions).

Gilbert, *The Student's Life of Jesus* (The Macmillan Co., New York).

Houghton, *The Life of Christ in Picture and Story* (American Tract Society, New York).

Phelps, *The Story of Jesus Christ* (Houghton, Mifflin & Co., Boston).

Stalker, *The Life of Jesus Christ* (F. H. Revell Co., Chicago).

Vincent, Lee, and Bain, *Earthly Footprints of the Man of Galilee* (N. D. Thompson Publishing Co., New York).

B. SUPPLEMENTAL READING FOR THE PUPIL

Endicott, *Stories of the Bible*, Vol. III (Educational Publishing Co., Boston).

Hoyt, *A Child's Story of the Life of Christ* (W. A. Wilde Co., Boston).

Hutchison, *The Gospel Story of Jesus Christ* (E. P. Dutton & Co., New York).

Proudfoot, *Child's Christ-Tales* (published by the author, Andrea Hofer Proudfoot, Chicago).

Tappan, *The Christ Story* (Houghton, Mifflin & Co., Boston).

PART II

THE BOYHOOD-GIRLHOOD PERIOD AND THE JUNIOR DEPARTMENT

CHAPTER V

SOME CHARACTERISTICS AND NEEDS OF THE PERIOD

ALTHOUGH the changes which occur during this period, from nine to thirteen years of age, are not so marked as those which make the following period one of exceptional interest and importance, they are of a character that indicate that there are special needs which must be met by new material and methods of instruction.

Physically the body grows very slowly in both height and weight. There seems to be a decided arrest of development at this time, for during the preceding and following periods the growth is rapid. The brain at the beginning of the period has attained nearly its full mature weight, and the subsequent increase is small and slow. All the period is probably given to growth of connecting or associative fibers. It is a time of co-ordination of muscular movements, with a great interest in plays and in manual work. During these years there is a decided lack of ability to concentrate attention for any length of time upon mental work, and too much must not be required of the boy or girl in the way of intellectual effort. It is a period which is not well known, but in general we may say that it is a time during which nature stores up energy in anticipation of and preparation for the new birth — that wonderful time when, on the one hand, the boy and girl are born out of childhood into manhood and womanhood, and, on the other hand, from egoism and isolation to altruism and society.

Some characteristics of the period.— The animistic tendencies already spoken of are very much weakened, disappearing at the close of the period, and may be left out of account in these years. The suggestibility of the boy and girl is still high in degree. They are strongly influenced by their companions. Dr. Street has shown that the age at which these influences are most felt is from ten to fifteen.[1] Because of this characteristic, careful suggestion on the part of the teacher may work wonders in the character and purposes of the pupils. Attention should also be given to their companions; evil habits should be eradicated and good ones formed; low ideals must be made to give place to high ones; and, in short, the boy or girl must be raised day by day to higher planes of living.

The altruistic impulses become somewhat stronger in all normal children, these tending to weaken the spirit of selfishness so manifest in early life. The teacher should do all in his power

---

[1] J. R. STREET, "A Study in Moral Education," *Pedagogical Seminary*, Vol. V, p. 15.

to foster these social impulses. During the latter part of the period class organization might prove helpful. The field for the manifestation of these impulses should be widened, and an attempt made to create an interest in the larger social life with which the child is surrounded.

Although no direct study of untruthfulness during the period has been made, the tendency is probably weaker in children whose social environment is normal. The development of conscience, slight as this is in many cases; the growth in unselfishness, and the development of the reflective powers, would all tend to produce a greater regard for the truth. The increasing interest in natural phenomena in the form of elementary science would also help in this direction. But if the boy or girl is thrown with companions who habitually disregard the truth, or is brought up in a home where truth-telling is not looked upon as of great importance, the comparatively slight growth in the above counteracting influences may not be sufficient to overcome the power of suggestion and imitation, and the natural selfishness of the child.

The respect for law in its general forms, not simply as embodied in personal commands, increases somewhat during these years, but the great awakening to the binding force of law does not come until after puberty.

All children continue to be fearful during this time, the source of the majority of boyhood-girlhood fears being the imagination. The teacher and the parent should be especially careful during these years not to excite fear through the imagination, and to guard the child in every way from possible enlargement of his stock of fears from this source.

With the increasing interest in the causal idea and in the idea that law rules in all things, superstition loses power, although the belief in some superstitions is not completely given up, and may remain, and in fact often does remain, through adult life. But both the science-teaching in the public school and the teaching about the rule of God in the Bible school help to give the child a right understanding of the happenings in this world.

Some interests of the period.— The interest in the causal idea increases, the fields in which it finds its best expression being science and history. The increasing interest in and knowledge of the rule of law in the physical realm may be used by the Bible-school teacher to help the pupils to an understanding of the rule of law in the world of history, and as a basis for his teaching concerning the relation of law to individual life and character. The literary interests change very decidedly during the period. The interest in fairy-stories begins to decline at the age of nine, and by thirteen is almost extinct. There grows up in its place a strong interest in history, in which

the main interest . . . . follows the strong lines of action and asks for a clear presentation of persons, places, relations of cause and effect; to which may be added, in due but slight proportion, time, ethics, and expansive detail.[2]

This interest begins in the last years of the primary period, for

from the age of seven onward we find them inquiring after time, cause, and effect, the social unit, and the truthful record — that is, all the elements of history lie within the field of the child's curiosity; and it is interesting to note how early they inquire after origin: Who made us? Where did we come from? The plain conclusion as to method here is that history is a suitable subject for children from the age of seven at least.[3]

One of Mrs. Barnes's conclusions from her study of the historic sense among children is as follows:

Introduce the subject of history into the curriculum as early as the age of seven or eight, or soon after children can count and read, making no difference between boys and girls. Up to the age of twelve or thirteen, history should be presented in a series of striking biographies and events, appearing as far as possible in contemporary ballads and chronicles, and illustrated by maps, chronologic charts, and as richly as possible by pictures of contemporary objects, buildings, and people. This series should appear in chrono-

[2] MARY SHELDON BARNES, "The Historic Sense Among Children," in *Studies in Education*, p. 47.
[3] *Ibid.*, p. 89.

logic order, the biographies themselves forming the basis of the chronology. These biographies should be chosen from the field of action and interest allied to children's lives; that is, they should be chosen from the personal, military, and cultural aspects of history, and scarcely at all from the political or intellectual life. Great pains should be taken with the first presentation, since it plays so important a part in the historic memory. The whole field of general history should be covered in this way, and should be taken from such sources as the Bible, Homer, Plutarch, the Norse sagas, tales of Indian warfare and pioneer life, voyages of great discoverers. These should be given in their original forms, only modified by such omissions as are demanded by youth and inexperience. These primitive texts should be illustrated as richly as possible by portraits, pictures of relics and monuments, maps, charts, ballads, stories.[4]

In Professor Wissler's very comprehensive study on "The Interest of Children in the Reading Work of the Elementary Schools,"[5] some interesting and helpful facts are presented. This study shows that the stories which are most certain to be remembered are of some length, are in terms of experience which the child can realize in himself or which he can appreciate, and which are especially natural or lifelike. The stories which are not remembered to any extent are the short story or the story in outline, those which treat of things the child cannot realize or appreciate, and those which are merely instructive, con-

[4] *Ibid.*, p. 92.
[5] CLARK WISSLER, *Pedagogical Seminary*, Vol. V, pp. 523 ff.

taining a moral and its setting, or which present abstract ideals of duty, happiness, etc. Prose is preferred to poetry by both boys and girls up to the age of thirteen, when there is a sudden and considerable increase in the interest in poetry. Stories of daily life, the usual rather than the unusual, those which are true to life and not fanciful in their construction, are preferred above all others. And again, what may appear strange to some, there is a strong preference, especially between the ages of eleven and thirteen, for stories which contain a moral lesson, but in which the moral is not obtrusive. Commenting upon these preferences, Professor Wissler says:

> From this it appears .... that even the moral lesson without the formal statement in conclusion, but bearing upon it the marks of a moral purpose, received less attention than the simple story whose moral force was felt and appreciated. It is further observed that the heroic in action is given more consideration than the formal hero, and that lessons designed to be instructive receive little regard from those whose preferences lean toward knowledge. The charge is often made that children have no regard for moral ideas, no feeling for the divinity of right action, and no love for knowledge; these results show that children do appreciate such things when presented in terms of their own experience. Take out of their text-books the sermon, the philosophical fable, and the cold stiff hero, and paint into them the good, the true, and the heroic in colors from life.[6]

[6] *Ibid.*, p. 535.

A "Study of Children's Reading Tastes," by Miss Clara Vostrovsky,[7] shows a marked increase in interest in works of general literature after the age of ten years, with a corresponding decline in interest in juvenile fiction. Of the four classes of books which she groups under the head of "general literature"—namely, history and historical biography, literature and literary biography, travel, and science—the interest is far stronger in history and historical biography among both the boys and the girls, although the boys lead somewhat. Of the children studied about 42 per cent. of the boys and 40 per cent. of the girls chose books of history or historical biography in preference to any one of the other three classes mentioned. A very large percentage of the boys, but a very much smaller percentage of the girls, chose books which contained stories full of adventure, of life, of action.

The theological interests and ideas of this period are very similar to those of the primary period. The conception of God as a sort of father is still dominant, and to this many children add the thought that God is watching them to insure obedience to his will. Heaven is still simply an improved earth, the following by a girl of twelve being a typical description:

[7] *Pedagogical Seminary*, Vol. VI, pp. 523 ff.

Heaven is a beautiful city high above the clouds, where everything is beautiful; I think that heaven must be perfect. The gates are pearls, and the walls are formed of jewels, and a beautiful, calm river, clear as crystal, flows through it, before the throne of the King of heaven. Our friends who have died and gone to live there now serve God, play harps, and sing praises to their Maker. The children sing songs of praise also, and serve Him.[8]

Their ideas concerning angels, Satan, hell, death, etc., remain practically unchanged, but from the age of ten to the close of the period there arises a spirit of questioning; the children try to reason things out and to relate their theology to what they have learned through experience and through their studies. This critical spirit seems to culminate at thirteen or fourteen; and the criticisms are far more persistent and severe at this time than later.[9] The development of the social or altruistic side of their nature, and the strengthening of their sense of justice, lead the boys and girls to try to harmonize their theological ideas with these newly aroused elements in their lives.

Frequently the children of this age say that they do not believe that savages and babies will go to hell, while very many who accept the standard theology for God, the angels, and heaven, declare that they do not believe that there is any devil in hell. This, of course, may be due simply to their teaching, but such sentiments seldom appear in compositions by children under eleven or twelve years old.[10]

[8] EARL BARNES, " Theological Life of a Child," *Pedagogical Seminary*, Vol. II, p. 443.
[9] *Ibid.*, p. 446. [10] *Ibid.*, p. 447.

This is the period when some of the cruder conceptions of the preceding years may be corrected, and when the government of God in love through law may be more clearly pointed out. The interest during the period in games, especially in the traditional games of boyhood and girlhood, may be used in connection with lessons which suggest teachings concerning right habits — temperance, self-control, etc.

The mental powers during the period.— The perceptive powers are still strong. The organs of sense attain to practical perfection about the beginning of the period, and from this time on the child is capable of close observation work. An appeal to the senses must continue in all work of instruction, that the ideas gained may have as concrete a content as possible. Memory is growing stronger, the maximum memory power being reached at about the close of the period.[11] This would indicate that this is the period for considerable memoriter work in connection with school instruction, the Bible passages selected being definitely related to the lesson work of the various grades; the selected passages not being memorized, however, until somewhat of an understanding of the matter has been given to the children. The imagination continues active and must be

[11] JOHN C. SHAW, " A Test of Memory in School Children," *Pedagogical Seminary*, Vol. IV, pp. 61 ff.

appealed to to get before the pupil's mind the setting of an historical event. Objective aids to the imagination, such as pictures, maps, charts, diagrams, objects, etc., must be freely used in all lesson work in this period. The reasoning powers are developing, but somewhat slowly. As has been already intimated, there is some evidence of a critical spirit toward the close of the period. The boys and girls are seeking for fuller and more correct information; hence they raise many questions, and demand some proof of the statements made. Wherever in the teaching work it is possible to present proofs, this should be done. Conscience is becoming more active, and in many cases is an important factor in moral and religious education, but the teacher's direct influence and example, in the majority of cases, and the example of companions, are more potent factors.

Some conclusions with reference to a course of study for the boy and girl from nine to thirteen years of age.—During these years God as a Worker in connection with human affairs is the general aspect of his nature which would appeal to the boy and girl. The great historical events of the Old and New Testaments, carefully selected and presented so as to show God at work among the nations of the world through his prophets, messengers, and ministers or missionaries, would appeal to the dominant literary interest of the period, *i. e.*, historical narrative; to the love of the heroic, the exciting, the adventuresome; and to the strong interest in personality, not from the standpoint of character, but from that of accomplishment. In this presentation care must be taken to make the persons, places, and causes and effects stand out prominently, as these are the elements in the historical story which appeal to the boy and girl; also to have each lesson a complete narrative, that the unity of the matter may make its own impression and be remembered. Following the Old and New Testament narratives, there should be given a year's study to the great events in the development of the kingdom of God since the time of the apostles; *i. e.*, a story-history of Christian missions. The child must be shown that God is still at work through his ministers and missionaries in all parts of the world today, and that he has been continuously at work since the beginning of the world.

In teaching the historical lessons indicated in the next chapter one must continue to appeal to the senses. Pictures, blackboard sketches and diagrams, maps, and other illustrative aids must be freely used. The use of some objective aid is especially called for in attempting to give the child any clear conception of the time periods studied and the chronological sequence of the lessons, as his time-sense is still weak. As verbal memory is strong during the period, the names of the books of the Bible, with certain facts concerning each one, together with various choice selections from those books, should be stored away in the memory. Whatever is selected to be thus memorized should be chosen with a view to its usefulness in further Bible study or for its moral-religious content.

An outline of a suggested course of study for the four years is given in the next chapter. In Grade A the story of the chosen people is given; in Grade B, the story of God's Son, Jesus Christ, who came to the world to bring the Message of Love and Light; in Grade C, the story of the early messengers, carrying the message Jesus brought, the Gospel of Love and Truth, to the nations of their time; and in Grade D, the story of the missionaries who have continued the work of the apostles, and who have carried the same message even to the "uttermost part of the earth." The boys and girls who finish this course of four years' study will have their vision of God enlarged, their sense of his loving interest in the affairs of men deepened, and their desire to be obedient to the message of Jesus strengthened.

CHAPTER VI
A COURSE OF STUDY FOR THE JUNIOR DEPARTMENT

GENERAL SUBJECT: GOD THE RULER — SEEKING TO BLESS THE WORLD

§ 1. OUTLINE OF THE COURSE FOR GRADE A

GRADE SUBJECT: THE STORY OF GOD'S PEOPLE — THE HEBREWS
(GOD CHOOSING AND BLESSING A PEOPLE)

Chapter 1 — The beginnings.
1. The call of Abram. *Gen 12.*
2. Abram and Lot. *Gen 13.*
3. Esau and Jacob. *Gen 25.*
4. Jacob the exile. *Gen 27.*
5. Joseph the dreamer. *Gen 37.*
6. Joseph the slave. *Gen 39.*
7. Joseph the ruler. *Gen 41, 42 etc.*
8. *Review.*

Chapter 2 — Seeking a new home.
9. The early life of Moses. *Exodus 2, 3*
10. Moses the leader. *Exodus 4*
11. Moses and Pharaoh. " *5 + 6, etc*
12. The exodus. " *13*
13. God's care in the wilderness. " *16, 17 etc.*
14. The law given at Sinai. " *19 + 20,*
15. The law broken at Sinai. " *32.*
16. The story of the spies and the wilderness wanderings. *Num. 13.*
17. Before the Jordan River. *Deut 1*
18. The last days of Moses. *Deut 34,*
19. Memory work: The Ten Commandments. Book work: The Pentateuch.
20. *Review.*

JUNIOR DEPARTMENT COURSE

Chapter 3 — Settlement in their new home.
21. Crossing the Jordan River. *Joshua 4.*
22. The fall of Jericho. *" 6, 7*
23. Joshua and the conquest. *" 7, 10*
24. Trouble in the land and the victory of Gideon. *Judg.*
25. The story of Ruth. *Ruth (whole book)*
26. The story of Samuel the teacher and judge. *Samuel*
27. *Review.* Also book work: Joshua, Judges, Ruth.

Chapter 4 — The united kingdom.
28. Saul the first king.
29. David's boyhood.
30. David the exile.
31. David the king.
    Memory work: Ps. 1.
32. Solomon the wise king.

Chapter 5 — The divided kingdom.
33. The new kingdoms and their first kings.
34. Elijah the prophet.
35. Elisha the prophet.
36. The story of the kings and the end of the kingdom of the North.
37. Joash the boy king.
38. The deliverance of Jerusalem.
39. Josiah the reformer.
    Memory work: Ps. 19.
40. The fall of Jerusalem and the end of the kingdom of the South.
41. Memory work reviewed.
    Book work: 1 and 2 Samuel, 1 and 2 Kings, 1 and 2 Chronicles, Isaiah, Jeremiah, Lamentations, Hosea, Amos, Obadiah, Jonah, Micah, Nahum, Zephaniah, Habbakuk, and the poetical books.
42. *Review.* Chaps. 4 and 5.

Chapter 6 — The people in exile.
  43. Their new home in exile.
  44. The story of Daniel's trials.
  45. The story of Daniel's reward.
  46. Esther the queen.

Chapter 7 — The return from exile.
  47. The journey home.
  48. The new temple.
  49. The work of Nehemiah and Ezra.
  50. Book work: Ezra, Nehemiah, Esther, Ezekiel, Daniel, Joel, Haggai, Zechariah, and Malachi.
  Review. Chaps. 6 and 7.

Special Lessons.
  51. Christmas lesson.
  52. Easter lesson.

---

§ 2. SUGGESTIVE LESSON PLANS FOR GRADE A
(Lessons 9–11)
Lesson 9
THE EARLY LIFE OF MOSES

Lesson Material.
  Exod. 1:22 — 2:10; Acts 7:20-22; Heb. 11:23.

Teacher's Study Material.
  Rawlinson, *Moses* in "Men of the Bible" series, chaps. ii, iii; Geikie, *Hours with the Bible,* Vol. II, pp. 114-30; Hastings, *Bible Dictionary,* art. "Moses;" a good critical commentary.

Illustrative Material.
  Outline map (blackboard), showing Egypt, Sinai, the wilderness or desert, and Palestine with the surrounding country. This map may be used in teaching all the les-

sons of this chapter. Locate Goshen, the home of the Hebrews. Pictures illustrating Egyptian life and civilization, such as the Perry, Nos. 1454-56, and the Wilde, Nos. 178-81. Picture for the Review Book, "The Finding of Moses," by Delaroche.

Connecting Links.
Review: As the last lesson was a full review of chap. 1, the teacher will give merely a simple review statement of that chapter. In our new chapter, chap. 2, we shall see how God's people, the Hebrews, got away from Egypt and found a new home.

Intervening events: Some time after the Hebrews went down into Egypt, Joseph the governor in Egypt, died. After some years a new King Pharaoh came to the throne. By this time the Egyptians had forgotten what Joseph had done for them, and hence the new king cared nothing for the Hebrew people. He made them his slaves and put them in charge of taskmasters, who stood over them while they worked and beat them cruelly with sticks. But, in spite of all this oppression, the Hebrews grew to be a great people, until finally King Pharaoh, fearing they would grow so strong that they might rebel against him, planned to stop their increasing in numbers and strength. What his plans were, and what the final result was, we shall find out from the stories of this new chapter.

Narrative Outline. (For the teacher. Language and detail to be adapted to the pupils.) .
1. Pharaoh and the Hebrews.
    a) The king's wicked command.
    b) Spies sent to watch the Hebrews.
2. Birth of the Hebrew child.
    a) The birth of the child brings joy into the home.
    b) Also distress because of the king's command.
    c) The child hidden for three months.

3. The plan to save the child.
    a) The making of the ark.
    b) The ark with the child set afloat on the Nile.
    c) The watching of sister Miriam.
4. Success of the plan.
    a) The child discovered by the king's daughter.
    b) She decides to adopt him.
    c) Through Miriam the mother is called as a nurse.
    d) He is given the name Moses.
5. The training of Moses.
    a) Brought up as the son of the princess.
    b) Taught in all the wisdom of the Egyptians.

Suggestions for Developing the Outline.

As the class is supposed to study the story material before coming to the session, develop the narrative as much as possible by questions, following the outline. Locate on the map the country of Egypt and the land of Goshen. What wicked decree or law did the king make? Why did he make this law? How did he try to make sure that the law was obeyed? Help the children to imagine the great distress and sorrow this caused in the homes of the Hebrews. Suppose something like this happened today, how should we all feel? What was the condition of the people at this time? Show pictures of the Hebrews working as slaves with the Egyptian taskmasters over them. What happened in one of the homes of the Hebrew people? How did the parents and the brother and sister feel? What do you suppose they talked about? How long did they manage to keep the child hidden? But he grew so big that they felt that they could hide him no longer. Picture the parents' anxiety. They talk over many plans, and finally agree upon one to save the baby boy. Describe the making of the ark. Show papyrus plant (see Bancroft's *Bible Objects*, or any other collection), and illustrate the weaving. Where did they place the ark with the child? What were they hoping for? Who watched? Describe the coming of the princess to bathe. What did she discover in the river? What did she decide to do? Why do you think she did this? Who was called as a nurse? Picture the mother's joy upon receiving her own baby to care for. Explain to the class that the baby was now safe, for the princess would protect him. What was the name given to the child? When Moses became old enough, where was he taken to live? Describe briefly a palace and life in a palace. Show pictures of such if you have them. Moses was sent to school and was taught many things. Tell something of the probable school life of Moses. Also tell the class about the civilization of Egypt at this time, that they may not think the people were ignorant and barbarous. Review the whole story, making sure that the class has a clear knowledge of the facts of the lesson. In this review try to arouse in the class some appreciation of the providential care of God which this lesson illustrates.

Suggested Generalization. (Adapt form of statement to pupils.)

God's providential care for his people.

How did Moses's parents plan to save him? Was their plan a good one? Could they have done anything more for the child? Did they know just how successful their plan would be? In whom did they put their trust? With what result? Through whom did God help them? God in similar ways is caring for his people today. We must do all we can; then trust the rest to God.

Memory Verse.

"By faith Moses, when he was born, was hid three months by his parents, because they saw he was a goodly child; and they were not afraid of the king's command" (Heb. 11:23).

Review Questions. (To be answered by the scholar at home.)

1. In what part of Egypt did the Hebrews live?
2. How did the king treat them?
3. What wicked law did the king make?
4. How did Moses's parents seek to save their child?
5. Who found Moses?
6. What did she decide to do with the child?
7. Whom did the princess secure for a nurse for him?
8. Where did Moses live and what was he taught?

Scholar's Home Work.

Advance work:

Study the text of the story, found in Exod. 1:22—2:10; Acts 7:20-22; and Heb. 11:23.

Review and constructive work:

Paste picture, "The Finding of Moses," by Delaroche, in the Review Book. Write over the picture the lesson subject, "The Early Life of Moses," and the place in the Bible where this story is found, Exod. 1:22—2:10. Beneath the picture write the memory verse. Answer the review questions, and when corrected by the teacher paste the sheet into the Review Book on the page opposite the picture.

LESSON 10
MOSES THE LEADER

Lesson Material.

Exod. 2: 16–22; 3: 1–12; 4: 1–21, 27–31.

Teacher's Study Material.

Exod. 2: 11 — 4: 31; Rawlinson, *Moses,* in "Men of the Bible" series, chaps. vi–viii; Geikie, *Hours with the Bible,* Vol. II, pp. 132–52; *Expositor's Bible,* "Exodus," chaps. ii–iv; Hastings, *Bible Dictionary,* art. "Moses;" a good critical commentary.

Illustrative Material.

Outline map showing Egypt and Midian. Trace journeys of Moses to and from Midian. Pictures of "A Shepherd and His Dog" (Wilde, No. 243), and "Jacob's Well" (Wilde, No. 312). Picture for the Review Book, "Moses and the Burning Bush," by D. Feti.

Connecting Links.

Review: Briefly review Moses's early life, questioning the class upon the chief elements of the story, and emphasizing the condition of the Hebrews at this time.

Intervening events: One day after Moses had grown to be a young man, he went to the place where the Hebrews were working for the Egyptians, and there he saw one of the cruel Egyptians beating a Hebrew. He tried to interfere, but the Egyptian persisted, and in a sudden burst of anger Moses struck him. He struck so hard that the blow killed the man. Moses was frightened when he saw what he had done, and hid the body in the sand for fear Pharaoh should find out about it. In some way Pharaoh did find out and sought to put Moses to death; so Moses fled into Midian to escape from the king. Our story begins at this point.

Narrative Outline. (For the teacher. Language and detail to be adapted to the pupils.)
1. Moses's life in Midian.
    a) His new home
    b) His occupation.
    c) His changed character.
2. Moses's call to leadership.
    a) God calls him to lead the Hebrew people.
    b) Moses's objections.
    c) God's promise of help.
    d) Aaron sent to help Moses.
3. Moses's return to Egypt.
    a) He starts with wife and children.
    b) The meeting with Aaron.
    c) Moses tells Aaron of his mission.
4. Moses's appearance before the Hebrew people.
    a) The people gather at his call.
    b) He tells of his mission.
    c) He proves his words by showing the signs.
    d) The people believe him and worship God.

Suggestions for Developing the Outline.

As the class is supposed to study the story material before coming to the session, develop the narrative as much as possible by questions, following the outline. Use the outline map showing Egypt and Midian. Describe Moses's condition when he reached the well — a fugitive, tired, friendless, without any place to go to. Show a picture of an ancient well, and explain how the flocks were brought there every night to be watered. Question the class about the events that led to Moses becoming a member of Jethro's household. Describe the country and Moses's life there. Show how in this life he was being trained further for his future great work. In what way did the knowledge of this future work come to him?

Question as to the unwillingness of Moses to undertake the work. How were his objections overcome? Why does he now leave Midian? Describe the preparations for the journey itself, using the map, and the meeting with Aaron. Note in this connection the early fulfilment of God's promise. What was the condition of the Hebrews when Moses came to them? Note that they had no army, no weapons, and had been slaves for many years. Would they be likely to believe Moses? Describe the way Moses and Aaron went about their work. In what way were they able to win the people? Did the people believe in them? How did they show their belief? Review the whole story (by questions, or by having one member of the class repeat the story while the others listen to correct), making sure that the class has a clear knowledge of the facts of the lesson. Try to present the narrative and to review it in such a way that the class may gain some idea of the relationship between God's work and his chosen workers. Moses's training in Egypt and in Midian fitted him to be a leader.

Suggested Generalization. (Adapt form of statement to pupils.)

God's work is to be done by those who are prepared to do it. What training did Moses receive in Egypt? What effect did the years spent in the desert of Midian have upon him? What kind of a man do you think would be required to become a leader of the Hebrews? Why did God call Moses to become their leader? It is so today: God calls those who are prepared to be leaders in doing his work.

Memory Verse.
"Come now therefore, and I will send thee unto Pharaoh, that thou mayest bring forth my people, the children of Israel, out of Egypt" (Exod. 3: 10).

Review Questions. (To be answered by the scholar at home.)
1. When Moses left Egypt, where did he go?
2. What was his occupation there?
3. What wonderful thing happened to him there?
4. What did God ask him to do?
5. What was Moses's reply?
6. What promise of help did God give him?
7. Who was sent to be Moses's helper?
8. What did Moses and Aaron do in Egypt?

Scholar's Home Work.
Advance work:
Study the text of the story, found in Exod. 3: 1-12; 4: 1-21, 27-31.
Review and constructive work:
Paste picture, "Moses and the Burning Bush" by D. Feti, in the Review Book. Write over the picture the lesson subject, "Moses the Leader," and the place in the Bible where this story is found, Exod. 2: 16-22, 3: 1-12, 4: 1-21, 27-31. Beneath the picture write the memory verse. Answer the review questions, and when corrected by the teacher paste the sheet into the Review Book on the page opposite the picture.

LESSON 11

MOSES AND PHARAOH

Lesson Material.
Exod. 5: 1-19; 6: 1-13; 7: 8-13, 20-24; 8: 6-15, 17-19, 24-32; 9: 1-12, 23-35; 10: 3-29; 11: 4-10; 12: 21-36.

Teacher's Study Material.
Exod. chaps. 5-12; Rawlinson, *Moses* in "Men of the Bible" series, chap. ix; Geikie, *Hours with the Bible*, Vol. II, pp. 152-87; *Expositor's Bible*, "Exodus," chaps.

v–xi; Price, *The Monuments and the Old Testament*, pp. 107–22; Hastings, *Bible Dictionary*, art. "Plagues of Egypt."

Illustrative Material.

Pictures of Egyptian temples and palaces. Picture, "Pharaoh Urging Moses to Leave Egypt," by Doré. Picture for the Review Book, "Moses and Aaron before Pharaoh," by Doré.

Connecting Links.

Review: Give a brief review of the last lesson and emphasize the difficult task Moses had undertaken — to get the consent of the king for the Hebrews to leave the land, and then to make all plans for the great multitude of people to take a long journey seeking a new home. The lesson today tells about Moses trying to get Pharaoh's permission for the Hebrews to leave Egypt.

Intervening events: After Moses had addressed the people, and had told them of how God had called him in the wilderness of Midian to return to Egypt to lead them to a new home where they would no longer be slaves but free, he and Aaron went before Pharaoh the king to ask his permission for the Hebrews to leave Egypt. Our narrative begins at this point.

Narrative Outline. (For the teacher. Language and detail to be adapted to the pupils.)

1. Moses's request of Pharaoh.
    a) Rejected by Pharaoh.
    b) Results in an increase of the Hebrews' burdens.
2. The encouraging message from God.
    a) His promise remembered.
    b) Deliverance assured.

3. The contest with Pharaoh.
    a) The sign of the rod.
    b) The first nine plagues.
        (1) The magicians try to imitate them.
        (2) Pharaoh promises to let the people go.
        (3) The plagues disappear — Pharaoh fails to keep his promise.
    c) The death of the first-born announced.
4. The Hebrews' preparation for leaving.
    a) Preparations for the journey.
    b) The Passover instituted.
5. The tenth plague inflicted.
    a) The first-born of all destroyed.
    b) Pharaoh's great distress.
    c) The Hebrews urged to leave.

Suggestions for Developing the Outline.

As the class is supposed to study the story material before coming to the session, develop the narrative as much as possible by questions, following the outline. Describe the first meeting of Pharaoh with Moses and Aaron. (Show picture.) For what did Moses and Aaron ask? How did Pharaoh treat them? What was the result to the people of this first request? Point out to the class the effect upon the Hebrews of this increase of their burdens. How did they change toward Moses and Aaron? What then did Moses do? What encouragement came to him? Describe the second meeting of the two leaders with King Pharaoh. Note the signs that were done in Pharaoh's presence. In what way did Moses and Aaron show themselves superior to the wise men of the king? What was the result of this meeting? Describe in order the first nine plagues. Note that they probably extended over quite a period of time, perhaps a year or more. Question the class as to the effect of each plague. What kind of a man does this part of the narrative show King Pharaoh to be? What did Moses finally threaten? Question the class about the preparations for the great journey. Describe briefly the institution of the Passover and explain its meaning. What great affliction finally came upon the Egyptians? Upon whom did it fall? How did this affect Pharaoh? What did the king's servants beg him to do? Picture the great distress throughout the city, and impress the thought that at last the great king had to recognize the God of the Hebrews. Note how eager the king and all his people were to have the Hebrews go. Why was this? Thus the promise of God was fulfilled, and the Israelites, under the leadership of Moses, started on their long journey to their new home in the Promised Land. Review the whole story, making sure that the class has a clear knowledge of the facts of the lesson narrative. Try to present the narrative and to review it in such a way that the class may be impressed with the certainty of the accomplishment of God's purposes which the lesson illustrates.

Suggested Generalization. (Adapt form of statement to pupils.)

God's purposes will be realized, although we may hasten or hinder such realization.

What did God promise to do for the Hebrews? Whom did he send as their leader? What did Pharaoh do when Moses asked for the release of the Hebrews? How did he act when one plague after another fell upon him and his people? What was he finally compelled to do? So today God has certain plans for our lives and for the lives of all people. We should try to find out what God wants, and then help and not hinder the good work.

Memory Verse.

"I am Jehovah, and I will bring you out from under the burdens of the Egyptians, and I will rid you out of their bondage" (Exod. 6:6a).

Review Questions. (To be answered by the scholar at home.)

1. What was the first request Moses made of Pharaoh?
2. What was the result of this request?
3. What promise did God make the Hebrews?
4. Name the first nine plagues.
5. What effect did these plagues have upon Pharaoh?
6. What great ceremonial feast was established at this time?
7. What was the tenth plague?
8. In what did this last plague result?

Scholar's Home Work.

Advance work:

Study the text of the story found in Exodus, portions of chaps. v to xii.

Review and constructive work:

Paste picture, "Moses and Aaron before Pharaoh" by Doré, in the Review Book. Write over the picture the lesson subject, "Moses and Pharaoh," and the place in the Bible where this story is found, Exod. chaps. v–xii. Beneath the picture write the memory verse. Answer the review questions, and when corrected by the teacher paste the sheet into the Review Book on the page opposite the picture.

JUNIOR DEPARTMENT COURSE 169

§ 3. BOOKS RELATING TO THE WORK OF GRADE A

A. REFERENCE READING FOR THE TEACHER

Bissell, *Biblical Antiquities* (American Sunday School Union, Philadelphia).
Geikie, *Hours with the Bible* (James Pott & Co., New York).
Geikie, *Old Testament Characters* (James Pott & Co., New York).
Kent, *A History of the Hebrew People*, 2 vols. (Charles Scribner's Sons, New York).
Kent, *A History of the Jewish People* (Charles Scribner's Sons, New York).
MacCoun, *The Holy Land in Geography and History*, 2 vols. (F. H. Revell Co., Chicago).
Ottley, *A History of the Hebrews* (The Macmillan Co., New York).
Price, *The Monuments and the Old Testament* (The Christian Culture Press, Chicago).
"Men of the Bible" series: 15 vols. on the Old Testament; Rev. J. S. Exell, M.A., editor (F. H. Revell Co., Chicago).

B. SUPPLEMENTAL READING FOR THE PUPIL

Baldwin, *Old Stories of the East* (American Book Co., New York).
Bennett and Adeney, *The Bible Story* (The Macmillan Co., New York).
Gaskoin, *Children's Treasury of Bible Stories*, Part I (The Macmillan Co., New York).
Gilder, *The Bible for Children* (The Century Co., New York).
Guerber, *The Story of the Chosen People* (American Book Co., New York).
Mackail, *The Little Bible* (Doubleday and McClure Co., New York).
Moulton, *The Modern Reader's Bible;* Children's series: Old Testament stories (The Macmillan Co., New York).

Ralph, *Step by Step through the Bible,* Parts I and II (Thomas Nelson & Sons, New York).

Sheldon, *Old Testament Stories* (W. W. Welch Co., Chicago).

---

§ 4. OUTLINE OF THE COURSE FOR GRADE B

GRADE SUBJECT: THE STORY OF GOD'S SON — JESUS CHRIST. (BRINGING GOD'S MESSAGE OF BLESSING FOR ALL)

Chapter 1 — The coming of Jesus.
1. Preparing for his coming — in the home of Zacharias.
2. Preparing for his coming — in the home of Joseph and Mary.
3. The lowly birth and heavenly announcement.
4. The wise men from the East.
5. Safety in Egypt.

Chapter 2 — The boyhood of Jesus.
6. Jesus' home and school training.
7. The first visit to Jerusalem.
8. *Review.* Chaps. 1 and 2.

Chapter 3 — Jesus begins his work.
9. The baptism of Jesus.
10. The temptation of Jesus.
11. Jesus announced by John.
12. Choosing the first disciples.
13. The first miracle.
14. Cleansing the temple.
15. *Review.*

Chapter 4 — Jesus and the people.
16. Winning a woman of Samaria.
17. A Sabbath-day's work.
18. A missionary journey.

Junior Department Course

19. Healing the paralytic.
20. The use of the Sabbath.
21. The sermon on the mount.
22. *Review.*
    Memory work: selections from the sermon on the mount.
23. Healing at a distance.
24. Raising the dead.
25. Answering John's messengers.
26. Forgiving the penitent.
27. Teaching by parables.
28. Stilling the tempest.
29. Casting out evil spirits.
30. Feeding five thousand.
31. *Review.*
    Memory work: selections from the sermon on the mount.

Chapter 5 — Jesus and his disciples.
32. Healing the foreigner.
33. Peter's confession.
34. A prophecy of what was to come.
35. The wonderful transfiguration.
36. Settling a dispute.
37. *Review.*
    Memory work: selections from the sermon on the mount.

Chapter 6 — Jesus completes his work.
38. Three stories of love.
39. The raising of Lazarus.
40. The rich young ruler.
41. Zaccheus the tax-collector.
42. The triumphal entry into Jerusalem.

43. *Review.*
   Memory work: selections from the sermon on the mount.

Chapter 7 — Jesus returns to his father.
44. The farewell to his disciples.
45. The arrest.
46. The trial.
47. The crucifixion and resurrection.
48. The appearances.
49. The ascension.
50. *Review.*
   Book work: the four gospels.

Special Lessons.
51. Christmas lesson.
52. Easter lesson.

---

§ 5. SUGGESTIVE LESSON PLANS FOR GRADE B
LESSONS 16–18
LESSON 16
WINNING A WOMAN OF SAMARIA

Lesson Material.
  John 4: 1-26, 28-30, 39-42.

Teacher's Study Material.
  Stevens and Burton, *A Harmony of the Gospels,* for the intervening events; Edersheim, *Life and Times of Jesus the Messiah,* Vol. I, pp. 394-418; Andrews, *Life of Christ,* pp. 183-86; Phelps, *The Story of Jesus Christ,* pp. 109-14; Farrar, *The Life of Christ,* pp. 110-15; Gilbert, *The Student's Life of Jesus,* pp. 104-9; a good critical commentary.

JUNIOR DEPARTMENT COURSE 173

Illustrative Material.

Outline map showing Jesus' journey from Jerusalem northward through Samaria to Galilee. On this map locate Jacob's well. General pictures: "Jacob's Well," "Woman Carrying Water-pot." Picture for the Review Book, "Christ and the Woman of Samaria," by Hofmann.

Connecting Links.

Review: As the last lesson was a full review of the lessons of chap. 3, a simple review statement by the teacher is all that is needed now. In our new chapter, in the story of God's Son, chap. 4, we shall learn of Jesus' work among the people; of how he taught them and helped them in many ways.

Intervening events: After the cleansing of the temple Jesus has a long talk with Nicodemus, a ruler of the Jews. He then leaves Jerusalem and preaches and works in Judea. After some months' work in Judea he starts north for Galilee, passing through Samaria, and it is here in Samaria that the events of our lesson happen.

Narrative Outline. (For the teacher. Language and detail to be adapted to the pupils.)

1. The weary travelers.
    a) Jesus and the disciples journey to Galilee.
    b) They reach Jacob's well tired and hungry.
    c) The disciples go for food.
    d) Jesus rests by the well-side.
2. The Samaritan woman.
    a) Comes to the well to draw water.
    b) Meets and talks with Jesus.
3. Jesus wins the woman to a better life.
    a) The woman's curiosity is aroused.
    b) Her desire is awakened

      c) Her real need is revealed to her.
      d) She finally believes in Jesus.
  4. The woman tells others the news.
      a) Many come from the city to see Jesus.
      b) He stays in the Samaritan city two days, teaching and helping the people.

Suggestions for Developing the Outline.

As the class is supposed to study the story material before coming to the session, develop the narrative as much as possible by questions, following the outline. After a brief review show on the map the road Jesus took on his journey to Galilee, and the position of Jacob's well. Tell of the origin of the well and its present condition, and show a picture of it as it is now. What was the condition of Jesus and his disciples when they reached the well? Picture to the class Jesus, tired and hungry, resting by the well-side, while his disciples sought food in the nearby town. Who comes to the well while Jesus is resting there? For what purpose? Show picture of woman carrying water. What did Jesus ask of her? Why was she so surprised at this? Tell the class something of the prejudice the Jews had against the Samaritans, and also of the way in which they regarded woman. Note that Jesus, although tired, was ever ready to help people. He could see that this woman, who had led an evil life, was discontented with that life, and even though she disliked Jews — for the Jews and the Samaritans had no dealings one with another — he wished to do something for her. He began in a perfectly natural way, by an ordinary request for a drink. Note how he aroused her curiosity, and then awakened a strong desire on her part for this wonderful water of which he spoke. But the woman did not understand Jesus' real meaning; she thought only of her physical needs. Now show the class how Jesus plainly revealed her needs by showing to her that she had been living a wrong life. What he wanted her to do was to change completely, and to begin to live a right life. Explain in this connection the meaning of Jesus' offer of "living water," as given in vs. 14. The woman was discontented with her past life and wished (thirsted) for something better; Jesus said that if she would believe in him and follow his teachings, she would never after be dissatisfied (never thirst again), but would be happy and contented. Question the class as to how the woman received Jesus' statement. What did she at first believe? Whom did she finally believe him to be? What does she then do? Why do the Samaritans at first believe? What do they ask of Jesus? With what result? Review the whole story, making sure that the class has a clear knowledge of the facts of the lesson narrative, and a grasp of the idea involved in the story. In connection with the review use Hofmann's picture, "Christ and the Woman of Samaria."

Suggested Generalization.

Every opportunity to do good is a call to do good.
In what condition was Jesus when he came to the well? Who came to the well while he was resting? What kind of a life had this woman led? What did Jesus do? But was he not very tired and desirous to rest? Why then did he speak to her? Was it worth while helping just one person? What was the result of their talk? How do you suppose Jesus felt at the close of the talk? So today we should use every opportunity to do good that comes to us, even though the service appears small.

Memory Verse.

"My meat is to do the will of him that sent me, and to accomplish his work" (John 4: 34).

Review Questions. (To be answered by the scholar at home.)
1. At what place did Jesus and his disciples rest on their journey to Galilee?
2. Who met him there?
3. What did Jesus ask of her?
4. What did Jesus say he could give her?
5. What did Jesus mean by these words?
6. Whom did the woman finally believe Jesus to be?
7. To whom did she carry the news?
8. What was the result of her message?

Scholar's Home Work.
  Advance work:
    Study the text of the story found in John 4: 1–26, 28–30, 39–42.
  Review and constructive work:
    Paste picture, "Christ and the Woman of Samaria," by Hofmann, in the Review Book. Write over the picture the lesson subject, "Winning a Woman of Samaria," and the place in the Bible where this story is found, John 4: 1–26. Beneath the picture write the memory verse. Answer the review questions, and when corrected by the teacher paste the sheet into the Review Book on the page opposite the picture. Trace the journeys of the lesson on the Progressive Outline Map of Palestine (published by D. C. Heath & Co., Boston).

LESSON 17
A SABBATH-DAY'S WORK

Lesson Material.
  Matt. 8: 14–17; Mark 1: 21–34; Luke 4: 31–41.

Teacher's Study Material.
  Stevens and Burton, *A Harmony of the Gospels,* for the intervening events; Gilbert, *The Student's Life of Jesus,*

pp. 114-29; Phelps, *The Story of Jesus Christ*, pp. 137-47; Farrar, *The Life of Christ*, pp. 125-29; Thomson, *The Land and the Book*, Vol. II, pp. 417-21; Edersheim, *Life and Times of Jesus the Messiah*, Vol. I, pp. 478-88; a good critical commentary.

Illustrative Material.

Trace on the blackboard outline map Jesus' journeys since the last lesson. General pictures: "Capernaum and the Sea of Galilee" (Wilde, No. 213), "The Book of the Law" (Wilde, No. 237), and "Jesus Preaching in the Synagogue," by Bida. Picture for the Review Book, "Christ Healing the Sick," by Hofmann.

Connecting Links.

Review: Briefly review the last lesson, laying emphasis upon the conditions under which the ministry of Jesus as there presented was accomplished.

Intervening events: As these are given trace the journeys on the map. Jesus continued his northward journey from Samaria and entered Galilee. The first note we have of him is at Cana, from which place he healed the nobleman's son who was lying sick at Capernaum. From there he went to Nazareth, his own city. A sermon which he preached in the Nazareth synagogue stirred the people against him, and he was forced to go to Capernaum, which he made his home. One day, walking by the Sea of Galilee, he saw four fishermen, Peter, Andrew, James, and John, fishing and mending their nets. These four men he called to be his first disciples. At this point our lesson of today begins.

Narrative Outline. (For the teacher. Language and detail to be adapted to the pupils.)

1. In the Capernaum synagogue.
    a) He teaches with authority.

  b) He heals with power.
   (1) A demoniac disturbs the meeting.
   (2) Jesus casts the evil spirit out of the man.
   (3) The people marvel at his power.
  c) His wonderful ministry is reported throughout the region.
 2. In Peter's home.
  a) They tell him of the sickness of Peter's wife's mother.
  b) He touches her and commands the fever to leave her.
  c) Her cure sudden and complete.
 3. In the city at sunset.
  a) After sundown many sick are brought to him.
  b) He lays his hands on them and heals them.
  c) He casts out the evil spirits from many.

Suggestions for Developing the Outline.

As the class is supposed to study the story material before coming to the session, develop the narrative as much as possible by questions, following the outline. Jesus now makes Capernaum his permanent home. On the Sabbath, as was his custom, he goes to the synagogue and is invited to teach the congregation. Describe a synagogue and its services. (See Thomson's *The Land and the Book*.) Show picture of a roll of the law and also Bida's picture, "Jesus Preaching in the Synagogue." What effect did his teaching have upon the people? Why? Explain to the class the difference between Jesus' teaching and that of the scribes. The scribes were continually quoting this, that, or the other Rabbi as authority for what they taught; Jesus said when he taught, "I say unto you." Question as to the disturbance caused by the possessed man. What was the trouble with him? We shall not be able to explain wholly this scene, as we do not understand just what demon-possession was; but such possessed persons acted as insane persons act, and many think that possession by an evil spirit, as it is called in the Bible, was a kind of insanity. Whatever the real trouble, Jesus heals the man. Question the class as to the means used. No medicine, no treatment; simply a word of command, and the man was healed. What was the effect of this upon the people? What question did they ask one another? To what extent did Jesus' wonderful work become known? Where did he go upon leaving the synagogue? What trouble did he find there? What do you suppose the disciples who told Jesus of the trouble expected of him? Did they have any right to expect this? Did they believe Jesus could cure the sick one? What led them to believe? What did Jesus do? With what result? How do we know that a cure was effected? Have the class compare these two miracles of healing; one physical, one mental; both by word of command; both sudden and complete. What effect did this ministry of healing have upon the four disciples? What happened in the city at sundown? Why did the people wait until sunset? Explain to the class the strict Sabbath-keeping practices of the Jews. They were so strict that they would not have cures wrought on the Sabbath day. Jesus held this to be wrong and he himself did cure sick people on the Sabbath, but the Jewish leaders condemned him for doing so. What diseases were healed by Jesus? What means did he use to heal? Try to have the class picture the scene: the divine minister, laying his hands of healing upon all who came to him and restoring them to health; speaking words of command with power, and thus curing the many afflicted with mental disease; speaking words of comfort and peace to those who were burdened with sorrows and troubles. Review the whole story, making sure that the class has a clear knowledge of the facts of the lesson narrative, and a grasp of the idea involved in the story. In connection with the review use Hofmann's picture, "Christ Healing the Sick."

Suggested Generalization.

> *To be helpful to others should be our highest aim.*

What did Jesus do as soon as he came to Capernaum? How did he seek to help the people? What did he do for the insane man? What for Peter's wife's mother? What for the many who were brought to him at sunset? Why did Jesus do all this? If this was Jesus' work, what does he expect of his disciples? There are many ways of being helpful to others, but the one who is not seeking at all times to be thus helpful is not living the highest and truest kind of a life.

Memory Verse.

"Whosoever would become great among you shall be your minister; and whosoever would be first among you shall be your servant" (Matt. 20:26, 27).

Review Questions. (To be answered by the scholar at home.)

1. What place did Jesus make his home after his rejection at Nazareth?
2. What was Jesus' Sabbath custom?
3. How did Jesus' teaching differ from that of the scribes?
4. What wonderful cure did Jesus perform in the synagogue?
5. What was the result of this miracle?
6. What other cure was done on the same day?
7. Who were brought to him at sunset?
8. What did he do for them?

Scholar's Home Work.

Advance work:

Study the text of the story found in Mark 1: 21-34 and in Luke 4: 31-41.

Review and constructive work:

Paste picture, "Christ Healing the Sick," by Hofmann, in the Review Book. Write over the picture the lesson subject, "A Sabbath-Day's Work," and the place in the Bible where this story is found, Mark 1: 21-34 and Luke 4: 31-41. Beneath the picture write the memory verse. Answer the review questions, and when corrected by the teacher paste the sheet into the Review Book on the page opposite the picture. Trace the journeys of the lesson on the Progressive Outline Map of Palestine.

LESSON 18

A MISSIONARY JOURNEY

Lesson Material.

Matt. 4: 23; 8: 1-4; Mark 1: 35-45; Luke 4: 42-44; 5: 12-16.

Teacher's Study Material.

Stevens and Burton, *A Harmony of the Gospels*, for the intervening events; Gilbert, *The Student's Life of Jesus*, pp. 129, 130; Phelps, *The Story of Jesus Christ*, pp. 146-54; Andrews, *The Life of Our Lord*, pp. 249-52; Edersheim, *Life and Times of Jesus the Messiah*, Vol. I, pp. 489-98; a good critical commentary.

Illustrative Material.

Trace on the blackboard outline map the probable route of the missionary journey. General pictures: "A Group of Lepers by the Roadside" (Wilde, No. 228), "Jesus

Healing the Leper," by Bida, and "Jesus Preaching in the Synagogue," by Bida. Picture for the Review Book, "Christ Preaching from a Boat," by Hofmann.

Connecting Links.

Review: Briefly review the last lesson, laying emphasis upon the compassion of Jesus and his readiness at all times to help the needy.

Intervening events: There are no events intervening between last lesson and the one for today. The missionary journey seems to have been begun immediately after the great day of healing in Capernaum.

Narrative Outline. (For the teacher. Language and detail to be adapted to the pupils.)

1. The reason for the journey.
    a) Jesus goes out early in the morning to pray.
    b) The multitude seek him.
    c) They desire him to remain with them.
    d) He answers that the Gospel must be preached to others.
    e) With his disciples he visits the towns of Galilee.
2. The work of the journey.
    a) Preaching the Gospel.
    b) Teaching the people.
    c) Healing all manner of disease.
3. An incident of the journey.
    a) A leper begs to be cured.
    b) Jesus cures him with a touch.
    c) The leper is commanded to tell no one, but to show himself to the priest.
    d) In his joy he tells everyone of the miracle.
    e) As a result great crowds come to Jesus for healing.

Suggestions for Developing the Outline.

As the class is supposed to study the story material before coming to the session, develop the narrative as much as possible by questions, following the outline. After the Sabbath day of healing Jesus goes out in the early morning to pray. Question the class about prayer. What is it? Why did Jesus pray? Try to impress the thought that if Jesus felt the need of prayer, how much more do we need it in our lives. Who came seeking Jesus? For what purpose? How did Jesus answer them? What does this answer teach us about the Gospel? What does it teach us about the work of Jesus? Jesus and a few of his disciples now start out upon a missionary journey throughout the province. Locate Galilee on the map. Point out and name to the class some of the principal villages and towns. Draw the journey line so as to include these. The evangelist tells us that Jesus' work was threefold: (1) Preaching the gospel in the synagogues. Show Bida's picture of Jesus preaching in the synagogue. Question about Jesus' preaching. What was the subject? Who heard him? What effect did it have? (2) Teaching the people. In the synagogue, upon the sea-shore, upon the hillside, or upon the plains, wherever Jesus could gather the people. Explain to the class the difference between teaching and preaching. (3) Healing the sick of all manner of disease, physical and mental. Jesus came to be a minister, to minister to man's needs, physical, mental, and spiritual. He was not only a preacher, proclaiming salvation, nor simply a teacher, pointing out to all the way of right living; he was also a healer of men's diseased bodies. Tell the class something of the great work of healing that is being carried on in our country and in mission lands, under the influence and inspiration of the spirit of Christianity. Somewhere on the journey a leper meets Jesus and beseeches him for healing. Leprosy was considered by the Jews to be incurable except by direct act of God. Question about the leper's faith. Did he believe that Jesus could cure him? Did he believe that Jesus would cure him? How did Jesus answer his petition? Show the class the difference between the way Jesus treated this leper and the way a Jew would have treated him. What command did Jesus give the leper? What did the leper do? What effect upon Jesus' missionary work did the report of this great miracle have? When Jesus was again alone what do we find him doing? Review the whole story, making sure that the class has a clear knowledge of the facts of the lesson narrative, and an understanding of the missionary spirit which the lesson expresses. In connection with the review use Hofmann's picture, "Christ Preaching from a Boat."

Suggested Generalization.
  The glad message of the Gospel is for all people.
For what did Jesus go away by himself in the early morning? Who followed after him? What did they want? What did Jesus propose to do? What reason did he give for doing this? What was his work while on the journey? What incident is given that illustrates one part of his work? Thus Jesus himself taught and illustrated his teaching by his actions, that "the good tidings of great joy" were to be carried to "all the people." We may not go away from home as missionaries, but we must have the missionary spirit if we are to be true disciples of Jesus.

Memory Verse.
  "But he said unto them, I must preach the good tidings of the kingdom of God to the other cities also: for therefore was I sent" (Luke 4: 43).

Review Questions. (To be answered by the scholar at home.)
1. For what purpose did Jesus go away by himself early in the morning?
2. Who followed him?
3. What did they desire?
4. How did Jesus answer them?
5. Where did he then go with his disciples?
6. For what purpose did he go on this missionary journey?
7. What wonderful miracle of healing did Jesus do?
8. How did the report of this miracle affect his missionary work?

Scholar's Home Work.
Advance work:
Study the text of the story found in Mark 1: 35-45.
Review and constructive work:
Paste picture, "Christ Preaching from a Boat," by Hofmann, in the Review Book. Write over the picture the lesson subject, "A Missionary Journey," and the place in the Bible where this story is found, Mark 1: 35-45. Beneath the picture write the memory verse. Answer the review questions, and when corrected by the teacher paste the sheet into the Review Book on the page opposite the picture. Trace the journeys of the lesson on the Progressive Outline Map of Palestine.

§ 6. BOOKS RELATING TO THE WORK OF GRADE B

A. REFERENCE READING FOR THE TEACHER

Edersheim, *The Life and Times of Jesus the Messiah*, 2 vols. (Longmans, Green & Co., New York).
Farrar, *The Life of Christ.* Various editions.
Geikie, *New Testament Hours* (James Pott & Co., New York).

Gilbert, *The Student's Life of Jesus* (The Macmillan Co., New York).

Gillie, *The Story of Stories* (The Macmillan Co., New York).

Phelps, *The Story of Jesus Christ* (Houghton, Mifflin & Co., Boston).

Rhees, *The Life of Jesus of Nazareth* (Charles Scribner's Sons, New York).

Stalker, *The Life of Jesus Christ* (F. H. Revell Co., Chicago).

Vincent, Lee & Bain, *Earthly Footprints of the Man of Galilee* (N. D. Thompson Publishing Co., New York).

B. SUPPLEMENTAL READING FOR THE PUPIL

Bennett & Adeney, *The Bible Story* (The Macmillan Co., New York).

Gaskoin, *Children's Treasury of Bible Stories,* Part II (The Macmillan Co., New York).

Gilder, *The Bible for Children* (The Century Co., New York).

Helm, *When Jesus Was here among Men* (F. H. Revell Co., Chicago).

Moulton, *The Modern Reader's Bible;* Children's series; New Testament stories (The Macmillan Co., New York).

Ralph, *Step by Step through the Bible,* Part III (Thomas Nelson & Sons, New York).

Weed, *A Life of Christ for the Young* (George W. Jacobs & Co., Philadelphia).

---

§ 7. OUTLINE OF THE COURSE FOR GRADE C

GRADE SUBJECT: THE STORY OF GOD'S EARLY MESSENGERS (CARRYING GOD'S MESSAGE OF BLESSING TO THE NATIONS)

Chapter 1 — The messengers at work in Jerusalem.

1. God preparing his messengers for their work.
2. Peter's first sermon.
3. Three thousand disciples won.
4. A lame man healed.
5. The messengers put into prison.

6. A lie and its consequences.
7. The messengers' boldness before the council.
8. The stoning of a messenger.
9. *Review.*

Chapter 2 — The messengers at work in Judea and Samaria.
10. The gospel story in Samaria.
11. Philip and the queen's treasurer.
12. The messengers' work of healing.
13. The visions of Peter and Cornelius.
14. Peter's visit to Cornelius.
15. Peter in trouble.
16. The messengers and the wicked king.
17. *Review.*

Chapter 3 — The messengers at work in Syria.
18. A new messenger appointed.
19. The new messenger beginning his work.
20. The messengers' work in Antioch.

Chapter 4 — The messengers at work in Asia Minor.
21. The messengers and the magician.
22. The messengers winning many disciples.
23. The messengers suffering persecution.
24. The church deciding what the messengers shall teach.
25. *Review.* Chaps. 3, 4.

Chapter 5 — The messengers at work in Europe.
26. Freeing a slave girl.
27. An earthquake and its results.
28. Forming new churches under difficulties.
29. Paul among idolaters.
30. The messengers in Corinth.
31. *Review.*
    Memory work: 1 Cor. 13: 1–7.

Chapter 6 — The messengers finishing their work in Asia Minor.
32. Paul at work in Ephesus.
33. The riot in Ephesus.
34. Raising the dead.
35. The homeward journey.
36. Paul's arrest in Jerusalem.
37. Paul's defense before the people.
38. *Review.*
    Memory work: 1 Cor. 13:8-13.

Chapter 7 — The messengers' closing days.
39. Paul tried by the Jewish rulers.
40. A plot and an escape.
41. Paul's trial before Governor Felix.
42. Paul's trial before Governor Festus.
43. Paul's trial before King Agrippa.
44. A storm and a shipwreck.
45. A winter on an island.
46. Two years in prison.
47. The last days of the messengers.
48. Book work: Paul's letters.
49. Book work: Acts, and the other New Testament letters and writings.
50. *Review.*

Special Lessons.
51. Christmas lesson.
52. Easter lesson.

---

§ 8. SUGGESTIVE LESSON PLANS FOR GRADE C
LESSONS 6-8
LESSON 6
A LIE AND ITS CONSEQUENCES

Lesson Material.
  Acts 4:34-37; 5:1-11.

JUNIOR DEPARTMENT COURSE 189

Teacher's Study Material.

Burton, *The Records and Letters of the Apostolic Age,* for the intervening events; *Expositor's Bible,* "The Acts of the Apostles," Vol. I, chap. xi; Purves, *The Apostolic Age,* pp. 35-41; Robinson, *The Life and Times of Peter;* Taylor, *Peter the Apostle;* Hastings, *Bible Dictionary,* art. "Ananias;" a good critical commentary.

Illustrative Material.

General pictures, "St. Peter Distributing Alms," by Masaccio, and "St. Peter" in Da Vinci's "Last Supper." Picture for the Review Book, "Death of Ananias" by Raphael.

Connecting Links.

Review: Briefly review the last lesson, emphasizing the refusal of the apostles to refrain from preaching about Jesus, because they considered that God had called them to this work and they must do what was "right in the sight of God." Have one of the pupils read his story of the last lesson.

Intervening events: After their release from imprisonment, the apostles reported all that had happened to the company of Christians in Jerusalem. They all joined in praising God for his goodness, and in prayer that they might be bold to speak about Jesus. They continued to witness to Jesus, and the church grew rapidly. Then follow the events of our lesson of today.

Narrative Outline. (For the teacher. Language and detail to be adapted to the pupils.)

1. The care of the early Christians for one another.
    a) Those with lands and houses sell them.
    b) The money thus received is distributed among the needy.
    c) No one lacks anything, all are supplied.

2. Ananias and his sin.
   a) Ananias and his wife sell their land.
   b) They plan to keep back part of the price.
   c) Ananias brings part to the apostles, making it appear as the whole.
   d) Peter condemns him for lying to God.
   e) He is suddenly stricken with death.
3. Sapphira and her sin.
   a) She joins the company later in ignorance of what has happened.
   b) Peter questions her as to the price of the land sold.
   c) Like her husband, she lies about the price.
   d) She also is condemned by Peter for lying to God.
   e) She is stricken with sudden death.

Suggestions for Developing the Outline.

As the class is supposed to study the story material before coming to the session, develop the narrative as much as possible by questions, following the outline. The early Christians were very closely united; we read they "were of one heart and soul." Being thus bound together like members of one family, they cared for one another as members of a family would. Question the class as to what the early Christians did for one another. What did the richer disciples do? Who received and distributed the money? To whom was the money given? What was the result? Who is mentioned by name as taking part in this good work? Were the disciples required to do this? (See Acts 5:4.) Why then did they do it? Impress here that this was purely an act of love. Who else is mentioned as selling their lands? What did they plan to do? Was this right? What did Ananias do? In what way did he try to deceive the apostles? Was he successful? We do not know how Peter knew of the sin of Ananias, but in some way it had been revealed to him. What did the apostle say he had done? Emphasize here Ananias's hypocrisy — he wanted to make it appear that he was very generous, that he brought the full price of the land to lay at the apostles' feet. Note that there was nothing to compel them to do what they had done. The land was theirs; the money received for the sale of the land was theirs; they could have kept it all, given a part, or given it all. Make it clear to the class that the sin of these two disciples was in giving a part and trying to make it appear that they had given the whole. The deed was all right, but the motive back of the deed was all wrong. What did Peter say Ananias had done? What was the effect upon Ananias of this discovery of his sin? (Concerning this sudden death see article in Hastings's *Bible Dictionary*, and the *Cambridge Bible* on "Acts.") Shortly after Ananias had been carried out by the young men for burial, Sapphira joins the group of disciples. Note her ignorance of what had taken place. What question did Peter ask her? To what did the "so much" refer? Note the fact that Peter's questioning about the price for which the land was sold might well have made her suspicious that the plan had in some way been discovered. But in spite of this, how does she answer Peter? How does Peter treat her answer? What judgment is passed upon her? What is the result? What was the effect of these two sudden deaths upon the young church in Jerusalem? Review the whole story, making sure that the class has a clear knowledge of the facts of the lesson, and an understanding of the hypocrisy in Ananias and Sapphira which the lesson reveals. In connection with this review use the pictures suggested.

Suggested Generalization.

To meet God's approval the heart (motive) as well as the deed must be right.

In the early church how did the disciples care for one another? What did Ananias and Sapphira do with their land? What did they plan to do with the money? What was wrong in this plan? What was their motive in doing this? Was this right? What judgment came upon them? What then does God require of all his disciples besides right deeds? We must be constantly on our guard to keep the heart pure as well as the outer life right. All that we do must be done from right motives.

Memory Verse.

"Man looketh on the outward appearance, but the Lord looketh on the heart" (1 Sam. 16:7*b*).

Review Questions. (To be answered by the scholar at home.)

1. How did the early Christians show their love for one another?
2. What did Ananias and his wife do with their land?
3. What did they plan to do with the money received?
4. What was wrong in this plan?
5. What did Peter condemn Ananias for doing?
6. What punishment came to Ananias because of his sin?
7. How was Sapphira punished?
8. What was the effect of these two punishments upon the disciples?

Scholar's Home Work.

Advance work:

Study the text of the story found in Acts 4:34—5:11.

Review and constructive work:

Paste picture, "Death of Ananias," by Raphael, in the Review Book. Write over the picture the lesson sub-

JUNIOR DEPARTMENT COURSE   193

ject, "A Lie and Its Consequences," and the place in the Bible where this story is found, Acts 4: 34–37; 5: 1–11. Beneath the picture write the memory verse. Answer the review questions, and when corrected by the teacher paste the sheet into the Review Book on the page opposite the picture. Write very briefly, in your own words, the story of the lesson.

LESSON 7

THE MESSENGERS' BOLDNESS BEFORE THE COUNCIL

Lesson Material.
Acts 5: 12–42.

Teacher's Study Material.
Burton, *The Records and Letters of the Apostolic Age,* for the intervening events; Robinson, *The Life and Times of Peter;* Taylor, *Peter the Apostle;* Purves, *The Apostolic Age,* pp. 41–51; *Expositor's Bible,* "The Acts of the Apostles," Vol. I, chap. xii; Hastings, *Bible Dictionary,* art. "Sanhedrin;" a good critical commentary.

Illustrative Material.
Show pictures of Herod's temple (Wilde, No. 385) and of Jerusalem (modern) showing the temple area. When speaking of the release from prison show Raphael's "The Deliverance of Peter." Sketch on the board the seating arrangements of the Sanhedrin in describing the council meeting. Picture for the Review Book, "The Apostles Preaching," by Doré.

Connecting Links.
Review: Briefly review the last lesson, emphasizing the truth that God considers *why* a deed was done as well as the deed itself. Have one of the pupils read his story of the last lesson.

Intervening events: The events of today's lesson are recorded immediately after those of last Sunday. The events recorded in the first part of the text, Acts 5: 12–16, probably extended over some days, if not weeks.

Narrative Outline. (For the teacher. Language and detail to be adapted to the pupils.)
1. The work of the apostles.
    a) Many signs and wonders are wrought.
    b) Many believers are added to the church.
    c) Many come for healing from the cities near Jerusalem.
2. The imprisonment and release of the apostles.
    a) The Jewish leaders imprison the apostles.
    b) An angel of the Lord delivers them.
    c) At daybreak they enter the temple and teach.
3. The meeting of the Jewish council.
    a) The keepers of the prison report the escape of the prisoners.
    b) The apostles are again brought before the council, but without violence.
    c) There they witness boldly for Jesus.
    d) The council wishes to put them to death.
    e) Gamaliel advises them not to do this rash thing.
    f) The apostles are then beaten and released.
    g) They rejoice in their sufferings and continue their teaching and preaching work.

Suggestions for Developing the Outline.

As the class is supposed to study the story material before coming to the session, develop the narrative as much as possible by questions, following the outline. Question the class concerning the threefold form of the apostles' activity — preaching, teaching, healing. What remarkable powers were manifested by the apostles? What were the results of this? What is said of the growth of the church? Who beside the dwellers in Jerusalem were helped? What two classes of diseases were healed? (On the question of miracles, see art. "Miracles," in Hastings's *Bible Dictionary*.) Picture to the class the excitement and questioning such signs and wonders would cause in Jerusalem. The popularity of the new preachers and teachers aroused the jealousy of the Jewish leaders, who arrested and imprisoned the apostles. How were the prisoners released? What command was given them? How was this command treated? What was the probable effect of this release upon the apostles and upon the people of the city? Describe a meeting of the council or Sanhedrin. Tell a little about the members, their qualifications and powers, and of the work the council was organized to do. When the council met, for whom did they send? Picture the astonishment of the officers when they found the prisoners gone. What was their report to the council? How did this report affect the Jewish leaders? What word came to them while they were wondering what to do? What was then done? When the apostles were brought before the council, what were they accused of doing? How did Peter and the others answer the charge? What was the effect upon the council of this bold witnessing for Jesus? Who sought to restrain them from their purpose? What was his advice? Of what possible evil did he warn them? Make clear to the class at this point the wisdom of Gamaliel's advice. Other leaders had arisen in the past whose claims were proven to be false by the failure of their plans. Let this new movement run its course: if it is of men, it will fail; if it is of God, it will succeed in spite of Jewish opposition. In this latter case the council will be found fighting against God. How did the council receive Gamaliel's advice? What did they do to the apostles? How did the apostles look upon their sufferings? Did they obey the command of the council? Was this right? Review the whole story, making sure that the class has a clear knowledge of the facts of the lesson and an appreciation of the courage of the apostles in boldly witnessing for Jesus before the council, although they knew that such a course would in all probability result in further punishment for them.

Suggested Generalization.

We must never be ashamed nor afraid to take a stand for the right.

What had the apostles been commanded by the council to refrain from doing? How did they treat this command? Why did they act as they did? What was the result of their action? When again brought before the council what did they say they must do? What result followed? Why did they think they must continue their work? What kind of men does this story show the apostles to have been? When the occasion comes we must be like the apostles, neither ashamed nor afraid to witness to what is right.

Memory Verse.

"We must obey God rather than men" (Acts 5:29).

Review Questions. (To be answered by the scholar at home.)

1. What was the work of the apostles in Jerusalem?
2. How did this work affect the Jewish leaders?
3. What did these leaders do?
4. Who released the apostles from prison, and what command did they receive at this time?
5. When again brought before the council what did they answer?

Junior Department Course

6. What did the council wish to do to the apostles?
7. What was Gamaliel's advice in the case?
8. What was the final action of the council?

Scholar's Home Work.

Advance work:

Study the text of the story found in Acts 5: 12-42.

Review and constructive work:

Paste picture, "The Apostles Preaching," by Doré, in the Review Book. Write over the picture the lesson subject, "The Messengers' Boldness before the Council," and the place in the Bible where this story is found, Acts 5: 12-42. Beneath the picture write the memory verse. Answer the review questions, and when corrected by the teacher paste the sheet into the Review Book on the page opposite the picture. Write very briefly, in your own words, the story of the lesson.

Lesson 8

THE STONING OF A MESSENGER

Lesson Material.

Acts 6: 8-15; 7: 1-60.

Teacher's Study Material.

Burton, *The Records and Letters of the Apostolic Age,* for the intervening events; Purves, *The Apostolic Age,* pp. 51-55; *Expositor's Bible,* "The Acts of the Apostles," Vol. I, chaps. xv and xvi; Conybeare and Howson, *Life and Epistles of St. Paul,* Vol. I, pp. 68-75; Hastings, *Bible Dictionary,* art. "Stephen;" a good critical commentary.

Illustrative Material.

General pictures, "St. Stephen," by Champaigne, "The Stoning of Stephen," by Beato Angelico, "St. Stephen before the Council" by Beato Angelico. Picture for the Review Book, "The Stoning of Stephen," by Rembrandt.

Connecting Links.

　Review: Briefly review the last lesson, emphasizing the courage shown by the apostles in the trying times in Jerusalem, and in spite of repeated punishment. Have one of the pupils read his story of the last lesson.

　Intervening events: After their release from prison the second time the apostles continued their teaching and preaching work in Jerusalem. The result was that the church grew very rapidly. In the distribution of the charity funds there was a complaint that the Greek Jews were neglected. To remedy the trouble and to leave the apostles free to give their entire time to the work of teaching and preaching, seven men were chosen to oversee this matter. One of these seven men was Stephen, about whom today's lesson tells.

Narrative Outline. (For the teacher. Language and detail to be adapted to the pupils.)

　1. The persecution of Stephen.
　　　a) Stephen's work accompanied by signs and wonders.
　　　b) Members of certain synagogues dispute with him but are unsuccessful.
　　　c) They stir up the people against Stephen.
　　　d) Stephen is finally brought before the council.
　2. Stephen before the council.
　　　a) False witnesses charge him with speaking against the temple and the law.
　　　b) The high-priest questions: "Are these things so?"
　　　c) Stephen denies that he has done wrong.
　　　d) He finally charges his hearers with disobedience to the law.
　　　e) He has a wonderful vision of Jesus.

JUNIOR DEPARTMENT COURSE 199

3. Stephen's death.
    a) He is cast out of the city and stoned.
    b) His last words a prayer for his slayers.

Suggestions for Developing the Outline.

As the class is supposed to study the story material before coming to the session, develop the narrative as much as possible by questions, following the outline. Describe briefly the growth of the church and the custom concerning the "daily ministration." Stephen, a man full of faith and with powers similar to those possessed by the apostles, did a prominent work in Jerusalem. Question the class about this work and its results. What was the effect of Stephen's work in Jerusalem? Who opposed him? With what success? What did they finally succeed in doing? By what means did they stir up the people and the Jewish leaders? Before whom was Stephen finally brought for trial? Describe briefly the Sanhedrin, and picture the scene of Stephen's trial. What kind of witnesses were secured? What was their charge against Stephen? What truth, if any, was in this charge? What remarkable change came over Stephen as he stood before the council? Have the class recall similar instances in the Bible. Give to the class a probable explanation of such changes of countenance. What does the high-priest demand? How does Stephen answer this demand? It will not be wise to go into the defense offered by Stephen at any length. Briefly explain to the class this defense, that it was a plea or argument intended to show that the new religion, which he and many others were preaching, was to be a universal religion, one for "all the people," and hence Judaism represented by the temple and the Mosaic law must give place to it. (See, in the *Cambridge Bible*, "The Acts of the Apostles," Introduction, pp. x, xi, xii.) At a certain point in his address, he breaks off abruptly and charges the council with having the same persecuting spirit as their fathers, and that they, not he, were breaking the law. Question the class about the effect of this last charge. What vision was granted at this time to Stephen? What did he say he saw? When the council heard this what did they do? How was Stephen put to death? Where? Why was he taken outside the city walls? Who were "the witnesses"? What spirit did Stephen show at his death? What were his last words? Try to impress upon the class at this point the beautiful character of this man Stephen, who could thus pray for forgiveness for those who were slaying him. Compare the spirit shown by Stephen with the spirit shown by Jesus upon the cross. Review the whole story, making sure that the class has a clear knowledge of the facts of the lesson, and some appreciation of the true courage shown by Stephen in his bold witnessing for the truth, and of his Christlike character, shown in the spirit of forgiveness toward his enemies. In connection with this review use Champaigne's picture of "St. Stephen." The other pictures may be used during the narrative development.

Suggested Generalization.

    To be Christlike we must learn to forgive.

What had Stephen done to arouse opposition? Before whom was he brought for trial? What kind of witnesses were secured? What was the charge against him? What was his answer to the charge? What effect did his reply have upon the council? How was Stephen put to death? What spirit did he show toward his slayers? In this respect whom was he like? If we would be Christlike, what spirit must we show?

Memory Verse.

"If ye forgive men their trespasses, your heavenly Father will also forgive you" (Matt. 6: 14).

Review Questions. (To be answered by the scholar at home.)

1. What opposition did Stephen meet with in Jerusalem?
2. What did his opposers finally succeed in doing?
3. What kind of witnesses were secured to testify against him?
4. What was the charge against him?
5. What was his answer to this charge?
6. At the close of his address what vision was granted him?
7. What was the council's final action?
8. What spirit did Stephen show toward his slayers?

Scholar's Home Work.

Advance work:

Study the text of the story found in Acts 6: 8-15; 7: 1-60.

Review and constructive work:

Paste picture, "The Stoning of Stephen" by Rembrandt, in the Review Book. Write over the picture the lesson subject, "The Stoning of a Messenger," and the place in the Bible where this story is found, Acts 6: 8-15; 7: 1-60. Beneath the picture write the memory verse. Answer the review questions, and when corrected by the teacher paste the sheet into the Review Book on the page opposite the picture. Write very briefly, in your own words, the story of the lesson.

---

§ 9. BOOKS RELATING TO THE WORK OF GRADE C

A. REFERENCE READING FOR THE TEACHER

Conybeare and Howson, *Life and Epistles of St. Paul* (Charles Scribner's Sons, New York).

202 BIBLE-SCHOOL CURRICULUM

Farrar, *The Life and Work of St. Paul* (E. P. Dutton & Co., New York).
Geikie, *New Testament Hours* (James Pott & Co., New York).
Gilbert, *The Student's Life of Paul* (The Macmillan Co., New York).
Purves, *The Apostolic Age* (Charles Scribner's Sons, New York).
Stalker, *The Life of Paul* (F. H. Revell Co., Chicago).
Taylor, *Paul the Missionary; Peter the Apostle* (Harper & Bros., New York).
Thatcher, *Sketch of the History of the Apostolic Age* (Houghton, Mifflin & Co., Boston).

B. SUPPLEMENTAL READING FOR THE PUPIL

Bennett and Adeney, *The Bible Story* (The Macmillan Co., New York).
Gaskoin, *Children's Treasury of Bible Stories*, Part III (The Macmillan Co., New York).
Gilder, *The Bible for Children* (The Century Co., New York).
Moulton, *The Modern Reader's Bible*; Children's series; New Testament stories (The Macmillan Co., New York).
Ralph, *Step by Step through the Bible*, Part III (Thomas Nelson & Sons, New York).
Weed, *A Life of St. Paul for the Young; A Life of St. John for the Young; A Life of St. Peter for the Young* (George W. Jacobs & Co., Philadelphia).

---

§ 10. OUTLINE OF THE COURSE FOR GRADE D

GRADE SUBJECT: THE STORY OF GOD'S LATER MESSENGERS
(CARRYING GOD'S MESSAGE OF BLESSING TO THE WORLD)

Chapter 1 — The messengers at work in India.
  1. What a cobbler did for God.
  2. How one life lighted up India.
  3. Winning the Hindus to Christ.
  4. Keeping pluckily at hard work.

5. How far one woman's work reached.
6. What one family did for missions.
7. *Review.*

Chapter 2 — The messengers at work in China.
8. Bringing the Bible to the people.
9. The pioneer work of the medical missionaries.
10. Giving a Christian education to the people.
11. The story of a great mission work.
12. Traveling among the villages.
13. The meaning of a Christian life in China.
14. *Review.*

Chapter 3 — The messengers at work in Japan.
15. Beginning the work under difficulties.
16. The story of a Japanese boy who started a university.
17. The story of a floating Bible.
18. At work for the orphans.
19. At work among the students.
20. The work of the medical missionaries.
21. *Review.*

Chapter 4 — The messengers at work in Africa.
22. Among the Hottentots in South Africa.
23. Freeing the slaves.
24. Bravely at work in Bechuanaland.
25. Blazing the way through "Darkest Africa."
26. Using the rivers as roads.
27. What an engineer did for Africa.
28. *Review.*

Chapter 5 — The messengers at work in the isles of the sea.
29. Showing the nobility of work.
30. Starting churches in Hawaii.
31. The martyr of Raratonga.
32. Transforming the Fiji cannibals.

33. Winning the New Hebrides for Christ.
34. Sailing about on the mission ships.
35. *Review.*

Chapter 6 — The messengers at work in Mohammedan lands.
36. Starting a Christian college in the Mohammedan capital.
37. How one woman started a school in Persia.
38. Bringing new light to the people.
39. Traveling in the deserts and villages of Arabia.
40. What one college man did for the Arabs.
41. At work in old Egypt.
42. *Review.*

Chapter 7 — The messengers at work in America.
43. On the Indian trail.
44. Fighting the saloon on the frontiers.
45. The story of the mission Sunday school.
46. Among the Alaskan Indians and the Esquimaux.
47. Teaching the neglected mountain whites.
48. Building up character among the negroes.
49. At work among the foreigners.
50. *Review.*

Special Lessons.
51. Christmas lesson.
52. Easter Lesson.

---

§ 11. SUGGESTIVE LESSON PLANS FOR GRADE D

LESSONS 1 AND 15

LESSON 1

WHAT A COBBLER DID FOR GOD

Lesson Material.
Myers, *William Carey: the Shoemaker Who Became a Missionary* (selected portions of the narrative); also see *Narrative Outline* below.

JUNIOR DEPARTMENT COURSE 205

Teacher's Study Material.

Beach, *India and Christian Opportunity*, chaps, i, iii, iv, v; *idem, The Cross in the Land of the Trident*, chaps. iii, iv, vi; *idem, A Geography and Atlas of Protestant Missions*, Vol. II (missionary maps); Sherring and Storrow, *The History of Protestant Missions in India;* Smith, *The Life of William Carey, D.D.;* Tisdall, *India: Its History, Darkness and Dawn*, pp. 52-119.

Illustrative Material.

Pictures showing the physical features of the country, its temples and other architectural features, and the manners and customs of the people. Many of these can be obtained from the Perry Picture Co., Malden, Mass., the Orient Picture Co., Mt. Vernon, N. Y., and the various denominational missionary boards. An outline map of India, sketched upon cloth or heavy paper, upon which the growth of missionary work may be traced. To be used for all the lessons of this chapter. Indian curios, especially those illustrating phases of the religious life of the people. For the Review Book, a picture of William Carey.

Connecting Links.

We have been studying for a year about the work of some of the early messengers of God, who carried the message of the gospel to the peoples of southern Europe. During this year we are to study about the work of other messengers of God, who have carried the good tidings to the peoples of India, China, Japan, and many other countries, so that now the gospel of Jesus is known in all countries of the world. The first country about which we are to study is India, and our first story is about "What a Cobbler Did for God."

Narrative Outline. (For the teacher. Language and detail to be adapted to the pupils.)
1. Carey the cobbler.
   a) Birth and early education.
   b) His work of preaching and teaching.
   c) His choice of a missionary life.
2. Carey the missionary.
   a) The journey to India.
   b) Beginning work under difficulties.
   c) Establishing the mission.
   d) Some gratifying results.
   e) Overcoming difficulties.
   f) Translating the Scriptures.
   g) Other forms of work.
   h) The closing days of his life.

Suggestions for Developing the Outline.

As many of the pupils may not have the opportunity to study the lesson material in advance, the question method of developing the lesson should not be used. Tell the story to the class, making as vivid a presentation as possible, using the map, the pictures, and the curios as suggested. Describe briefly Carey's home and his meager early education. Note especially his eagerness as well as his aptitude for learning, as illustrated by the way he began the study of Greek. His early work of shoemaking, teaching in an evening school, and preaching may be very briefly touched upon. Tell of the formation of the missionary society, largely through Carey's efforts, and put on the board the motto of the society, "*Expect great things from God. Attempt great things for God*" — words taken from Mr. Carey's address which finally led to the organization of the missionary society which sent him to India as a missionary. When this society decided to send two missionaries to India, Carey offered to go as one. Point out the difficulties met at this time; the objection of his wife to go with him, lack of funds, the difficulty in securing a passage, etc. Finally the journey is begun. Contrast the ease of travel now with the inconvenience and tediousness in those days. Describe the life on shipboard. India was finally reached. Show the outline map and mark upon it the places connected with the life and work of Carey as they are told about in the story. Show the pictures of India and Indian life as you tell very briefly about the country and the people. Picture the condition of the people, their poverty and degradation. Tell a little of their religion and of some of their religious rites. Also speak of the missionary work which had been done before Carey's time. (See Beach, *The Cross in the Land of the Trident*, chaps. iii, iv, vi.) Picture the difficulties which Carey met in beginning his work (see Myers, chap. iv), and contrast with the difficulties and discouragements which Paul met with in his missionary labors. Finally a permanent mission was established at Serampore, and results began to show. A brief description of the life at this place would prove interesting. Compare with the community life of the early church (see Grade C, Lesson 6). Now speak with some detail of the three events of importance which occurred during the early residence at Serampore: (1) the baptism of the first convert, (2) the publication of the New Testament in the language of the people, and (3) Dr. Carey's appointment as professor in the college at Fort William (see Myers, chap. vii). Note the importance of each of these, especially the translation and publication of the New Testament. Show at this time specimens of the Scriptures printed in various languages and dialects (these can be obtained from the American Bible Society, New York). Although the work was now well established it still met with opposition, both in India and in England, from people who did not believe in mission work of this character; but this was finally all overcome, and the missionaries enjoyed liberty of action. Now tell with as much detail as time allows about the great work of translation undertaken and successfully carried on by Dr. Carey, trying to have the class realize the great importance of this branch of missionary activity. Carey's other work, philanthropic, benevolent, and educational, should be briefly pointed out, that the class may gain an idea of the true character of mission work abroad. For forty-one years Carey worked in India, dying there in June, 1834, at the age of seventy-three years. In closing, rapidly review the outline, which may be put on the board as the story is told, and emphasize the more important parts of the great work Dr. Carey was enabled to do for the people of India.

Suggested Generalization.

The lowliest servant of God may do a great work for him.

Where was Carey born? What humble trade did he learn? What did he long to do? To what country did he go as a missionary? What obstacles did he meet there? How did they affect him? What kept him at his work in spite of hardships? What did he accomplish in India? How important was this work? How long did he labor there? Thus we see that although he was an humble cobbler, his faith, energy, and ability enabled him to do splendid service for God.

Memory Verse.

"Expect great things from God. Attempt great things for God" (from Carey's address).

Review Questions. (To be answered by the scholar at home.)
1. What was Carey's trade?
2. What other work did he do in his native village and and in nearby towns?
3. What did he finally choose to do, and why?
4. To what country did he go?
5. What difficulties did he meet in his work?
6. What was perhaps the most important work he did?
7. In what other ways did he help the people of India?
8. How long did he labor in India?

Scholar's Home Work.

Advance work:
If possible to secure the book, study the suggested lesson material.

Review and constructive work:
Paste picture, "William Carey," in the Review Book. Write over the picture the lesson subject, "What a Cobbler Did for God." Beneath the picture write the memory verse. Answer the review questions, and when corrected by the teacher paste the sheet into the Review Book on the page opposite the picture. Write very briefly, in your own words, the story of the lesson.

LESSON 15

BEGINNING THE WORK UNDER DIFFICULTIES

Lesson Material.

Cary, *Japan and Its Regeneration*, pp. 51-57, 75-98; also see *Narrative Outline* below.

Teacher's Study Material.

Cary, *Japan and Its Regeneration;* Gordon, *An American Missionary in Japan,* chaps. iv, v, vi; Peery, *The*

Gist of Japan, chaps. i, iii, iv, viii, ix, x; Ritter, *A History of Protestant Missions in Japan;* Casartelli, *The Catholic Church in Japan.*

Illustrative Material.

Pictures showing the physical features of Japan, its temples and other architectural features, and the manners and customs of the people. Many of these can be obtained from the Perry Picture Co., Malden, Mass., the Orient Picture Co., Mt. Vernon, N. Y., and the various denominational missionary boards. An outline map of the Japanese islands, sketched upon cloth or heavy paper, upon which the growth of missionary work may be traced. To be used for all the lessons of this chapter. Japanese curios, especially those illustrating phases of the religious life of the people. For the Review Book, a picture of Yokohama (Perry, No. 1912).

Connecting Links.

Review very briefly the work done in China. For the next two months we are to study about the messengers at work in a neighboring empire, Japan, a country in which we are all very much interested at the present time. Show on the map its position with reference to China and India. Briefly describe the country and its people, and give a little of its history. Our first story is about how the messengers began their work, and the difficulties they had to meet.

Narrative Outline. (For the teacher. Language and detail to be adapted to the pupils.)

 1. The early Jesuit missions.
    a) The work of Xavier and his successors.
    b) Persecutions of the Christians.
    c) Final banishment of all foreigners.

JUNIOR DEPARTMENT COURSE 211

2. The expeditions of Commodore Perry.
3. The beginnings of modern Roman Catholic missions.
4. The beginnings of modern Protestant missions.
   a) The first missionaries and their work.
   b) Early persecutions.
   c) The period of popularity.
   d) Later opposition.

Suggestions for Developing the Outline.
As many of the pupils may not have the opportunity to study the lesson material, the question method of developing the lesson should not be used. This lesson is not as interesting as some of those which come later, but in telling the story try to make as vivid a presentation as possible, using the map, the pictures, and the curios as suggested. In describing the work of the Jesuit missionary, Francis Xavier, bring out clearly his zeal and devotion to the cause. Also impress upon the class the courage required to undertake such a work in a strange country where he was certain to meet hardship. Although Xavier himself did not succeed in accomplishing much, others who went with him and those who followed after him were enabled to do a great deal (see Cary, *Japan*, p. 52). Tell briefly of the persecutions to which these early Christians were subjected, and of the causes which led to such persecutions. Compare with the persecutions of the early Christians by the Jews and the Romans. But the same spirit of faithfulness which characterized the early Christians in the Roman empire when they were persecuted marked the lives of many of these Japanese Christians during the days of their trial (see Cary, p. 55). Finally in 1624 all foreigners, except the Dutch and the Chinese, were banished from the country, and for over two centuries Japan was closed to the outer world. Next describe the visit of Commodore Perry with

his naval vessels in 1853, and the second visit eight months later. Note the final result of these two visits, and explain the treaties and their important bearing upon mission work. The work of the Roman Catholic priests sent as missionaries to Japan as soon as it was open to foreigners may be briefly spoken of, noting especially the joy of some of these priests when they found many Christian families as the result of the work of the Jesuit missionaries more than two centuries before. (See Cary, pp. 79, 80.) These missionaries shared in the general persecution which came upon all missionaries, and showed the same spirit of zeal and courage as did their Protestant brethren. The work of the Protestant missionaries may be described in more detail, as it is their work in which we are especially interested. Note the coming of the first missionaries. Show on the map the places to which they went. Then speak of the difficulties they met with in attempting to give the message of the gospel to the people; the unfriendliness of the government, the indifference of the people, the opposition of the priests and leaders of the religions of the country. But in spite of these obstacles and difficulties, and of the fact that they could not openly preach about Jesus Christ, they did what they could by circulating the Bible in Chinese, which the educated Japanese could read, and in teaching many to read and speak English. This latter work gave the missionaries many opportunities to speak to their students about Christianity. Now tell the story of the first convert to be baptized, Yano Riyu, who was baptized in 1864 in Yokohama, and of the first Japanese Christian church, organized in Yokohama in 1872. Briefly describe the persecutions to which they were now subjected and quote some of the instances given by Cary in *Japan*, pp. 85–88. Gradually opposition lessened, and the work made great progress from 1873 to 1888. This was the great period of popularity. But again persecution arose, and many false charges were made against the Japanese Christians (see Cary, pp. 97, 98). But in spite of this second period of opposition the work has grown, and we shall learn more about the wonderful results in the lessons which are to follow. In closing, rapidly review the outline, which may be put upon the board as the story is told, and emphasize the more important parts of the work of these early missionaries.

Suggested Generalization.

God's messengers and workers should not be daunted by opposition.

Who were the first missionaries to Japan? How were they treated? When Japan was again open to foreigners who came at once to its shores? What did they attempt to do? How were they treated? Did they give up their work? What did they do? What was the result of their work? If they had given up because of opposition, the work in Japan would have been greatly delayed. As workers for God, then, we must never give up our work because of difficulties or opposition we may meet.

Memory Verse.

"All believers on earth belong to the family of Christ in the bonds of brotherly love" (from the constitution of the first Japanese Christian church).

Review Questions. (To be answered by the scholar at home.)

1. Who were the first missionaries to Japan?
2. What did they accomplish?
3. How were they treated?

4. Who succeeded in getting Japan to allow foreigners to live in the country?
5. As soon as the treaties were made who came to Japan?
6. What difficulties did they meet in their work?
7. When and in what place was the first church organized?
8. How successful were these early missionaries?

Scholar's Home Work.

Advance work:

If possible to secure the book, study the suggested lesson material.

Review and constructive work:

Paste picture, "The City of Yokohama," in the Review Book. Write over the picture the lesson subject, "Beginning the Work in Japan under Difficulties." Beneath the picture write the words, "The First Convert Baptized (1864) and the First Japanese Christian Church Organized (1872) in This City." Under this line write the memory verse. Answer the review questions, and when corrected by the teacher paste the sheet into the Review Book on the page opposite the picture. Write very briefly, in your own words, the story of the lesson.

---

§ 12. BOOKS RELATING TO THE WORK OF GRADE D

A. REFERENCE READING FOR THE TEACHER

Barrows, *The Christian Conquest of Asia* (Charles Scribner's Sons, New York).

Beach, *The Cross in the Land of the Trident* (F. H. Revell Co., Chicago).

Bliss, *A Concise History of Missions* (F. H. Revell Co., Chicago).

Clark, *Leavening the Nation* (The Baker, Taylor Co., New York).

Crosby, *With South-Sea Folk* (Pilgrim Press, Boston).

Gordon, *The American Missionary in Japan* (Houghton, Mifflin & Co., Boston).

Graham, *The Missionary Expansion since the Reformation* (F. H. Revell Co., Chicago).

Guernsey, *Under Our Flag* (F. H. Revell Co., Chicago).

Guinness, *The Story of the China Inland Mission* (F. H. Revell Co., Chicago).

Jackson, *Alaska and Missions on the North-Pacific Coast* (Dodd, Mead & Co., New York).

Paton, *John G. Paton: An Autobiography*, 3 vols. (F. H. Revell Co., Chicago).

Pierson, *The New Acts of the Apostles* (The Baker, Taylor Co., New York).

Puddefoot, *Minute-Men on the Frontier* (T. Crowell & Co., New York).

Stewart, *Dawn in the Dark Continent* (F. H. Revell Co., Chicago).

Tristam, *Rambles in Japan* (F. H. Revell Co., Chicago).

Zwemer, *Arabia the Cradle of Islam* (F. H. Revell Co., Chicago).

B. SUPPLEMENTAL READING FOR THE PUPIL

Ballard, *Fairy Tales from Far Japan* (F. H. Revell Co., Chicago).

Banks, *Heroes of the South-Sea Islands* (American Tract Society, New York).

Barrett, *The Child of the Ganges* (F. H. Revell Co., Chicago).

Brain, *The Transformation of Hawaii* (F. H. Revell Co., Chicago).

Bryson, *Child Life in Chinese Homes* (American Tract Society, New York).

Chamberlain, *The Cobra's Den*, and *In the Tiger Jungle* (F. H. Revell Co., Chicago).

Drummond, *Tropical Africa* (Charles Scribner's Sons, New York).

Duggan, *A Mexican Ranch* (American Baptist Publication Society, Philadelphia).

Page, *Amid Greenland Snows* (F. H. Revell Co., Chicago).

Young, *On the Indian Trail* (F. H. Revell Co., Chicago).

PART III
THE YOUTH PERIOD AND THE INTERMEDI-
ATE DEPARTMENT

CHAPTER VII

SOME CHARACTERISTICS AND NEEDS OF THE PERIOD

THE period from twelve or thirteen to sixteen or seventeen is one of the most important periods of life, for changes take place at this time in both the physical and psychical natures which permanently affect the whole after life.

Physically it is a time of rapid growth, both in height and weight of body. The bones may grow so fast that the muscles cannot keep pace with them, the result being a stretching of the muscles, causing "growing pains." On the other hand the muscular system may grow faster than the bones and as a result the boy becomes clumsy, lacks control of his movements, and "runs against everything, drops whatever he touches, and tumbles over it in trying to pick it up." It is the awkward age, and the boy or girl needs to be understood and sympathetically treated by teacher and parent. The general health is better in the majority of cases; but with many it is poorer. There are marked changes of features, for it is during this period that the final type of features is determined. These changes are important to the teacher, for as Lancaster says,[1] "The features

[1] *Pedagogical Seminary*, Vol. V, p. 127.

and countenance are the best indices of character and disposition. If these change radically we may look for a change in character, which will necessitate a change in treatment or injury will result. . . . . Many a life tragedy starts with the misunderstanding of the boy or girl at adolescence." There are probably important changes in the brain, "for the shape of the head changes and the new intellectual and emotional activities of this period must be accompanied by the functioning of cerebral centers that have lain dormant before."[2] During this period there comes a physiological new birth, when the boy and girl are born "out of childhood into manhood and womanhood;" and again there comes a psychological new birth when they are born from "egoism and isolation to altruism and society."

Some characteristics of the period.— We now have the beginnings of new sensations, and the rapid development of many of the characteristics noted in the earlier periods, along with the complete or almost complete disappearance of others.

The animistic tendencies, which grew weaker in the last period, finally disappearing at its close, now give place to what we might call a poetic imagination. It is just at this time that there is a very marked increase in the interest shown in poetry.

[2] BURNHAM, *Pedagogical Seminary*, Vol. I, p. 176.

Suggestibility is still high in degree, and the influence of the teacher during the period is marked, especially during the latter part. When we consider this fact in connection with that other fact, that the youth is most open to religious conviction at this time, the importance of the two becomes at once apparent.

There is a change and an advance from selfishness to unselfishness, and a decided development of general social and altruistic impulses. President G. Stanley Hall says in this connection:[3]

> Before this age the child lives in the present, is normally selfish, deficient in sympathy, but frank and confidential, obedient upon authority, and without affectation save the supreme affectation of childhood, viz., assuming the words, manners, habits, etc., of those older than himself. . . . . There is now a longing for that kind of close sympathy and friendship which makes cronies and intimates; there is a craving for strong emotions which give pleasure in exaggeration; and there are nameless longings for what is far, remote, strange, which emphasizes the self-estrangement which Hegel so well describes, and which marks the normal rise of the presentiment of something higher than self. . . . . There is often a strong instinct of devotion and self-sacrifice toward some, perhaps almost any, object or in almost any cause which circumstances may present. . . . . The life of the mere individual ceases and that of the person or, better, of the race, begins.

During this period some find it very hard to

[3] *Loc. cit.*, Vol. I, pp. 205, 206.

tell the truth; others find the slightest deviation from the truth very painful.

There is a great increase in the regard for law in its general forms, and by the end of the period practically all recognize its binding force.

Although the imitative tendency is still strong, there is a change in the activities imitated. There is a strong tendency to imitate now those actions which it is thought will make the boys and girls appear more manly and womanly. During this unsettled time the boys should have male teachers and the girls female teachers, not only that they may be taught both by precept and example what true manliness and womanliness are, but also because of the peculiar temptations which come to the young people during this period. President G. Stanley Hall says of the peculiar dangers of the period:[4]

> The dangers of this period are great and manifest. The chief of these, far greater even than the dangers of intemperance, is that the sexual elements of soul and body will be developed prematurely and disproportionately. Indeed early maturity in this respect is itself bad. If it occurs before other compensating and controlling powers are unfolded, this element is hypertrophied and absorbs and dwarfs their energy and it is then more likely to be uninstructed and to suck up all that is vile in the environment. . . . . Quite apart, therefore, from its intrinsic value, education should serve the purpose of preoccupation, and

[4] *Ibid.*, Vol. I, p. 207.

CHARACTERISTICS AND NEEDS 223

should divert attention from an element of our nature the premature or excessive development of which dwarfs every part of soul and body. Intellectual interests, athleticism, social and æsthetic tastes, should be cultivated. There should be some change in external life. Previous routine and drill work must be broken through and new occupations resorted to, that the mind may not be left idle while the hands are mechanically employed. Attractive home life, friendships well chosen and on a high plane, and regular habits should of course be cultivated. Now, too, though the intellect is not frequently judged insane, so that pubescent insanity is comparatively rare, the feelings which are yet more fundamental to mental sanity are most often perverted, and lack of emotional steadiness, violent and dangerous impulses, unreasonable conduct, lack of enthusiasm and sympathy, are very commonly caused by abnormities here. . . . . In short, the previous selfhood is broken up like the regulation copy handwriting of early school years, and a new individual is in process of crystallization. All is solvent, plastic, peculiarly susceptible to external influences.

There are other characteristics which are more or less marked and which belong distinctively to this unsettled period of life. One of these is the showing forth of ancestral ways. Dr. Burnham says in this connection:[5]

At adolescence there seems to be a great influx of hereditary strength and character. The boy of good blood who has been lazy, perverse, or reckless before, often becomes serious now and develops his latent manhood. For the boy with evil hereditary tendencies it is a dangerous

[5] *Ibid.*, Vol. I, p. 180.

period. One's inheritance from the past is the anchor which holds him in the storms of adolescence, or the impulse which drives him on to perversity and sometimes to insanity. At present, however, our knowledge upon this point is very general and indefinite.

There is a great increase of vitality and energy at this time which objectifies itself in many ways, physical and mental. "It is clear," to again quote Professor Burnham,[6] "that at this period education must no longer be mere acquisition, it must give outlet for action. Youth must be given an opportunity to do something." But this activity is subjected to great changes, spells of languor and inertia alternating with spells of intense energy and activity. As in all development, progress seems to be irregular, periods of advancement alternating with periods of rest.

The period is also one during which young people are subject to varying moods, spells of elation alternating with spells of despondency. Dr. Lancaster says in his study of this period[7] that

thoughts of suicide were very common. . . . . Feelings are reported as being much more intense and wider ranged. Anger and pride are usually intensified but kept under better control, while fear is usually reported as much less intense, except of a moral nature or fear of some secret disease. . . . . The curve of despondency starts at eleven, and rises steadily and rapidly till fifteen, and culminates at

[6] *Ibid.*, p. 193.   [7] *Ibid.*, Vol. V, p. 92.

CHARACTERISTICS AND NEEDS 225

seventeen, then falls steadily till twenty-three, where it reaches the base line.

The spirit of leadership manifests itself very strongly, this spirit showing itself concretely in the various clubs. societies, and young people's organizations.

Religion begins now to take on a new meaning. The mere forms of religion, which satisfied the child, now lose their attractiveness, and the youth seeks for the inner, spiritual meaning of true religion. "It is a new interest and very many speak of it as a sudden awakening. It is spontaneous, like the interest in art or music, or the love of nature. Where no set forms have been urged, the religious emotion comes forth as naturally as the sun rises." Dr. Starbuck has shown [8] that the greatest number of conversions, so called, occur at about sixteen. The curve rises rapidly from twelve to sixteen and falls quite rapidly from sixteen to twenty.

Some interests of the period.— The predominant literary interest now comes to be in legendary heroes, pioneers, and heroes in history. The social interest in historical study also develops to a marked degree. From Professor Wissler's study [9] we learn that boys and girls from thirteen to fifteen years of age prefer stories of daily life,

[8] *The Psychology of Religion,* chap. iii.
[9] *Pedagogical Seminary,* Vol. V, pp. 523 ff.

moral precepts, and description. The basis of their preference is given as "because true to life," and "because of moral lessons." The selected material must then be made lifelike and must suggest moral lessons. Miss Vostrovsky's study[10] shows a growing interest during this period in works which are classified under the head of General Literature, such books being preferred by 34 per cent. of the boys fourteen years old, by 39 per cent. of the boys fifteen years old, by 44 per cent. of the boys sixteen years old, by 48 per cent. of the boys seventeen years old, and by 85 per cent. of the boys eighteen years old. Of the works classed as General Literature, nearly 50 per cent. of the boys of all ages from thirteen to seventeen preferred historical biography, the other 50 per cent. being divided among books of science, travel, history, literature, and literary biography. Professor Dawson, in his study of "Children's Interest in the Bible," says, with reference to the gospel books,[11] that

> This is pre-eminently the choice of the adolescent. . . . . It is evident that adolescence needs, and seeks, above everything else, some kind of a philosophy and regimen of life. Life has become a thing fraught with a new but vague meaning; the struggle is to make its meaning clear. Life has become a larger, richer thing; the struggle is to learn the method by which its largeness and richness may be

[10] *Ibid.*, Vol. VI, pp. 523 ff.
[11] *Ibid.*, Vol. VII, p. 166.

personally realized. The quickening of moral feeling leads to self-scrutiny and an apprehension of more or less friction between the self and the best environments. The quickening of the religious feelings begets a desire to get adjusted to the largest and best ideals. The quickening of the sense of life, as lived through others and for others, awakens the impulse to become a part of the great cosmic struggle for more complete existence. In the gospels is found the Christian philosophy of life; and in the gospels is found the Christian regimen of life, in its broad outlines. For the gospels reveal the personality of One who "came that they might have life and that they might have it more abundantly," and Christian philosophy sums itself up in personal character. And the gospels reveal broadly the Christian regimen of life, for this is simply to follow where He leads. It is not surprising, therefore, that, when the meaning and method of life are sought with such earnest zest as during the adolescent years, the Christian explanation of what life is, and how it may be lived, should be of interest.

This period is one of strong theological convictions. The questioning tendency concerning theological matters reaches its maximum at about fourteen, slowly declining after that time. This questioning, however, is largely for information. During the early part of the next period there comes into the life of the thinking person a time of storm and stress, a time of doubt more or less prolonged and severe, when the young man seeks to know the "reason for the faith that is within."

There are many other interests, such as that in nature, art, music, reading, poetry, etc. These interests are varying but should be appealed to so far as possible.

The mental powers during the period.—Memory increases in strength, and what is called verbal memory reaches its maximum strength in the first half of the period. The power of inference develops strongly and rapidly, and interest in classification increases. Imagination, true creative imagination, now begins to manifest itself strongly. It is the great time for the creating of ideals. These ideals change frequently, and as Lancaster says,[12] "One's stage of development can be marked quite accurately by his ideal. The manners and ways of speaking, walking, and dressing indicate closely the ideal that the boy or girl is following." These ideals awaken longings to be like the ideal. There is a strong tendency to plan the future, this being one of the results of the widening of the mental horizon, with the rush of new ideas, new longings, and the change of thought and ideals. The emotional activity throughout the period is intense, and there are strong impulses to do great things. Speaking of the religious emotions, Lancaster says:

> It is the natural time for the growth of the religious emotions which are the only basis of a healthy, moral nature. Aside from all relations to a future life, the religious emotions should be regarded as the most valuable of all for

[12] *Ibid.*, Vol. V, pp. 127, 128.

immediate results in character. . . . . The worst thing that can happen is early forcing of the religious emotions and the subsequent relapse. The religious feeling often comes in waves of increasing intensity. The first may appear in very early childhood, but they reach their maximum about sixteen with the average person. . . . . Each religious wave should be treated sympathetically, but public expression of any particular belief should not be urged before fifteen to twenty.

Conscience is more of a factor in the educational work of this period, although it is not a fixed quantity, being well developed in some boys and girls and seemingly almost wanting in others.

Some conclusions with reference to a course of study for the youth from thirteen to seventeen years of age.— From the foregoing consideration of the characteristics, powers, and interests of the youth period of life, it would seem that biographical matter was best adapted to the ends in view and to the conditions of the youth. His chief literary interest is in great historic characters, his imagination is actively forming ideals and making plans for the future, and it is the time for the natural development of the religious emotion. If we present to him in concrete form the essentials of an ideal human character, this will tend to stir the emotional side of his nature and eventually win him to a natural expression of allegiance to Him who combines all these elements in his person — the typical man, Jesus. In presenting this form of material the teacher should seek to emphasize those elements in the characters studied which tend to objectify themselves in social service, that thus the pupils in forming their ideals may see clearly that the highest type of Christian character is that expressed in the life of Jesus, who "came not to be ministered unto, but to minister." Such a method of presentation will also suggestively guide the pupil's activities into the most helpful channels. The great men and women of the Old Testament, those who present helpful elements of character worthy of study; the great characters of the New Testament, including an extended study of the life of the ideal character, Jesus; and a number of carefully selected great characters in the various periods of the world's history, illustrating a high type of manhood and womanhood in various walks of life, would be the biographies suggested for the course of study in this department of the Bible school.

An outline of a suggested course of study for the four years spent in the Intermediate Department of the Bible school is given in the next chapter. In Grade A, the most important Old Testament characters who lived in the historic periods of the migrations, the settlement, the kingdom, and the province, are chosen for study. In Grade B, a full year is given to the study of the ideal man, Jesus, considered from the standpoint of one who ministers. In Grade C, the larger part of the year's work is given to the study of the lives of the two great apostles, Peter and Paul. In Grade D, we go outside the Bible and select some of the world's great characters, as found in the early church, in modern missions, and in the wider service of mankind. In this last grade there is of course great difficulty in selecting a list of characters to be studied that will commend itself to all; but the difficulty lies rather in the abundance of suitable material at hand, than in any question of fitness in the characters chosen.

The youth of both sexes, pursuing such a course for four years under competent teachers, ought to form a noble conception of the meaning of true Christian character, and be won to a hearty, whole-souled, and open allegiance to the One who manifested forth the glory of God in a perfect human life — Jesus Christ, the Son of God, the ideal man.

CHAPTER VIII
A COURSE OF STUDY FOR THE INTERMEDIATE DEPARTMENT

GENERAL SUBJECT: GREAT MEN AND WOMEN AND THEIR DEEDS
(REVEALING GOD A FORMER OF CHARACTER)

§ 1. OUTLINE OF THE COURSE FOR GRADE A

GRADE SUBJECT: GREAT CHARACTERS IN THE OLD TESTAMENT

Part 1 — During the period of the migrations.
1. Abram the pioneer.
   a) Wandering life.
2. *b)* Settled life.
3. Jacob the prince.
4. Joseph the prime minister.
   a) The child and slave.
5. *b)* Ruler in Egypt.
6. *c)* Savior of his people.
7. Moses the liberator.
   a) Preparing for his mission.
8. *b)* Liberating a people.
9. *c)* Making a nation.
10. Miriam the prophetess.
11. *Review. Memory work.*

Part 2 — During the period of the settlement.
12. Joshua the soldier.
    a) Entering the promised land.
13. *b)* Conquering the country.
14. Deborah the woman-judge.
15. Gideon the warrior-judge.
16. Ruth the model daughter.
17. Hannah the model mother.

Intermediate Department Course

18. Samuel the prophet-judge.
    a) His training under Eli.
19. *b)* Establishing the kingdom.
20. *Review. Memory work.*

Part 3 — During the period of the kingdom.
21. Saul the wilful king.
22. David the godly king.
    a) His shepherd and soldier life.
23. *b)* An exile from home.
24. *c)* Reigning in Israel.
25. *d)* His old age.
26. Jonathan the friend.
27. Solomon the magnificent king.
    a) The early rule in wisdom.
28. *b)* The later years of folly.
29. *Review. Memory work.*
30. Elijah the prophet of fire.
    a) Predicting God's judgment.
31. *b)* Upholding God's glory.
32. Elisha the prophet of peace.
    a) Showing kindness to the people.
33. *b)* Aiding the king.
34. Joash the boy-king.
35. Amos the prophet of righteousness.
36. Hosea the prophet of love.
37. Isaiah the statesman-prophet.
    a) His political work for Judah.
38. *b)* His religious work for Judah.
39. Josiah the reformer-king.
40. Jeremiah the prophet of tears.
    a) Trying to save the nation.
41. *b)* Closing years of his life.
42. *Review. Memory work.*

Part 4 — During the period of the province.
  43. Ezekiel the prophet of visions.
  44. Daniel the captive prince.
      a) His rise to power.
  45. *b)* Triumph in temptation.
  46. Zerubbabel the leader of the return.
  47. Ezra the scribe.
  48. Nehemiah the governor.
      a) Repairing the city.
  49. *b)* Reforming the customs of the people.
  50. *Review. Memory work.*

Special Lessons.
  51. Christmas lesson.
  52. Easter lesson.

---

§ 2. SUGGESTIVE LESSON PLANS FOR GRADE A
Lessons 21 and 26
Lesson 21
SAUL THE WILFUL KING

Lesson Material.
  1 Sam., chaps. ix to xxi.

Teacher's Study Material.
  Deane, *Samuel and Saul: Their Lives and Times,* in " Men of the Bible " series, chaps. iv to xiv; Geikie, *Hours with the Bible,* Vol. III, chaps. iv and v; *idem, Old Testament Characters,* chap. on " Saul;" Kent, *A History of the Hebrew People,* Vol. I, pp. 113-35; Kittel, *History of the Hebrews,* Vol. II, pp. 103-37; Hastings, *Bible Dictionary,* art. " Saul."

Illustrative Material.
  Use the blackboard for the outline of the lesson material. Locate on the map as the lesson progresses the

important places connected with Saul's life. Pictures of Palestine, showing the character of the country, the cities and towns, and the manners and customs of the people would be helpful. Also select from the following pictures: "Samuel Anointing and Blessing Saul," "Saul Attempts the Life of David," and "David Spares Saul's Life," all by Doré; "Samuel Anointing Saul," and "Saul's Rejection," by von Schnorr. At the lesson close write upon the board the plan for the scholar's "Life of Saul the Wilful King."

Organization of Material.
1. The times in which Saul lived.
    a) Politically — a period of foreign oppression.
    b) Socially — a period of transition to agricultural life.
    c) Religiously — a period of irreligion.
2. Saul's early life.
    a) Son of Kish, tribe of Benjamin.
    b) Home — Gibeah.
    c) Occupation — farmer.
3. Saul's public life.
    a) His rise to power.
    b) His decline.
    c) His fall.
4. Work accomplished.
    a) Partially unified the tribes.
    b) Inspired a hope of freedom.
    c) Created the beginning of a military organization.
5. Marked traits of character.
    a) True patriotism.
    b) Considerable organizing ability.
    c) Impatience and wilfulness.
    d) Without a deep religious nature.

Presentation of Material.

Develop by questions the various sections as outlined under the heading "Organization of Material." Locate on the map the sections of Palestine occupied by the various tribes of Israel. Give the class as clear a picture as possible in a brief presentation of the times in which Saul lived. The tribes were scattered and practically independent, there being an apparent lack of any unity of feeling, and of any union of effort to throw off the oppressive yoke of the Philistine rule. This was due partly to the scattered condition of the tribes, and partly to the lack of a capable leader. Socially the period was one of transition from the nomadic to the agricultural life. The towns grew in importance and became the centers of tribal life. The law of blood revenge was in force and the moral condition of the people was very low. The masses of the people were irreligious, there being no center of worship, and the influence of prophets like Samuel was scarcely felt except through a small section of the land. It was into such times that Saul was born and grew up to young manhood. Question the class about the little that is known of Saul before he is chosen king. Of what family? Of what tribe? Where was his home? What was his occupation (1 Sam. 11:5)? What was his appearance (1 Sam. 9:2)? Then develop by questions the steps in Saul's rise to power, noting (1) the private anointing by Samuel; (2) the public choosing by the people at the great assembly at Mizpah; (3) the assumption of the position of king by Saul at Jabesh-gilead, in connection with the demand of Nahash the Ammonite; and (4) the solemn establishment of the kingdom by Samuel at Gilgal. As each one of these points is brought out, dwell upon it briefly, drawing out by further questions the facts connected with it. Then

INTERMEDIATE DEPARTMENT COURSE 237

question the class upon Saul's decline in power, noting the first step taken in connection with the Philistine war. Describe the circumstances, picturing Saul's growing impatience at the delay of Samuel, and his final offering of the required sacrifices at Gilgal. Then comes Samuel and condemns Saul for this act. Show the significance of the scene. This was the first break with the ruling religious party represented by Samuel, and was the first step downward in Saul's public career. (See 1 Sam. 13: 11–14.) The second downward step was taken in connection with the war against the Amalekites. What was the nature of the war? Who commanded it to be undertaken? What were the special obligations and restrictions placed upon Saul? With what success does he meet? Describe his disobedience. Upon whom does he attempt to shift the blame for his action? What was the result of this disobedience? After this final break with Saul, Samuel leaves him and sees him no more. From this time on we have what some scholars have called "Saul's insane career." During this period Saul seeks constantly the life of David, who had been anointed by Samuel as Saul's successor. Finally very briefly question the class concerning Saul's fall, death, and burial, noting (1) the war with the Philistines, (2) the disastrous battle of Gilboa, and (3) Saul's death, and his burial by the grateful people of Jabesh-gilead. Next present the work Saul accomplished, bringing out as much as possible from the class by questions. The people did rally about Saul and felt, as they had not felt for a long time, that they were one people. In Saul's successes they saw the possibility of freedom, and so were more ready to unite under a new leader, David, to make this freedom real. Further than this the beginning had been made in organizing a standing army, which became the nucleus of David's more complete military organization. Thus Saul did a good work for his people, and prepared the way for the wonderful progress under David. Then briefly point out the marked elements of character in Saul, showing how the first two contributed to his success, and how the last two brought his rejection and final downfall. In closing, review the whole outline, emphasizing the good that Saul did, but showing that a large and permanent success could not result from the work of a man who was so lacking in important character elements.

Points to Emphasize.
1. Observance of forms will not take the place of obedience to principles.
2. The meanness of any attempt to shift responsibility for our wrong-doing upon others.
3. Life tests character; we cannot always predict the end from a knowledge of the beginning.

Scholar's Home Work.
Advance work: A careful study of the lesson material.
Review work: Questions for written answers to be returned to the teacher:
1. What were the political conditions of Saul's time?
2. What were the social conditions of Saul's time?
3. What were the religious conditions of Saul's time?
4. To what tribe did Saul belong and where did he live?
5. What were the steps in his rise to power?
6. What caused his decline and fall?
7. In what war and at what place was he slain?
8. By whom was he buried? Why by them?
9. What work did he accomplish?
10. What are the most marked traits in his character?

Constructive work: Write a short Life of Saul, the Wilful King, upon the following plan:

SAUL THE WILFUL KING

§ 1. The times in which he lived.
§ 2. How he became king.
§ 3. His life as a king.
§ 4. What he did for Israel.
§ 5. Traits of character.

Illustrative picture for the chapter, either Doré's "Samuel Anointing and Blessing Saul," or von Schnorr's "Samuel Anointing Saul."

Verses for memorizing: 1 Sam. 12:24; 15:22b.

LESSON 26
JONATHAN THE FRIEND

Lesson Material.

1 Sam. 13:1-23; 14:1-52; 18:1-4; 19:1-7; 20:1-42; 23:16-18; 31:1-13; 2 Sam. 1:1-27.

Teacher's Study Material.

Deane, *Samuel and Saul: Their Lives and Times*, in "Men of the Bible" series, chaps. viii, x, xii, and xiv; *idem, David: His Life and Times*, in "Men of the Bible" series, chaps. ii, iii, iv, and v; Geikie, *Hours with the Bible*, Vol. III, chaps. iv and v; Whyte, *Bible Characters*, Vol. II; Mathison, *Representative Men of the Bible;* Hastings, *Bible Dictionary*, art. "Jonathan."

Illustrative Material.

Use the blackboard for the outline of the lesson material. Locate on the map, as the lesson progresses, the more important places connected with Jonathan's life. Pictures of Palestine showing the character of the country and the manners and customs of the people would be helpful. The picture by Doré, "David and Jonathan," may also be used. At the lesson close write upon the board the plan for the scholar's "Life of Jonathan the Friend."

Organization of Material.
  1. Jonathan the prince.
      a) Son of Saul the king.
      b) Noted for his strength and grace.
      c) Loyal to his father.
  2. Jonathan's military exploits.
      a) Smites the Philistine garrison in Geba.
      b) Leads the assault at Michmash.
          (1) His daring exploit.
          (2) Saul's foolish vow and its consequences.
  3. Jonathan and David.
      a) The first meeting.
      b) The first covenant.
      c) His friendly services to David.
      d) Character of his friendship for David.
  4. Jonathan's death and burial.
  5. Marked traits of Jonathan's character.
      a) Courage.
      b) Loyalty.
      c) Unselfishness.
      d) Constancy.
      e) Affectionateness.

Presentation of Material.
Develop by questions the various sections as outlined under the heading "Organization of Material." Jonathan was Saul's eldest son (1 Sam. 14: 49) and shared "in the perils and enterprises of his father's stormy reign, and was involved in his ruin." His friendship for David was noteworthy, and undoubtedly was a factor in David's advancement. Question the class concerning Jonathan's personal characteristics: (1) his physical

INTERMEDIATE DEPARTMENT COURSE 241

strength and fleetness of foot (2 Sam. 1:23); (2) his skill as an archer, as became a Benjamite (2 Sam. 1:22); and (3) his beauty and grace (2 Sam. 1:19). Throughout the record we have him presented as a courageous captain, skilful, bold, and exceedingly practical (*e. g.*, *cf.* 1 Sam. 14:24 and 1 Sam. 14:29, 30). And although a friend of David, we have no hint that he was disloyal to his father, but rather that he was in his father's confidence (see 1 Sam. 19:2, 3 and 20:2). Next note Jonathan's military exploits, his smiting of the garrison in Geba, and especially the daring assault upon the Philistines at Michmash. Question the class about the Michmash campaign, noting especially (1) the daring exploit of Jonathan and his armor-bearer; (2) Saul's foolish order and vow, in which connection show the contrast between the foolishness of Saul and the practical wisdom of Jonathan (*cf.* 1 Sam. 14:24 and 14:29, 30); and (3) the rescue of Jonathan by the people from the penalty imposed by Saul in his vow. Some explain this rescue as brought about by a ransom, and others by the offering of a vicarious sacrifice. In developing this section of the outline, describe the topography of this part of the country, and supplement the questions by bits of word-picturing, that the courage and daring of Jonathan may be thoroughly apppreciated by the class. Now develop the more important part of the story, the remarkable relations existing between Jonathan and David. Describe their first meeting (1 Sam. 18:1-4) and the resulting covenant. Then take up the various services rendered by Jonathan to David from time to time: (1) he intercedes with Saul on David's behalf (1 Sam. 19:1-7); (2) he discovers Saul's evil purpose against David, at which time he risks his own life (1 Sam. 20:25-34); and (3) he warns David of his great danger and bids him leave (1 Sam. 20: 35-42). These services are evidences of true love and friendship, for Jonathan had nothing to gain but everything to lose from thus befriending David. At this point question the class concerning the character of this friendship which Jonathan showed for David, showing that it was (1) entirely unselfish and disinterested, as Jonathan could gain no material advantage from it; (2) expressed in deeds of helpfulness, although at great risk to Jonathan; and (3) that it resulted in complete confidence between the two. In connection with the question of Jonathan's possible knowledge of David's future, or at least of his ambitions for the future, see the article in Hastings's *Bible Dictionary*. Then question concerning Jonathan's death and burial, emphasizing again, as in the lesson on Saul, the gratitude of the people of Jabesh-gilead. Read David's eulogy from the Revised Version, or better from Moulton's *Modern Reader's Bible*. Read this impressively, and without comment, letting the poem itself show forth the great love, friendship-love, of David and Jonathan. Lastly bring out by questions the most marked traits in Jonathan's character: (1) his courage, shown both in battle and in his befriending of David; (2) his loyalty, both to his father and to the friendship which he had formed for David; (3) his unselfishness, manifested not only in his friendship for David but in his never seeking to take advantage of the conditions of the times (*cf*. Absalom's conduct with Jonathan's); (4) his constancy; and (5) his affectionateness, manifested in all his relations with David. In closing, review the whole outline, and try to have the class appreciate somewhat the beauty of Jonathan's character, impressing the thought that a winsome, lovable character may be one also characterized by courage and strength.

Points to Emphasize.
1. True friendship is unselfish, seeking not her own.
2. True friendship is unchangeable, the same in adversity as in prosperity.
3. True friendship is expressive, seeking opportunities of helpfulness.

Scholar's Home Work.
Advance work: A careful study of the lesson material.
Review work: Questions for written answers to be returned to the teacher:
1. For what physical characteristics was Jonathan noted?
2. Name his most famous military exploits.
3. What incident in the Michmash campaign showed his practical wisdom?
4. Under what circumstances did Jonathan and David meet?
5. What resulted from this meeting?
6. What services did Jonathan render to David?
7. What was the character of his friendship for David?
8. Describe his death and burial.
9. What evidence have we of David's love for Jonathan?
10. What are the most marked traits of Jonathan's character?

Constructive work: Write a short *Life of Jonathan the Friend* upon the following plan:

JONATHAN THE FRIEND

§ 1. His personal characteristics.
§ 2. His military career.
§ 3. His friendship for David.
§ 4. Marked traits of character.

Illustrative picture for the chapter, Doré's "David and Jonathan.'

Verses for memorizing: 2 Sam. 1 : 19–27.

---

§ 3. BOOKS RELATING TO THE WORK OF GRADE A

A. REFERENCE READING FOR THE TEACHER

Geikie, *The Holy Land and the Bible*, 2 vols. (James Pott & Co., New York).

Kent, *A History of the Hebrew People* (Charles Scribner's Sons, New York).

Kent, *A History of the Jewish People* (Charles Scribner's Sons, New York).

Kittel, *A History of the Hebrews*, 2 vols. (Williams and Norgate, London).

McCurdy, *History, Prophecy and the Monuments*, 3 vols. (The Macmillan Co., New York).

Mathison, *Representative Men of the Bible*, Series I and II (A. C. Armstrong & Son, New York).

"Men of the Bible: Their Lives and Times." Edited by Rev. J. S. Excell, M.A.; 15 vols. on the Old Testament (F. H. Revell Co., Chicago): (1) *Abraham*, by Deane; (2) *Isaac and Jacob*, by Rawlinson; (3) *Moses*, by Rawlinson; (4) *Joshua*, by Deane; (5) *Gideon and the Judges*, by Lang; (6) *Samuel and Saul*, by Deane; (7) *David*, by Deane; (8) *Solomon*, by Farrar; (9) *Elijah*, by Milligan; (10) *Kings of Israel and Judah*, by Rawlinson; (11) *Isaiah*, by Driver; (12) *Jeremiah*, by Cheyne; (13) *Ezra and Nehemiah*, by Rawlinson; (14) *Daniel*, by Deane; (15) *Minor Prophets*, by Farrar.

Meyer, *Old Testament Heroes*, 10 vols. (F. H. Revell Co., Chicago); the following characters are included: Abraham, Joseph, Moses, Joshua, Israel, Samuel, Elijah, David, Jeremiah, and Zechariah.

Smith, *The Historical Geography of the Holy Land* (A. C. Armstrong & Son, New York).

Whyte, *Bible Characters,* 3 vols. on Old Testament characters (F. H. Revell Co., Chicago): Vol. I, Adam to Achan; Vol. II, Gideon to Absalom; Vol. III, Ahithophel to Nehemiah.

B. READING AND REFERENCE BOOKS FOR THE PUPIL

Banks, *Hero Tales from Sacred Story* (Funk and Wagnalls Co., New York).

Willett, *The Prophets of Israel* (F. H. Revell Co., Chicago).

"The Clark Bible Primers" (Charles Scribner's Sons, New York): (1) *Life of Abraham,* by Scott; (2) *Period of the Judges,* by Paterson; (3) *Life of Moses,* by Iverach; (4) *Joshua and the Conquest,* by Croskery; (5) *Life of David,* by Thomson; (6) *Life and Reign of Solomon,* by Winterbotham; (7) *The Kings of Israel,* by Walker; (8) *The Kings of Judah,* by Given.

§ 4. OUTLINE OF THE COURSE FOR GRADE B

GRADE SUBJECT: GREAT CHARACTERS IN THE NEW TESTAMENT

A. *The Life of Jesus the Ideal Man*

THE SON OF MAN CAME NOT TO BE MINISTERED UNTO, BUT TO MINISTER

Part 1 — Jesus and his ministry.

1. Prophecies concerning Jesus.
    a) Selected Old Testament prophecies.
    b) Annunciation to Zacharias.
    c) Annunciation to Mary and Joseph.
    d) Mary's visit to Elizabeth.
2. Events in fulfilment of these prophecies.
    a) The birth stories.
    b) Circumcision and presentation.
    c) Visit of the Magi.
    d) The Egyptian sojourn.

3. The training of Jesus for his ministry.
   a) His childhood.
   b) Visit to Jerusalem at 12 years.
   c) The eighteen silent years at Nazareth.
4. The baptism — Jesus accepts his ministry.
5. The temptation — Jesus proves his fitness for his ministry.
6. Jesus' ministry announced.
   a) John's testimony to the priests.
   b) John's testimony to certain disciples.
7. Jesus' ministry begun.
   a) The miracle at Cana.
   b) The first disciples chosen.
8. *Review. Memory work.*

Part 2 — Jesus' ministry to the religious leaders.
9. The cleansing of the temple.
10. The discourse with Nicodemus.
11. John's testimony at Ænon.

Part 3 — Jesus' ministry to the common people. (Galilean ministry — 1st period.)
12. Discourse with the woman of Samaria.
13. A day of miracles in Capernaum, and the first preaching tour.
14. Healing of the paralytic.
15. Teaching concerning the Sabbath.
16. *Review. Memory work.*

Part 4 — Jesus' ministry to the common people. (Galilean ministry — 2d period.)
17. Choosing the Twelve.
18. The sermon on the mount.
19. The answer to John's messengers.
20. Jesus in the house of Simon.
21. The parables by the sea.

INTERMEDIATE DEPARTMENT COURSE 247

22. The parables by the sea.
23. A day of miracles by the sea.
24. The Twelve sent forth.
25. Feeding the five thousand.
26. Discourse on the bread of life.
27. *Review. Memory work.*

Part 5 — Jesus' special ministry to the apostles. (Galilean ministry — 3d period.)

28. The first northern journey for retirement.
29. The second journey, and Peter's confession.
30. Jesus foretells his death and resurrection.
31. The transfiguration.
32. Discourse on humility and forgiveness.
33. An autumn visit to Jerusalem.
34. *Review. Memory work.*

Part 6 — Jesus' ministry drawing to a close. (Perean ministry.)

35. The mission of the Seventy.
36. Ministering and teaching in Jerusalem.
37. Parables of grace and warning.
38. The raising of Lazarus.
39. Jesus and the rich young ruler.
40. The ambition of James and John.
41. The visit to Zaccheus.
42. *Review. Memory work.*

Part 7 — The triumphant close of Jesus' ministry. (Passion Week.)

43. The triumphal entry into Jerusalem.
44. A day of conflicts and victories.
45. Farewell discourses to his disciples.
46. The trials and crucifixion.
47. The resurrection.

Part 8 — The disciples commissioned to continue Jesus' ministry. (The Forty Days.)
48. The appearances to the disciples.
49. The great commission and the ascension.
50. *Review. Memory work.*

Special Lessons.
51. Christmas lesson.
52. Easter lesson.

---

§ 5. SUGGESTIVE LESSON PLANS FOR GRADE B
LESSONS 1 TO 7
LESSON 1
PROPHECIES CONCERNING JESUS

Lesson Material.

Isa. 9:2-7; 11:1-9; 42:1-4; 53:1-12; 61:1-3; Jer. 31:31-34; Mic. 5:2-5a; Luke 1:5-23, 26-56; Matt. 1:18-25.

Teacher's Study Material.

Wenley, *The Preparation for Christianity*, pp. 93-112, 143-82; Edersheim, *The Temple and its Services*, pp. 58-78, 112-23; "Expositor's Bible," *Luke,* pp. 15-46; related sections in the various standard lives of Jesus Christ; a good critical commentary.

Illustrative Material.

Use the blackboard for the outline of the lesson material. Sketch the ground plan of the temple when describing the vision of Zacharias. At the lesson close write upon the board the plan for chap. i of the scholar's *Life of Christ.* If the class is fortunate enough to have a room, hang upon the walls one of the large reproductions of Hofmann's "Head of Christ," and let it remain there during the year's study. If the class does not have a room, use a smaller picture mounted upon a stiff cardboard which can be passed around among the members.

Organization of Material.
1. The revelations of some Old Testament prophecies.
    a) Office of Jesus.
    b) Ancestry and birthplace.
    c) Personal equipment of Jesus.
    d) The ministry of Jesus. Characteristics and purpose.
    e) Humiliating treatment of Jesus.
    f) Ultimate success of his ministry.
2. Revelation to Zacharias.
    a) Zacharias and Elizabeth. Character and condition.
    b) The revelation in the temple to Zacharias.
    c) Zacharias's unbelief and punishment.
3. Revelation to Mary.
    a) The angel's glad message to Mary.
    b) The child Jesus to be the Son of God.
    c) Mary's humble acceptance of the promise.
4. Revelation to Joseph.
    a) The vision or dream.
    b) Joseph's belief.
5. Mary's visit to Elizabeth.
    a) Elizabeth's song of blessing.
    b) Mary's song of praise.

Presentation of Material.

Develop by questions the various sections as outlined under the heading "Organization of Material." Note the double office of Jesus as given in Isa. 9: 2–7, viz., light-giver (teacher?) and world-ruler. See the genealogical table in the first chapter of Matt. and have the class note some of the more important names in the ancestral line of Jesus. Also note the prophecy in Micah giving his birthplace. Explain and indicate the value of the various elements of the personal equipment of Jesus as prophesied, viz., wisdom and understanding, counsel and might, knowledge and fear of the Lord (Isa. 11:2). Question concerning the characteristics of the ministry of Jesus, namely: righteousness and justice (Isa. 11:3, 4), faithfulness (Isa. 11:5), meekness and compassion (Isa. 42: 2, 3). Also the purpose of his ministry as clearly presented in Isa. 61:1–3. But in spite of such a ministry of joy and helpfulness, he was not to be received by his own people. Note their prophesied treatment of him; despised, rejected, wounded, oppressed, imprisoned, and slain (Isa. 53:1–9). Nevertheless his ministry was ultimately to succeed. Note in this connection the prophecy of joy in the outcome (Isa. 53:11), and of the needful strength and inspiration for the work (Isa. 42:4). His great purpose was finally to be accomplished, and the new law of love to reign in the hearts of men, accompanied by the spreading abroad of the knowledge of the Father (Jer. 31:31–34). Such was to be the minister and his ministry. Explain in a few words the temple service and the arrangement of the priests in courses. Question as to the character of Zacharias and Elizabeth, and their great desire. Show what was revealed to Zacharias, namely: a son, his office and greatness, and in this an indirect prophecy of the Christ (Luke 1:17). Bring out Zacharias's unbelief to contrast later with Mary's belief. The vision to Mary distinctly revealed (1) the birth of a son, God to be his Father; (2) a command to name him Jesus, Savior, thus indicating office; (3) this son to be recognized as the Messiah, and (4) to receive for all time the throne of David (Luke 1:31–33). Bring out all these facts by questions. Contrast Mary's humble faith with the unbelief of Zacharias. The revelation to Joseph was practically the same as that to Mary. Joseph also believed, and thus these two, in perfect harmony, waited for the fulfilment of their hopes. Mary and Elizabeth meet and rejoice together in the wonderful things which are about to take place. Have the class read Mary's hymn of praise from the Revised Version. Show in this hymn Mary's joy (1) in what the Lord has done for her, (2) in what he will do for his people, and that all this was (3) in remembrance of promises made centuries before to Abraham. In closing review the entire lesson, unitizing the various prophecies into one picture, showing clearly Jesus, the world's coming minister and savior.

Points to Emphasize.
1. The equipment of Jesus.
2. The type of service he was to render to man (Isa. 61: 1-3).
3. The blessing of God upon such service, bringing ultimate success to his ministry.

Scholar's Home Work.
Advance work: A careful study of the lesson material.
Review work: Questions for written answers to be returned to the teacher:
1. What was to be the great work of Jesus?
2. Where was he to be born, and of what family?
3. In what way was he to be fitted for his work?
4. To what classes of people was he to minister?
5. What was prophesied concerning the treatment he would receive?
6. What success would he attain?
7. What was revealed to Zacharias?
8. What was revealed to Mary and Joseph?

9. What was the difference in the way the heavenly message was treated by Zacharias and by Mary and Joseph?

10. In Mary's hymn of praise for what did she thank God?

Constructive work: Write the first chapter for the *Life of Christ,* upon the following plan:

JESUS THE IDEAL CHARACTER
Part I. *Jesus and His Ministry*
Chapter I. *Prophecies concerning Jesus*

§ 1. The Old Testament picture of Jesus.
§ 2. Zacharias's vision in the temple.
§ 3. The wonderful dreams of Mary and Joseph.
§ 4. The story of the *Magnificat.*

Illustrative picture for the chapter, Hofmann's "Head of Christ."

LESSON 2

EVENTS IN FULFILMENT OF THESE PROPHECIES

Lesson Material.
Luke 2: 1–38; Matt. 2: 1–23.

Teacher's Study Material.
Exod. 13: 2, 13–15; Lev. 12: 2–4, 6–8; Numb. 3: 44–51; Fairbairn, *Studies in the Life of Christ,* pp. 30–45; Smith, *Historical Geography of the Holy Land,* pp. 318–20, 432–35; Edersheim, *The Temple and its Ministry,* pp. 301–303; *idem, Sketches of Jewish Social Life,* pp, 42–51; related sections in the various standard lives of Jesus Christ; a good critical commentary.

Illustrative Material.
Use the blackboard for the outline of the lesson material. Draw upon the board an outline map of Palestine and trace the journey from Nazareth to Bethlehem, from

Bethlehem to Jerusalem and return, and from Bethlehem to Egypt and return to Nazareth. Locate on enlarged map-section the following places: Jerusalem, Nazareth, and Bethlehem. At the lesson close write upon the board the plan for chap. ii of the scholar's *Life of Christ*. Show pictures of the places mentioned in the lesson, and also of Raphael's " Sistine Madonna."

Organization of Material.
1. Events connected with Jesus' birth.
    a) The journey to Bethlehem.
    b) The birth in Bethlehem.
    c) The heavenly announcement to the shepherds.
    d) The shepherds' visit to the child.
2. Circumcision and presentation in the temple.
    a) The child circumcised and named Jesus.
    b) Brought to the temple at Jerusalem for redemption.
    c) Simeon's thanksgiving and prophecy.
    d) Anna's thanksgiving and prophecy.
3. The visit of the Magi.
    a) The heavenly sign and the journey to Jerusalem.
    b) Herod's inquiry and commission.
    c) The Magi journey to Bethlehem.
    d) They worship the child Jesus and present their gifts.
    e) God's warning and their return to their own country.
4. The Egyptian sojourn.
    a) Herod's evil design.
    b) God's warning to Joseph.
    c) The flight into Egypt.
    d) Herod's cruelty.
    e) The return to Nazareth of Galilee.

Presentation of Material.

Develop by questions the various sections as outlined under the heading "Organization of Material." Describe Bethlehem and the journey thither, and explain to the class the reasons which led to its undertaking. Picture the birth scene. Show the significance of the lowly birth of Jesus. Note here the fulfilment of phophecy. In the announcement from heaven bring out the following facts concerning the good tidings or "Gospel" : (1) It was universal in extent — "to all the people;" (2) It consisted in salvation — "born this day .... a savior;" (3) The savior a specially equipped person — "Christ the Lord" (the anointed one). The ceremony of circumcision brought the Jewish child under the old Abrahamic covenant with all of its privileges, and made him heir to all its promises. At this time — the eighth day — it was usual to name the child. Jesus, Savior, was not an uncommon name among the Jews, but in this case it was destined to be a most significant one. Explain the ceremony of redemption, and have the class read the Old Testament passages bearing upon this requirement. Note that the parents of Jesus, although with the memories of the wonderful visions granted to them concerning this child fresh in their minds, carefully fulfilled all the requirements of the Mosaic law. Have the class read Simeon's prophecy and burst of praise, noting (1) Simeon's spiritual enlightenment which enabled him to see the future work of the babe Jesus; (2) again the prophecy of the universality of this work; (3) the reflected glory of this work upon the nation of Jesus. Anna's prophecy was similar to Simeon's. Explain the character of the Magi, and describe their journey to Jerusalem. This journey occasioned by (1) the widespread knowledge in the East of Jewish messianic

INTERMEDIATE DEPARTMENT COURSE 255

prophecy; (2) the general expectancy that the time for its fulfilment was near at hand; (3) the extraordinary heavenly sign. Question concerning Herod's trouble of mind. Note the source of information, the priests and scribes, and the reference to the prophecy in Micah. Question concerning the real reasons for Herod's interest in the birth of Jesus. Note how Herod's evil design at this time was frustrated by (1) a direct warning to the Magi, and (2) a direct warning to Joseph. But although Jesus was saved Herod's cruel command was carried out. Question concerning (1) the stay in Egypt (many Jews there, hence he was probably among friends); (2) the signal for the return (the death of Herod); (3) the permanent home in Nazareth of Galilee (describe Nazareth). In closing review the entire lesson, uniting the various parts into a connected narrative, that the class may have a clear picture of the first few months of Jesus' life.

Points to Emphasize.
1. Universality of the coming ministry of Jesus — "to all the people."
2. Significance of the lowly birth of Jesus.
3. The careful observance of all the requirements of the law by the parents of Jesus.
4. God's care for the young child.

Scholar's Home Work.
Advance work: A careful study of the lesson material.
Review work: Questions for written answers to be returned to the teacher:
1. Why was the journey of Mary and Joseph to Bethlehem undertaken?
2. What does the lowly birth of Jesus signify to us?
3. What were the "glad tidings" which were brought to the shepherds?

4. How did the shepherds prove the truth of the angel's message?
5. Why was Jesus taken to the temple?
6. For what did Simeon praise God?
7. What was Simeon's prophecy concerning Jesus?
8. What occasioned the Magi's journey to Jerusalem?
9. Why was Herod so troubled over the news of the birth of Jesus?
10. In what way were Herod's evil plans brought to naught?

Constructive work: Write the second chapter for the *Life of Christ*, upon the following plan:

JESUS THE IDEAL CHARACTER

Part I. Jesus and His Ministry

Chapter II. Events in Fulfilment of these Prophecies

§ 1. The birth story.
§ 2. The wonderful temple scene.
§ 3. The Magi and their visit.
§ 4. The divine care for the young child.

Illustrative picture for the chapter, Raphael's "Sistine Madonna."

Lesson 3

THE TRAINING OF JESUS FOR HIS MINISTRY

Lesson Material.

Luke 2: 40-52; 4: 16; John 7: 15.

Teacher's Study Material. (To be used also as lesson material.)

Edersheim, *Life and Times of Jesus the Messiah*, Vol. I, pp. 223-54; Stapfer, *Jesus Christ before His Ministry*, pp. 5-90; Schurer, *The Jewish People in the Time of Jesus Christ*, Part II, Vol. II, pp. 46-52, 75-83;

Fairbairn, *Studies in the Life of Christ*, pp. 46–63; Edersheim, *Sketches of Jewish Social Life*, pp. 103–138; related sections in the various standard lives of Jesus Christ; a good critical commentary.

Illustrative Material.

Use the blackboard for the outline of the lesson material. At the lesson close write upon the board the plan for chap. iii of the scholar's *Life of Christ*. Show pictures of an oriental house of the poorer class, an oriental roll of the law, an Arab school of today, and an oriental carpenter's shop. Also show a picture of Hofmann's "Christ in the Temple."

Organization of Material.
1. Home training.
   a) The godly parents.
   b) The humble, happy home.
2. School training.
   a) The elementary school.
   b) The synagogue school training. (Deprived of training in the schools of the rabbis. See John 7:15.)
3. Training from private study.
   a) Thorough student of the scriptures.
   b) Sympathetic student of nature.
   c) Careful student of men.
4. Industrial training.
   a) Learned the trade of carpenter.
   b) In sympathy with the workers — the common people.
5. Social training.
   a) The social life of the home — Jesus among his brothers.
   b) The social life of the town — he mingled with men.

6. Religious training.
   a) The home atmosphere and training.
   b) Influence of the synagogue services at Nazareth.
   c) Influence of the feast and festival days at Jerusalem.

Presentation of Material.

Develop by questions the various sections as outlined under the heading "Organization of Material." As there is so little biblical matter bearing upon this lesson, the teacher should assign for study at home and report in class selected sections from the books noted under the heading "Teacher's Study Material." Describe the home in Nazareth into which Jesus was born. Call from the class their ideas as to what such a home must have been. Question concerning the character of Mary and Joseph. What would be the influence of such a home upon Jesus? (See Luke 2:51.) Describe the elementary-school system of Palestine in the time of Christ. We may suppose that Jesus attended such a school because (1) it was required of all Jewish boys, and Jesus' parents were strict Jews; and (2) Jesus being able to read and write probably learned to do so at such a school. It is probable that he also attended the synagogue school, but not the higher schools of the rabbis. Jesus was a thorough student of the Old Testament scriptures. Possibly his parents possessed a copy of the scriptures from which he studied. Have the class read passages showing Jesus' accurate knowledge of the scriptures, such as Matt. 4:4, 7, 10; 12:3; 19:4; 21:16, 42; 22:31; Mark 2:25; 12:10, 16. Show Jesus' intimate knowledge of nature, reading such passages as Matt. 6:26–29; 13:3–8; 21:19; Mark 4:28; John 15:1–8. But he was also acquainted with men; he knew what was in human nature. Let the class read John 2:25; Luke 12:13–15. According to Jewish custom

Jesus learned a trade, that of carpenter. Note that this brought him into sympathetic touch with the worker. If Joseph died during the early childhood of Jesus, he as the eldest son would be called upon to support the family. This would be ennobling, for as Fairbairn says, "Work for home is a noble education. It makes men forethoughtful, unselfish, dutiful to the weak, tender to the sorrowful, mindful of the loving. It had been a calamity to Himself and His mission had our Christ been deprived of so grand yet so universal a discipline." Show the social training Jesus had. Describe the life in the home with the brothers. Question as to the qualities this would tend to develop in him. He was not an ascetic nor a recluse like John the Baptist, but mingled freely with men (see Matt. 11:18, 19). The most important part of his training was his religious training. Picture to the class the influence of the home atmosphere and the home religious ceremonies. Question concerning the habits of Jesus on the Sabbath (Luke 4:16-20), and his probable atendance upon the more important feasts at Jerusalem (Luke 2:41, 42). Show the effect of these services upon his religious nature. In closing review the entire lesson, uniting the various parts into a connected narrative, that the class may have a clear idea of the thoroughness and breadth of the training which Jesus had for his ministry.

Points to Emphasize.

1. The need of careful study and training for all who would render a large service to mankind.
2. The thoroughness and breadth of Jesus' training.
3. The naturalness of Jesus' development in all aspects of his nature. "And Jesus increased in wisdom and stature, and in favor with God and man."

Scholar's Home Work.

Advance work: A careful study of the lesson material.
Review work: Questions for written answers to be returned to the teacher:

1. What kind of parents did Jesus have?
2. Describe Jesus' home.
3. What kind of a boy is Jesus shown to be in the record of his visit to Jerusalem?
4. What was Jesus' school training?
5. What subjects did he privately study?
6. What trade did Jesus learn?
7. What was the effect upon his character of his learning a trade?
8. In what did Jesus' social life differ from that of John the Baptist?
9. What was Jesus' custom on the Sabbath day?
10. What other influences helped to develop his religious nature?

Constructive work: Write the third chapter for the *Life of Christ* upon the following plan:

JESUS THE IDEAL CHARACTER

Part I. Jesus and His Ministry

Chapter III. The Training of Jesus for his Ministry

§ 1. Jesus' home life.
§ 2. His school life.
§ 3. His private study.
§ 4. Jesus the carpenter.
§ 5. Jesus among men.
§ 6. Development of his religious nature.

Illustrative picture for the chapter, Hofmann's "Christ in the Temple."

LESSON 4
THE BAPTISM — JESUS ACCEPTS HIS MINISTRY

Lesson Material.

Matt. 3: 1-17; Mark 1: 1-11; Luke 1: 57-80; 3: 1-18, 21, 22.

Teacher's Study Material.

Fairbairn, *Studies in the Life of Christ*, pp. 64-79; Stapfer, *Jesus Christ before His Ministry*, pp. 121-33; Phelps, *The Story of Jesus Christ*, pp. 62-76; Hastings, *Bible Dictionary*, Vol. I, art. "Baptism," and Vol. II, art. "John the Baptist;" related sections in the various standard lives of Jesus Christ; a good critical commentary.

Illustrative Material.

Use the blackboard for the outline of the lesson material. Trace on the board map the journey of Jesus from Nazareth to the Jordan banks near Bethabara. Show pictures of the fords of the Jordan near Jericho. Also pictures of the rugged hill-country of Judea. In this connection speak of the influence of environment upon character. At the lesson close write upon the board the plan for chap. iv of the scholar's *Life of Christ*. Show a picture of Du Mond's "The Baptism of Jesus."

Organization of Material.

1. Birth of John the Baptist.
    a) Prophecy to Zacharias fulfilled.
    b) The child circumcised and named.
    c) Prophecies of Zacharias concerning Jesus and John.
2. Ministry of John the Baptist.
    a) Called from the wilderness by God.
    b) Proclaims the nearness of the kingdom.
    c) Preaches remission of sin through repentance.
    d) Baptizes believers.

3. The baptism of Jesus by John.
   a) Jesus comes from Galilee.
   b) Jesus baptized by John in the Jordan.
   c) The miraculous manifestations at the baptism.

Presentation of Material.

Develop by questions the various sections as outlined under the heading "Organization of Material." Jesus had been in retirement in Nazareth, but now at the age of thirty, he prepares to enter upon his ministry. Recall from the class by questions the angel's annunciation to Zacharias in the temple (see Lesson 1), Zacharias's unbelief and its punishment. The time for the fulfilment of this prophecy had now come and a child was born to Elizabeth and Zacharias. The neighbors and kinsfolk rejoice with the parents. Note in connection with the ceremony of circumcision and naming (1) the astonishment of the friends at the naming of the child John — why? (2) the ending of Zacharias's punishment at the moment of the complete fulfilment of the prophecy, and (3) the widespread knowledge of these things among the people of the hill-country. This may have been a factor in the great popularity which John gained at the very outset of his preaching. Bring out by questions the elements of the prophecy of Zacharias concerning Jesus, that he was (1) the prophesied "horn of salvation" of Israel (explain meaning of term), and (2) a light-giver and guide to all (see Luke 1:79); and in the prophecy concerning John that he was to be (1) the Messiah's forerunner or herald, announcing the coming of the Lord, and (2) a preacher preparing the hearts of many for the teachings of salvation (Mal. 3:1 and Isa. 40:3). Describe the wilderness hill-country of Judea, and briefly sketch John's probable preparation for his work. When about thirty years of age John is called by God from the wilderness to begin his mission. Describe his appearance and picture the effect of his sudden coming. Question the class concerning his relation (1) to prophecy — a fulfilment of Isa. 40:3, (2) to the Messiah — the forerunner, making ready the way and announcing the nearness of the kingdom, and (3) to salvation — a preacher of repentance as a condition of the remission of sins. Develop by questions the practical character of John's preaching (see Luke 3:8, 10-14). John baptized many who accepted his teachings. Explain the meaning of John's baptism of water — a symbol of cleansing. While John was preaching and baptizing near the lower fords of the Jordan, Jesus comes to him from Galilee. Recall from the class some of the facts (1) concerning the messianic prophecies, (2) their remarkable fulfilment, and (3) the thirty years of training which Jesus had received. He now believed that he was the Messiah of the Jews and the Savior of the world. He comes now to signify his acceptance of his mission. Picture the baptismal scene — the broad, shallow fords, the crowds, the stern preacher of righteousness, the baptisms in the waters of the Jordan. Note the colloquy between Jesus and John. John saw the beauty of Jesus' character in his face, and testified to his own need of baptism at the hands of Jesus. Note Jesus' answer and explain its meaning. Also note the miraculous manifestations (probably seen and heard only by Jesus and John) — manifestations of God's approval of the life of Jesus up to this time. These manifestations of approval confirmed Jesus' belief, which had been growing in clearness for many years, that he was the chosen one of God for the salvation of the world. Thus did Jesus accept his great mission, and thus was he consecrated to his work. In closing, review the entire lesson, unitizing the various parts into a connected narrative, emphasizing the faithfulness of Jesus and John to their ideals, and the approval of God upon such lives.

Points to Emphasize.
1. The faithfulness and humility of John.
2. The emphasis which Jesus placed upon the careful following of the law.
3. God's approval of a life resulting from a loving acceptance of his law.

Scholar's Home Work.

Advance work: A careful study of the lesson material.
Review work: Questions for written answers to be returned to the teacher:
1. What remarkable thing happened at the naming of the child John?
2. What did Zacharias prophesy concerning Jesus?
3. What did Zacharias prophesy concerning John?
4. What kind of a training did John have for his work?
5. What was the great subject of all John's preaching?
6. What new ceremony did John introduce?
7. What success did John have in his work?
8. Why did Jesus come to be baptized by John?
9. In what manner did God show his approval of Jesus' life?
10. What effect did these miracles at the baptism have upon Jesus?

Constructive work: Write the fourth chapter for the *Life of Christ* upon the following plan:

INTERMEDIATE DEPARTMENT COURSE 265

JESUS THE IDEAL CHARACTER
Part I. *Jesus and His Ministry*
Chapter IV. *The Baptism of Jesus*

§ 1. John the Baptist's early life and training.
§ 2. The ministry of John.
§ 3. The baptism of Jesus by John.

Illustrative picture for the chapter, Du Mond's "The Baptism of Jesus."

LESSON 5

THE TEMPTATION — JESUS PROVES HIS FITNESS FOR HIS MINISTRY

Lesson Material.
Matt. 4: 1-11; Mark 1: 12, 13; Luke 4: 1-13.

Teacher's Study Material.
Heb. 4: 15; Jas. 1: 2, 3, 12-15; Gilbert, *The Student's Life of Jesus*, pp. 57-66; Weiss, *The Life of Christ*, Vol. I, pp. 337-55; Wendt, *The Teaching of Jesus*, Vol. I, pp. 101-6; "Expositor's Bible" series, *Matthew*, pp. 39-47; related sections in the various standard lives of Jesus Christ; a good critical commentary.

Illustrative Material.
Use the blackboard for the outline of the lesson material. Show a picture of Mt. Quarantana, the traditional site of the temptation. At the lesson close write upon the board the plan for chap. v of the scholar's *Life of Christ*. Also show a picture of Brünewald's "Christ Standing by the Sea."

Organization of Material.
1. The first temptation.
   a) An appeal to appetite — hunger.
   b) A temptation to distrust God's providential care.
   c) Victory through reliance upon God's truth.

2. The second temptation.
   a) An appeal to pride of position and calling.
   b) A temptation to trust to God's promises without fulfilling their conditions.
   c) Victory through reliance upon God's truth.
3. The third temptation.
   a) An appeal to the highest ambition — world conquest.
   b) A temptation to distrust God's power and the efficacy of his methods.
   c) Victory through reliance upon God's truth.

Presentation of Material.

Develop by questions the various sections as outlined under the heading "Organization of Material." Immediately following the baptism Jesus was "led up of the Spirit into the wilderness." This wilderness of Judea, near the northern end of the Dead Sea, the traditional site being Mt. Quarantana, was the scene of the present lesson. Explain to the class very briefly the possibility of Jesus being tempted, there being no sin in temptation but only in yielding to it. Also impress the reality of the temptation, although in the form of mental experiences and not in that of physical reality, as the narrative would seem to imply if taken literally (see Gilbert's *Life of Jesus*). After a period of more or less complete fasting due to absorption in thought concerning his Messianic work, the temptation came through a mental suggestion to supply himself with food by the use of his power as the Son of God. Note here that this temptation came through that which is in itself good — hunger. Hunger is to be gratified. Question as to when such action is justifiable. Have class read Matt. 12: 1–8. Explain the passage. Why not justifiable in the case of Jesus? The suggestion was, "Because thou art the Son of God, do this;" Jesus' reply was, "Because I am the Son of God, I will not distrust his providential care." What passage in the Bible came to Jesus' mind? Note in this connection (1) the relative values Jesus places upon the lower and the higher life, (2) the duty of obedience to the higher law, (3) the value of a knowledge of fundamental truths as helps to discern and to overcome evil. Try to impress these thoughts upon the class, especially the one that the needs of the lower nature are no excuse for breaking the law of the higher nature. Illustrate by examples. In the second temptation the very trust Jesus had in God is put to the test. Note the appeal — to Jesus' position as the Son of God. The suggestion came to test the promises. Have the class read Ps. 91:9-16. What are the conditions under which such promises apply? (See vs. 9.) Only when danger threatens while in the line of duty. Was Jesus called upon at any time to manifest his Messiahship in any miraculous way? (See Matt. 12:39.) How was his work to be accomplished? (See Zech. 4:6 and John 4:25, 26.) What passage in the Bible came to Jesus' mind at this time? Explain meaning. Impress the thought that God's promises are sure to those who fulfil the conditions attached. If we break God's laws, physical, mental, spiritual, we cannot expect him to overrule the results. We cannot expect preservation if we run into needless danger. Illustrate by other examples. In the third temptation there came a suggestion to Jesus that his work might be the better and more quickly done if he made use of worldly powers, methods, and means. Note the appeal — to Jesus' great hope and desire to win the world to himself and thus to God. But this work was to be done by God's power and in God's way. Explain the meaning of the temptation — the use of worldly means and powers to acomplish the end. This was, then, a temptation to distrust (1) God's wisdom, (2) his love, and (3) the efficacy of his methods. What passage from the Bible came to Jesus' mind at this time? Explain the meaning of this, that using wrong means and methods to do God's work is like bowing down to or worshiping evil. Impress the thought that if we are to be coworkers with God in the betterment of the world we must always seek to do our work in the right way and by the use of the right means. Principle, not policy, must guide us. Illustrate by examples. In closing review the entire lesson, uniting the various parts into a connected narrative, emphasizing the keenness of Jesus in seing the evil in the various suggestions, and the power he received to cast them aside.

Points to Emphasize.
1. The apparently innocent form of some temptations.
2. The value of a knowledge of God's truth, to help to detect and to overcome temptation.
3. The value of early training in times of crises.

Scholar's Home Work.
Advance work: A careful study of the lesson material.
Review work: Questions for written answers to be returned to the teacher:
1. Where did Jesus go immediately after the baptism, and what impelled him?
2. In the first temptation to what was the appeal made?
3. Why would it have been wrong to yield to the suggestion?
4. What helped Jesus to see the evil in this suggestion and to cast it aside?
5. In the second temptation to what was the appeal made?

INTERMEDIATE DEPARTMENT COURSE 269

6. Why would it have been wrong to yield to this suggestion?
7. What helped Jesus to see the evil in this suggestion and to cast it aside?
8. In the third temptation to what was the appeal made?
9. Why would it have been wrong to yield to the suggestion?
10. What helped Jesus to see the evil in the suggestion and to cast it aside?

Constructive work: Write the fifth chapter for the *Life of Christ* upon the following plan:

> JESUS THE IDEAL CHARACTER
> Part I. Jesus and His Ministry
> Chapter V. The Temptation of Jesus

§ 1. The wilderness scene.
§ 2. The first temptation and its meaning.
§ 3. The second temptation and its meaning.
§ 4. The third temptation and its meaning.

Illustrative picture for the chapter, Grünewald's "Christ Standing by the Sea."

LESSON 6
THE MINISTRY OF JESUS ANNOUNCED

Lesson Material.

John 1: 19–37.

Teacher's Study Material.

Matt. 17: 10–13; Isa. 53: 1–12; Mathews, *History of New Testament Times in Palestine*, pp. 159–73; Edersheim, *Life and Times of Jesus the Messiah*, Vol. I, pp. 160–79; Andrews, *The Life of Our Lord*, pp. 154–57; Hastings,

Bible Dictionary, art. "Forerunner;" related sections in the various standard lives of Jesus Christ; a good critical commentary.

Illustrative Material.

Use the blackboard for the outline of the lesson material. At the lesson close write upon the board the plan for chap. vi of the scholar's *Life of Christ*. Show a picture of Bida's "Behold the Lamb of God."

Organization of Material.

1. The official announcement to the Jerusalem deputation.
   a) The committee from Jerusalem.
   b) John's testimony concerning himself.
   c) John's testimony concerning Jesus.
2. The general announcement to the people.
   a) Jesus proclaimed as the Lamb of God.
   b) John's witness to Jesus as the Son of God.
3. The special announcement to two disciples.
   a) Jesus again proclaimed as the Lamb of God.
   b) The response of the two disciples.

Presentation of Material.

Develop by questions the various sections as outlined under the heading "Organization of Material." The scenes of this lesson come very shortly after the last lesson on the Temptation of Jesus. John was still preaching and baptizing on the east banks of the Jordan, just north of the Dead Sea. Note the interest John had awakened by his preaching, and the following he had gained. Let the class read from Matt. 3: 5-12 and Luke 3: 1-18. Question concerning the effect of his preaching upon different classes of people (Luke 3: 10 ff.). Picture the Messianic hopes of the people at this time. What expectation had John's preaching aroused? What was the teaching of the scribes concerning Elijah? Read

Matt. 17:10. John's work and his increasing following led the Pharisees of Jerusalem to send a semi-official deputation to him. Develop the interview by questions, noting (1) the makeup of the committee, (2) the questions they asked John, and (3) their earnestness and perseverance in seeking a definite answer. Then bring out the elements of John's answer, calling attention first to the positive assertions that he was not (1) the Christ, nor (2) Elijah, nor (3) even the Prophet, but only a Voice, a herald of the Lord. Describe the oriental customs relating to heralds and forerunners. Also note the homage implied in John's words in vs. 27. A teacher could require of a scholar any work of a servant except to unloose the latchet of his shoe. Finally emphasize John's testimony concerning Jesus the Messiah that he was even then "in their midst." The next day Jesus is openly pointed out to the people. Explain briefly the picture of the Messiah as given in the fifty-third chapter of Isaiah. This picture may have been in John's mind, or he may have been thinking of the paschal lamb when he said, "Behold the Lamb of God which taketh away the sin of the world." Note in this phrase a prophecy of Jesus' great work — to take away the world's sin. Recall by questions the scenes of the baptism, especially the revelations given at that time. John again witnesses to these revelations and testifies (1) that this Jesus is he that baptizes with the Holy Spirit, and (2) that he is the Son of God. Note here the second aspect of Jesus' work, to baptize with the spirit, to give power, strength for daily living. Again opportunity offers and for the third time John gladly testifies concerning Jesus, again proclaiming him as the Lamb of God. Two of John's immediate disciples respond to his words and follow Jesus. Emphasize here (1) John's faithful witnessing, (2) the two disciples' open-mindedness, and (3) John's greatness in joyfully subordinating himself. In closing review the entire lesson, uniting the various parts into a connected narrative, bringing into bold relief the faithful testimony of John and the revealed twofold function of the ministry of Jesus as announced by John.

Points to Emphasize.
1. John's repeated faithful witnessing to Jesus.
2. The double aspect of Jesus' ministry — to forgive sin and to give strength for daily living.
3. The possible rewards of faithful witnessing.

Scholar's Home Work.
Advance work: A careful study of the lesson material.
Review work: Questions for written answers to be returned to the teacher:
1. What expectation had John's preaching and work raised in the minds of the people?
2. What did the leaders in Jerusalem do to settle this matter?
3. What was John's testimony to the committee concerning himself?
4. What did he testify to the committee concerning Jesus?
5. What in this lesson shows John's wonderful humility?
6. What did John testify to the people concerning Jesus?
7. What does John say is the work Jesus is to do for all?
8. To what two disciples was Jesus especially pointed out?
9. What did these disciples do when they saw Jesus?
10. How do you think John felt to have some of his disciples leave him?

Constructive work: Write the sixth chapter for the *Life of Christ* upon the following plan:

> JESUS THE IDEAL CHARACTER
> Part I. *Jesus and His Ministry*
> *Chapter VI. The Ministry of Jesus Announced*
> § 1. John and the Jerusalem committee.
> § 2. John and the people.
> § 3. John and the two disciples.

Illustrative picture for the chapter, Bida's "Behold the Lamb of God."

LESSON 7
THE MINISTRY OF JESUS BEGUN

Lesson Material.

John 1:38—2:12.

Teacher's Study Material.

Luke 24:13-32; John 7:52; "Expositor's Bible" series, *John*, pp. 55-84; Edersheim, *Life and Times of Jesus the Messiah*, Vol. I, pp. 346-63; Gilbert, *The Student's Life of Jesus*, pp. 84-90; Edersheim, *Sketches of Jewish Social Life*, pp. 150-55; related sections in the various standard lives of Jesus Christ; a good critical commentary.

Illustrative Material.

Use the blackboard for the outline of the lesson material. Trace on the board the journey of Jesus from Bethabara near the Jordan to Cana of Galilee, and thence to Capernaum. Show pictures of Cana, Capernaum (ruins) and surrounding country. At the lesson close write upon the board the plan for chap. vii of the scholar's *Life of Christ*. Show a picture of Bonifazio's "Christ and Philip."

Organization of Material.

1. Revealing himself.
    a) Jesus' invitation.
    b) The revelation of his Messiahship.

2. Gaining disciples.
    a) The result of the two disciples' testimony.
    b) The direct call of Philip by Jesus.
    c) The calling of Nathanael.
3. Ministering to the home life.
    a) The marriage feast.
    b) The opportunity for service.
    c) The service rendered.

Presentation of Material.
Develop by questions the various sections as outlined under the heading "Organization of Material." Recall the testimony of John to his disciples and the effect upon them. Point out some of the characteristics of these two disciples of John. Their inquiry as to Jesus' home may mean that they will not detain him now, but will seek him out later to become more intimately acquainted. He asks them to come with him *now*, and this is the beginning of the long companionship. Try to picture this first interview with Jesus; the eager questions of the disciples, the Master's answers, the quotations from prophecy, the growing interest as he opens up to them something of his hopes and plans, which finally leads to the firm conviction in the disciples' minds that he is indeed the Messiah. Have the class read Luke 24: 13-32, and compare this account with their mental picture of the first interview of Jesus with the two disciples of John. What did Andrew's belief lead him to do? What did John do? Refer to the importance attached to the meaning of names, and show the significance of Simon's new name. By questions develop the events following, the direct call of Philip and the result. Explain the prejudice against Galilee, and the belief that the Messiah must come from Judea. See John 7: 52. Recall the fact that Jesus was born in Judea in accordance with prophecy. Note the

character of Nathanael and explain the phrase "in whom is no guile." In developing the interview note (1) the doubt of Nathanael and to what it was due, (2) the supernatural knowledge shown by Jesus, (3) Nathanael's acknowledgment of Jesus, and (4) Jesus' promise of greater revelations. Describe an oriental house, the festive preparations for a wedding, the manner of sitting and serving at table, the gathering of the guests, etc. What guests were present at this time? Why were Jesus and his disciples invited? Note Mary's interest when the wine failed. What may be a reasonable explanation of this interest? Question the class as to (1) Mary's request — why made of Jesus? (2) Jesus' reply — its meaning and (3) Mary's order to the servants — what did it show? Question on the facts of the miracle and the testimony of the ruler to its genuineness. This first miracle of Jesus was (1) one of humble service in the home, (2) done in accordance with the known will of God, (vs. 4), and was (3) a setting forth of the divine nature of Jesus which confirmed the belief of the disciples in him. Emphasize these thoughts. Jesus shortly after left Cana and went down to Capernaum. In closing review the entire lesson, uniting the various parts into a connected narrative, emphasizing the service which Jesus rendered in revealing himself, in calling coworkers, and in ministering to the home life in Cana.

Points to Emphasize.

1. The willingness of Jesus to reveal the truth to those who are willing to learn.
2. The inspiration to service which comes from a personal knowledge of Jesus the Christ.
3. The interest of Jesus in our daily affairs.
4. The testimony which our deeds bear to our character.

Scholar's Home Work.

Advance work: A careful study of the lesson material.
Review work: Questions for written answers to be returned to the teacher:

1. What led Jesus to invite the two disciples to his home?
2. What did Jesus reveal to them that day?
3. What did John and Andrew do immediately upon leaving Jesus?
4. Whom did Jesus himself call to be a disciple?
5. Whom did Philip bring to Jesus?
6. Why did Jesus attend the wedding at Cana?
7. What opportunity for service came to him while there?
8. Why did he not perform the miracle at once when asked?
9. How do we know that it was a real miracle?
10. What was the effect of the miracle?

Constructive work: Write the seventh chapter for the *Life of Christ* upon the following plan:

JESUS THE IDEAL CHARACTER
Part I. Jesus and His Ministry

Chapter VII. The Ministry of Jesus Begun

§ 1. The remarkable interview.
§ 2. The calling of the disciples.
§ 3. Jesus at the wedding in Cana.

Illustrative picture for the chapter, Bonifazio's "Christ and Philip."

§ 6. BOOKS RELATING TO THE WORK OF GRADE B

A. REFERENCE READING FOR THE TEACHER

Andrews, *The Life of Our Lord* (Charles Scribner's Sons, New York).

Bruce, *The Miraculous Element in the Gospels*, and *The Parabolic Teaching of Christ* (A. C. Armstrong & Son, New York).

Edersheim, *The Life and Times of Jesus the Messiah*, 2 vols. (A. D. F. Randolph & Co., New York).

Fairbairn, *Studies in the Life of Christ* (Hodder & Stoughton, London).

Gilbert, *The Student's Life of Jesus* (The Macmillan Co., New York).

Ramsay, *The Education of Christ* (G. P. Putnam's Sons, New York).

Rhees, *The Life of Jesus of Nazareth* (Charles Scribner's Sons, New York).

Sanday, art. "Jesus Christ," in Hastings's *Bible Dictionary*.

Schürer, *The Jewish People in the Time of Jesus Christ*, 5 vols. (Charles Scribner's Sons, New York).

Smith, *The Historical Geography of the Holy Land* (A. C. Armstrong & Son, New York).

Stalker, *Imago Christi* (American Tract Society, New York).

Stapfer, *Jesus Christ: His Person, His Authority, and His Work*, 3 vols. (Charles Scribner's Sons, New York).

Stevens and Burton, *A Harmony of the Gospels* (Charles Scribner's Sons, New York).

Watson, *The Life of the Master* (McClure, Phillips & Co., New York).

Weiss, *The Life of Christ*, 3 vols. (T. & T. Clark, Edinburgh).

Wendt, *The Teaching of Jesus*, 2 vols. (Charles Scribner's Sons, New York).

Wenley, *The Preparation for Christianity in the Ancient World* (F. H. Revell Co., Chicago).

Whyte, *Our Lord's Characters*, Vol. VI in the series "Bible Characters" (F. H. Revell Co., Chicago).

B. READING AND REFERENCE BOOKS FOR THE PUPIL

Barton, *Jesus of Nazareth: The Story of His Life and the Scenes of His Ministry* (The Pilgrim Press, Boston).

Bird, *Jesus the Carpenter of Nazareth* (Charles Scribner's Sons, New York).

Phelps, *The Story of Jesus Christ* (Houghton, Mifflin & Co., Boston).

Stalker, *Life of Christ* (F. H. Revell Co., Chicago).

Willett, *Life and Teachings of Jesus* (F. H. Revell Co., Chicago).

"The Clark Bible Primers" (Charles Scribner's Sons, New York): (1) *Life of Christ*, by Salmond; (2) *Parables of Our Lord*, by Salmond.

---

§ 7. OUTLINE OF THE COURSE FOR GRADE C

GRADE SUBJECT: GREAT CHARACTERS IN THE NEW TESTAMENT (CONTINUED)

B. *Other New Testament Characters*

Part 1 — The forerunner and the lesser apostles.

1. John the Baptist.
   a) Early life and training.
2. *b*) His ministry.
3. The apostolic band.
4. John the Beloved.
   a) Early life and training.
5. *b*) Period of discipleship.
6. *c*) Closing years.
7. *Review. Memory work.*

Part 2 — The life of Peter.

8. Peter's early life and training.
9. Peter's fall and reinstatement.
10. Peter's first sermon.

Intermediate Department Course

11. Peter's first miracle.
12. Peter's first testimony before the rulers.
13. Peter rebuking Ananias and Sapphira.
14. Peter's vision at Joppa.
15. Peter and Cornelius.
16. Peter's imprisonment and release.
17. Closing years of Peter's life.
18. *Review. Memory work.*

Part 3 — The life of Paul.

19. Paul's early life and training.
20. Paul the inquisitor and persecutor.
21. Paul the convert.
22. Paul's first Christian activity.
23. Paul's first missionary journey — outward.
24. Paul's first missionary journey — homeward.
25. Paul at the Jerusalem council.
26. *Review. Memory work.*
27. Paul strengthening the churches.
28. Paul's vision at Troas.
29. Paul beginning his work in Europe.
30. Paul at work in Thessalonica, Berea, and Athens.
31. Paul's first ministry in Corinth.
32. Paul and the Thessalonians.
33. Paul's return and the letter to the Galatians.
34. *Review. Memory work.*
35. Paul's ministry in Ephesus.
36. Paul and the Corinthian church.
37. Paul and the Roman church.
38. Paul's journey to Jerusalem.
39. Paul's arrest in Jerusalem.
40. Paul's address to the people.
41. Paul before the Sanhedrin.
42. *Review. Memory work.*
43. Paul before Felix.

44. Paul's appear to Cæsar.
45. Paul's defense before Agrippa.
46. Paul's voyage to Rome.
47. Paul's labors in Rome.
48. Paul's later work.
49. Paul's second imprisonment and martyrdom.
50. *Review. Memory work.*

Special Lessons.
51. Christmas lesson.
52. Easter lesson.

---

§ 8. SUGGESTIVE LESSON PLANS FOR GRADE C
Lessons 1 and 2
Lesson 1
JOHN THE BAPTIST — HIS EARLY LIFE AND TRAINING

Lesson Material.

Luke 1: 5–25, 57–80; 3: 1–6.

Teacher's Study Material.

Rhees, *The Life of Jesus of Nazareth,* pp. 3–20, 70–78; Edersheim, *Life and Times of Jesus the Messiah,* Vol. I, pp. 133–43, 157–59; Mathews, *A History of New Testament Times in Palestine,* pp. 159–71; Riggs, *A History of the Jewish People,* pp. 213–31; Fairbairn, *Studies in the Life of Christ,* pp. 64–79; Smith, *The Historical Geography of the Holy Land,* pp. 312–17; Hastings, *Bible Dictionary,* arts. "John the Baptist," and "Forerunner."

Illustrative Material.

Use the blackboard for the outline of the lesson material. Locate on map (blackboard outline) the Wilderness, Jordan, Jerusalem. Also the political divisions of the country under the sons of Herod. The following pictures may prove helpful: "The Wilderness," "An Arab School," and "John the Baptist" by del Sarto. At the lesson close write upon the board the plan for chap. i of the scholar's *Life of John the Baptist.*

Organization of Material.
1. The times in which he lived.
   a) Political conditions.
   b) Social divisions.
   c) Religious life.
2. His ancestry and birth.
   a) Character of parents.
   b) Birth in the hill-country of Judea.
      (1) The prophecy.
      (2) The announcement.
      (3) The fulfilment.
3. His early environment and training.
   a) Desert surroundings.
   b) Strict Jewish training.
4. His office and call.
   a) The herald of Christ.
   b) Divinely called to this work.

Presentation of Material.
Develop by questions the various sections as outlined under the heading "Organization of Material." Seek to give as clear an idea as possible of the times in which John lived. Recall the fact that Palestine had been under Roman rule since the victory of Pompey in 63 B. C. Since then the Roman emperors had directed affairs in Palestine. Herod the Great reigned, under the emperor, over all Palestine at the time of John's birth. Show by use of map how kingdom was divided among his sons at his death. Note the most important social divisions or classes: (1) the Sadducees, representing the aristocratic,

priestly party, who maintained the ritual and the customs but had little real interest in religion; (2) the Pharisees, representing the religious party, devoted to the observance of the law in all its minor points, and very strict in all religious duties; (3) the Essenes, a strict ascetic order; (4) the Samaritans, living in Samaria, a mixed people, part Jew, part foreigner, despised by all orthodox Jews since the time of Ezra; (5) the unnamed and uninfluential company of devout, pious people who were looking for the Messiah. Show how the reverence for the law was followed by reverence for man's interpretation of the law — the traditions of men; and again how the separation from the nations around them had developed into a hatred for other peoples. Thus a mere form of worship had gradually replaced true zeal and piety. Note the exception — the few who were striving to live true lives, and who were looking for the coming of the Messiah. Though briefly presented, try to leave a clear picture of the times in the minds of the pupils. Question the class in regard to the parents of John, their names, age, character, etc., and the office of Zacharias. Explain the courses of the priests and their temple duties. Have the class read the prophecies concerning John (Mal. 4: 5, 6; *cf.* Isa. 40:3). Question the class concerning the facts of the annunciation, Zacharias's unbelief and punishment, and the fulfilment of the promise. Note the restoration of the power of speech to Zacharias at the naming of John. In the psalm of thanksgiving note the two elements of (1) thanksgiving for the promised redemption and (2) prophecy concerning John's office and work. We do not know the exact place where John's early life was spent. Have class read Luke 1:80. Note the natural and uneventful childhood. Describe the desert or wilderness of Judea. Area of about thirty-five by fifteen miles, barren, rugged, unattractive in appearance, still only a short distance from Jerusalem and Hebron. So while he was trained amid hard and austere surroundings, he was not ignorant of the life of his fellow-men in the cities, of their needs and their activities. Picture the religious training of a Jewish boy, beginning, as soon as he learned to speak, to study the Bible, the only text-book used up to the age of ten. After this came the traditional law, and if the education was carried still farther there followed the rabbinic comments. Every part of the life, even the eating and drinking, was regulated by the law. Show how John's separation in the desert from the formalism and cant of the religious teachers kept him pure and developed in him the Old Testament prophetic type of character. His training opened his eyes to the hypocrisy and hollowness of the scribes and Pharisees, and led him to demand truth and simplicity of living. He was not trained to belong to any sect or school, but was the product of the old and simple Jewish faith, reared by pious parents, devout, earnest, a student of the Scriptures, and thoughtful and original as regards its application to life. The time of preparation now fully completed, fix the attention of the class on the central thought in the lesson, the call to service. From what? At about what age? From where? To what? Have class read Luke 3:4-6; compare the promise made to Zacharias in Luke 1:13-17. What custom interprets his office of forerunner? Picture the oriental forerunner and show application in the illustration to John's work. What would the forerunner seek to accomplish? What was to be John's work? In closing, review the whole outline, emphasizing the ancestry, training, and office of John, that the pupils may be made to understand the close relationship between good birth and careful training, and a large service to mankind.

Points to Emphasize.
1. The need of "forerunners," "preparers of the way" of every reform.
2. The close relationship existing between preparation and service.
3. That back of every opportunity is the divine call.

Scholar's Home Work.
Advance work: A careful study of the lesson material.
Review work: Questions for written answers to be returned to the teacher:
1. By whom was Palestine ruled when John was born?
2. What were the two most important religious parties?
3. What was the religious condition of the people?
4. Who were the parents of John and what was their character?
5. What wonderful circumstances attended John's birth?
6. What was the promise in regard to his future?
7. Where was his early life spent?
8. What training did he have?
9. How old was he when he received his call?
10. What word is used to describe his office?

Constructive work: Write the first chapter for the *Life of John the Baptist* upon the following plan:

JOHN THE BAPTIST
Chapter I. His Early Life and Training

§ 1. Palestine and its people.
§ 2. The wonders of John's birth.
§ 3. His home life and training.
§ 4. The divine call.

Illustrative picture for the chapter, Andrea del Sarto's "John the Baptist."

INTERMEDIATE DEPARTMENT COURSE

LESSON 2
JOHN THE BAPTIST — HIS MINISTRY

Lesson Material.

Matt. 3:1-12; 11:2-19; 14:3-12; Mark 1:9-11; John 1:19-35; 3:23-30.

Teacher's Study Material.

Mark 1:1-8; 6:14-29; Luke 3:7-20; 7:19-23; Rhees, *Life of Jesus of Nazareth,* pp. 79-86, 92, 93; Edersheim, *Life and Times of Jesus the Messiah,* Vol. I, pp. 264-74, 278-87, 336-44, 654-75; Weiss, *The Life of Christ,* Vol. I, pp. 307-18, 355-64; Stalker, *The Life of Christ,* pp. 40-44; Smith, *The Historical Geography of the Holy Land,* pp. 482-96; Fairbairn, *Studies in the Life of Christ,* pp. 64-79; Hastings, *Bible Dictionary,* art. "John the Baptist."

Illustrative Material.

Use the blackboard for the outline of the lesson material. Locate on the blackboard map the places in the lesson — Wilderness, Fords of Jordan, Castle of Macherus. Pictures: "The Fords of the Jordan," and "John the Baptist Preaching" by Titian. At the lesson close write upon the board the plan for chap. ii of the scholar's *Life of John the Baptist.*

Organization of Material.

1. John's ministry.
    a) Place, near the Jordan.
    b) Aim — a preparation for the Coming One.
    c) Theme — Repent, for the kingdom of heaven is at hand.
    d) Results.
        (1) Crowds hear him.
        (2) Many are baptized.

2. Significant events in John's career.
    a) The baptism of Jesus.
    b) His glorious witness to Jesus.
    c) The message to Jesus from prison and the answer.
    d) His martyrdom.
3. Work accomplished.
    a) Heralded the coming of the Messiah.
    b) Prepared men's hearts for the kingdom of heaven.
4. Marked characteristics of John.
    a) Singleness of purpose.
    b) Fearlessness.
    c) Insight into character.
    d) Humility.

Presentation of Material.

Develop by questions the various sections as outlined under the heading "Organization of Material." Show on the map the place of John's ministry, the "region round about Jordan" and the wilderness near. Also show pictures of this region. The Jordan was probably the scene of the many baptisms. Describe the preacher, his dress, manner of life, probable style of preaching, etc. Question the class as to the great aim John had in view. Have some one read Luke 3:4-6 and John 1:22, 23. Question the class on the theme and the chief features of John's preaching, bringing out the following thoughts: (1) the coming of the kingdom; (2) the need of repentance and reformation in every class and individual as a preparation for that kingdom; (3) the sign of repentance and consecration to the new idea — baptism; (4) the prediction of the Coming One. Also question on the results of his ministry, showing that many repented and thus became prepared for the kingdom, but that many were offended by the strictness of John's requirements. Rapidly glance at the remaining years of John's life, noting some of the

INTERMEDIATE DEPARTMENT COURSE 287

more significant events. After John had been preaching for perhaps six to nine months, Jesus came to him to be baptized. Bring out by questions the more significant details of the scene. Note that this event brought to John the assurance that the One for whom he had been preparing the way had come. Question the class concerning the facts connected with the visit of the committee from the Jerusalem leaders. As each point comes up explain the Jewish view in regard to Christ, Elijah, and the prophet. Explain the meaning of John's answer. Note and emphasize John's testimony to the people and to the disciples concerning Jesus, "He must increase but I must decrease." Question the class as to the cause of John's imprisonment (Matt. 14:3, 4). Point out how Christ's work had made great progress by this time. Note the effect of Jesus' ministry upon John's disciples (Matt. 11:16–19; John 3:23–30). Why did John question whether he had not been mistaken? He, in prison, was seemingly set aside; many things were so different from what he had anticipated. Question as to John's inquiry and Jesus' reply. Show how this was the true fulfilment of prophecy in contrast to what they expected. Read Isa. 61:1, 2. Briefly note the details of John's martyrdom. Looking back over both lessons what do we find John accomplished? What was his life work? In what different ways did he accomplish this? Note that (1) by preaching he reached a large number among all classes; (2) he prophesied the coming of the Messiah and warned of the coming judgment; (3) he prepared men's hearts by (*a*) convincing of sin, (*b*) leading to repentance, and (*c*) consecrating them to the kingdom of the Christ by the ordinance of baptism. Make clear to the class that John accomplished the work he came to do although his life was short. Question the class as to their impressions of John's character. Try to have the class see clearly the following characteristics: (1) singleness of purpose, as shown in his complete freedom from all self-seeking or desire for favor among the powerful; (2) fearlessness in attacking the sins of all classes, Pharisees and Sadducees (Matt. 3:7), publicans and soldiers (Luke 3:12-14), the royal family (Matt. 14:3, 4); (3) insight into character (Matt. 3:14; *cf.* John 1:31); (4) humility as shown in his words to the Jerusalem committee (John 1:27) and to his disciples who were troubled over the growing popularity of Jesus (John 3:28-30). In summing up show that John's strength was that of a great pioneer, a great reformer who must surmount difficulty and prepare the way for a new and better order of things. Review the outline, emphasizing the work of John and the characteristics which made him so successful in accomplishing it.

Points to Emphasize.

1. The need of fearless champions of the right at all times.
2. A noble service rendered for others is greater than any mere personal achievement.
3. The proof of a true preparation for the kingdom of God is a changed life.

Scholar's Home Work.

Advance work: A careful study of the lesson material.
Review work: Questions for written answers to be returned to the teacher:
1. What did John aim to do?
2. How did he seek to accomplish this aim?
3. What was the theme of his preaching?
4. What rite did he observe in connection with his work?
5. What did his baptism mean?

INTERMEDIATE DEPARTMENT COURSE

6. What were the immediate results of his preaching?
7. What were the significant events of his life?
8. What was his testimony concerning Jesus.
9. How did Jesus satisfy John's doubts concerning himself?
10. What are the most marked traits in John's character?

Constructive work: Write the second chapter for the *Life of John the Baptist* upon the following plan:

JOHN THE BAPTIST
Chapter II. His Ministry

§ 1. His work as a preacher.
§ 2. Great events in his life.
§ 3. What he did.
§ 4. Traits of character.

Illustrative picture for the chapter, Titian's "John the Baptist Preaching."

Verses for memorizing: John 3:28, 30, 31; Matt. 3:1, 2, 5-8.

---

§ 9. BOOKS RELATING TO THE WORK OF GRADE C
A. REFERENCE READING FOR THE TEACHER

Bartlet, *The Apostolic Age* (Charles Scribner's Sons, New York).

Burton, *The Records and Letters of the Apostolic Age* (Charles Scribner's Sons, New York).

Conybeare and Howson, *Life and Epistles of St. Paul*, 2 vols. (Charles Scribner's Sons, New York).

Farrar, *Life and Work of St. Paul* (E. P. Dutton & Co., New York).

Geikie, *New Testament Hours* (James Pott & Co., New York).

Iverach, *St. Paul: His Life and Times* (F. H. Revell Co., Chicago).

Macdonald, *Life and Writings of St. John* (Charles Scribner's Sons, New York).

Matheson, *Spiritual Development of St. Paul* (A. D. F. Randolph & Co., New York).

Meyer, *John the Baptist* and *Paul: a Servant of Jesus Christ;* in the series "New Testament Heroes" (F. H. Revell Co., Chicago).

Purves, *The Apostolic Age* (Charles Scribner's Sons, New York).

Ramsay, *Paul the Traveler and Roman Citizen* (G. P. Putnam's Sons, New York).

Robinson, *Life and Times of Peter* (American Tract Society, New York).

Whyte, *Joseph and Mary to James* and *Stephen to Timothy;* in the series "Bible Characters" (F. H. Revell Co., Chicago).

B. READING AND REFERENCE BOOKS FOR THE PUPIL

Bird, *Paul of Tarsus* (Charles Scribner's Sons, New York).

Gilbert, *The Student's Life of Paul* (The Macmillan Co., New York).

Stalker, *The Two St. Johns of the New Testament* (American Tract Society, New York).

Stalker, *Life of Paul* (F. H. Revell Co., Chicago).

Taylor, *Paul the Missionary* and *Peter the Apostle* (Harper and Bros., New York).

"The Clark Bible Primers" (Charles Scribner's Sons, New York): (1) *Life of John*, by Gloag; (2) *Life of Paul*, by Gloag; (3) *Life of Peter*, by Salmond.

§ 10. OUTLINE OF THE COURSE FOR GRADE D

GRADE SUBJECT: GREAT CHARACTERS OF POST-APOSTOLIC TIMES

Part 1 — Great characters in the early church.
1. St. Francis of Assisi.
2. St. Francis of Assisi.
3. Savonarola.

4. Savonarola.
5. Savonarola.
6. Martin Luther.
7. Martin Luther.
8. Martin Luther.
9. *Review. Memory work.*

Part 2 — Great characters in modern missions.
10. Zinzendorf.
11. John Eliot.
12. William Carey.
13. William Carey.
14. Livingstone.
15. Livingstone.
16. Livingstone.
17. *Review. Memory work.*
18. John G. Paton.
19. John G. Paton.
20. John G. Paton.
21. Neesima.
22. Neesima.
23. Mackenzie.
24. Fidelia Fiske.
25. *Review. Memory work.*

Part 3 — Great characters in the world's service.
26. Queen Louise of Prussia.
27. Washington.
28. Washington.
29. Mary Lyon.
30. Mary Lyon.
31. Lincoln.
32. Lincoln.
33. Lincoln.
34. *Review. Memory work.*

35. Louis Agassiz.
36. George Peabody.
37. Florence Nightingale.
38. Frances Willard.
39. Henry Drummond.
40. Henry Drummond.
41. Bishop Brooks.
42. Bishop Brooks.
43. *Review. Memory work.*
44. Queen Victoria.
45. Queen Victoria.
46. Dwight L. Moody.
47. Dwight L. Moody.
48. Booker T. Washington.
49. Booker T. Washington.
50. *Review. Memory work.*

Special Lessons.
51. Christmas lesson.
52. Easter lesson.

---

§ 11. SUGGESTIVE LESSON PLANS FOR GRADE D

LESSONS 29 AND 30

LESSON 29

MARY MASON LYON — A SKETCH OF HER LIFE

Lesson Material.
Have the pupils read the story of Mary Lyon in Bolton's "Girls Who Became Famous," and also the accounts in the various biographical encyclopædias.

Teacher's Study Material.
Hitchcock, *The Power of Christian Benevolence Illustrated in the Life and Labors of Mary Lyon,* and *History of Mt. Holyoke Seminary during the First Half-Century;* Nichols, *Reminiscences of Mary Lyon* (pamphlet);

Bolton, *Girls Who Became Famous*, pp. 122-40; North, *Mary Lyon Year Book;* Dunning, "The Inner Life of Mary Lyon," in the *Chautauquan* for January, 1900; biographical encyclopædias.

Illustrative Material.

Use the blackboard for the outline of the lesson material. Show pictures of Mary Lyon, and also of the seminary, and later pictures of the college, arranging the latter so as to show the development of the college. At the lesson close write upon the board the plan for chap. i of the scholar's *Life of Mary Mason Lyon.*

Organization of Material.
1. Educational ideals of her time.
    a) The higher education of women not approved.
    b) The common school elements of an education considered sufficient for girls.
    c) Private schools for girls aimed at accomplishments, not development.
2. Birth and ancestry.
    a) Date and place of birth — February 28, 1797; Buckland, Mass.
    b) Parents — both strong Christian characters.
    c) Ancestors — "of irreproachable character and noted for piety."
3. Early environment and training.
    a) Influence of the simple farm life and work.
    b) Careful parental training.
    c) Development through dependence upon self.
4. Life events.
    a) Work as a student.
    b) Work as a teacher.
    c) The founding of Mt. Holyoke Seminary.
    d) In the seminary as teacher and principal.
5. Death on March 5, 1849.

Presentation of Material.

Develop by questions so far as possible, the various sections as outlined under the heading "Organization of Material." Seek to give a clear idea of the educational ideals concerning girls which prevailed at this time. The average New Englander did not believe the education of women was worth its cost. It was unfashionable for girls to know more than the three R's. In the schools of the time accomplishments were sought for more than mental development. Some member of the class might have as an assigned topic for presentation, "The Education of Women in the First Part of the Nineteenth Century." A clear understanding of the unfavorable conditions existing at this time will make Miss Lyon's work stand out all the more sharply. Question the class as to the date and place of her birth. Locate place on map. Also question as to her parents. The father, Aaron Lyon, was a godly man, sometimes called "the peace-maker;" the mother, Jemima Shepard, was a person of strong mind and active piety. Also question the class as to the line of ancestors from which she came. What was their character? What would be their influence upon her? Picture the life on the farm, the simple surroundings, the burden of work laid upon all the members of the household. What kind of training would she receive from her parents? Note the character of the home, rich in affection, with all the rugged virtues showing forth constantly. Finally speak of the development that would come from the necessity, soon forced upon her, of dependence upon self. Impress the thought of the value of such a birth, environment, and training for the great work which she was later permitted to do. Describe her life as a student at the district school, at Sanderson Academy, at Conway with Dr. Hitchcock (later the president of Amherst College), and

INTERMEDIATE DEPARTMENT COURSE

at Byfield in the famous school of Rev. Joseph Emerson. This topic might also be given to a student for class report. Then describe her life as a teacher at various places; at Sanderson Academy, Adams Academy, and at Ipswich. Locate these places on the map. She was by nature a born teacher. What success did she have? Then describe the beginnings of her great work — the founding of Mt. Holyoke Seminary for the higher education of women. Note her steadfast purpose which did not change in spite of the indifference and opposition of some. She gained help and interest from many, went around soliciting funds, and finally raised the necessary amount. A site was selected, and the corner-stone of the building was laid October 3, 1836. Repeat to the class her remark in this connection: "It was a day of deep interest. The stones and brick and mortar speak a language which vibrates through my very soul." When the seminary opened in the fall of 1837, her life as a teacher and principal began. Note the immediate success of the enterprise; accommodations were provided for eighty and one hundred and sixteen came. Note also the underlying principles of the seminary as given by Miss Lyon herself. Question the class about her life in connection with the seminary, bringing out her deep interest in the religious life of the students, and her great interest in missions, which stirred others to a like interest, and which at this day is a characteristic of the life at Mt. Holyoke College. Finally describe briefly her death and the burial on the college campus. In closing, review the whole outline, emphasizing the unfavorable conditions for any educational enterprise at the time, and Miss Lyon's unwavering purpose, her deep interest in the welfare of young women, and her tireless energy which finally enabled her to accomplish so much for higher education.

Points to Emphasize.
1. The blessings from godly parents and a Christian home.
2. The development that comes from the use of one's own powers.
3. The value of an ideal clearly seen and tenaciously held.

Scholar's Home Work.
Advance work: A careful study of the lesson material.
Review work: Questions for written answers to be returned to the teacher:
1. In Mary Lyon's time what was thought of the higher education of girls?
2. When and where was Mary Lyon born?
3. What kind of parents did she have?
4. What was her home training?
5. Where did she study?
6. Where did she teach?
7. When did she found Mt. Holyoke Seminary?
8. With what success did her plan meet?
9. What were the principles upon which the seminary work was to be conducted?
10. When did she die and where was she buried?

Constructive work: Write the first chapter for the *Life of Mary Lyon* on the following plan:

MARY MASON LYON
Chapter I. A Short Sketch of Her Life

§ 1. The early life of Mary Lyon.
§ 2. Her life as a student and teacher.
§ 3. The founding of Mt. Holyoke Seminary.
§ 4. Her work in the seminary.

Illustrative picture for the chapter, any good picture of Mary Mason Lyon.

Lesson 30
MARY MASON LYON — HER WORK AND CHARACTER

Lesson Material.

The same as in the preceding lesson, with the addition of assigned topics for class report.

Teacher's Study Material.

See preceding lesson.

Illustrative Material.

Use the blackboard for the outline of the lesson material. Use the pictures suggested in the preceding lesson, and also pictures, when obtainable, of the various schools noted under the heading "Work accomplished." At the lesson close write upon the board the plan for chap. ii of the scholar's *Life of Mary Mason Lyon.*

Organization of Material.

1. Work accomplished.
    a) The first woman to found a woman's college.
    b) Aroused a sense of the need of higher education for women.
    c) Inspired the founding of other women's colleges.
    d) Furnished a model for many girls' schools.
    e) Aroused a great interest in missions.
    f) Started the movement for the training of women for teaching.
2. Marked traits of character.
    a) Great intellectual ability.
    b) Invincible perseverance.
    c) Intense enthusiasm for her work.
    d) Great discernment in judging character.
    e) Rare administrative talent.
    f) Deep religious nature.

Presentation of Material.

Develop by questions, so far as possible, the various sections as outlines under the heading "Organization of Material." Rapidly review the last lesson, so as to freshen the pupil's mind upon the main facts in the life of Mary Lyon. Then question the class upon the work accomplished, developing the outline on the board as the answers are given, and supply information where lacking. She not only inspired the founding of other women's colleges, such as Smith, Vassar, and Wellesley, but she inspired many of her graduates to found schools and colleges upon the principles underlying Mt. Holyoke. Among these are: Lake Erie Seminary and College at Painesville, Ohio; Western College at Oxford, Ohio; Mills Seminary and College in California; the Persian Seminary in Persia; a school in Bitlis, Turkey, for Kurdish girls; a Huguenot seminary at Wellington, South Africa; and a girls' school at San Sebastian, Spain. Tell a little of the work and influence of these schools, thus showing the wide influence for good of such a consecrated life as the one we are studying. Note next a most remarkable characteristic of Mt. Holyoke Seminary, and afterwards also of the college, namely: the wonderful missionary interest and spirit which was aroused and which has remained to this day. One-half of her own pupils became foreign missionaries; nearly three hundred missionaries have gone out from the seminary and college. Finally note the starting of the movement for the training of women teachers. About 75 per cent. of the graduates of Mt. Holyoke have been teachers. Mary Lyon herself was a teacher by nature, and she seemed to have the power to inspire others with the teaching spirit. Next discuss the marked traits in her character, trying to draw from the class by questions the character elements noted under section two in the outline. As each of these characteristics is brought out in answer to questions, dwell upon it for a moment, showing its importance as a character element, and its bearing upon success in life. That she possessed a deeply religious nature is shown by her (1) unwavering trust in an overruling Providence, (2) feeling of personal responsibility for the salvation of her pupils, and (3) intense interest in missions. A quotation from Dr. Dunning's article well sums up her life: "No fuller or more fruitful life has been lived by any woman in this century than that of Mary Lyon." In closing, review the whole outline, emphasizing the work accomplished and the character-traits which rendered such a large service possible.

Points to Emphasize.
1. A life of consecrated service is a wonderfully powerful "center of influence."
2. Our chosen work demands the development and undivided service of all our powers.
3. Those who make life larger, truer, more beautiful, are God's noblemen and noblewomen.

Scholar's Home Work.
Advance work: A review of last lesson and a further study of suggested material.
Review work: Questions for written answers to be returned to the teacher:
1. What was the immediate result of Mary Lyon's active interest in the higher education of women?
2. In what way did the work of Mary Lyon further contribute to the higher education of women?
3. What were some of the more direct results of her work?
4. What spirit is specially characteristic of Mt. Holyoke?

5. How has this been concretely manifested?
6. What contribution did Mary Lyon make to the training of teachers?
7. What intellectual capacity did she possess?
8. What other qualities did she possess which contributed to her success?
9. In what ways was her religious nature shown?
10. What estimate do you place upon her life?

Constructive work: Write the second chapter for the *Life of Mary Lyon* on the following plan:

MARY MASON LYON
Chapter II. Her Work and Character

§ 1. The direct work accomplished.
§ 2. The results of her influence.
§ 3. Marked traits of her character.
§ 4. An estimate of her life.

Illustrative picture for the chapter, the Mt. Holyoke College buildings of today.

Quotations from her pen for memorizing:

"If anyone thinks he has no responsibilities it is because he has not sought them out."

"There is nothing in the universe that I fear except that I may not know all my duty or may fail to do it."

---

§ 12. BOOKS RELATING TO THE WORK OF GRADE D

A. REFERENCE READING FOR THE TEACHER

Allen, *Life and Letters of Phillips Brooks* (E. P. Dutton & Co., New York).

Agassiz, *Life and Correspondence of Louis Agassiz* (Houghton, Mifflin & Co., Boston).

Blaikie, *The Personal Life of David Livingstone* (F. H. Revell Co., Chicago).

INTERMEDIATE DEPARTMENT COURSE 301

Bryson, *The Life of John Kenneth Mackenzie* (F. H. Revell Co., Chicago).
Gordon, *Life of Frances E. Willard* (People's Publishing Co., Philadelphia).
Hardy, *Life and Letters of Joseph Hardy Neesima* (Houghton, Mifflin & Co., Boston).
Hitchcock, *Life and Labors of Mary Lyon* (American Tract Society, New York).
Jacobs, *Martin Luther* (G. P. Putnam's Sons, New York).
Lee, *Queen Victoria: a Biography* (The Macmillan Co., New York).
Lodge, *Life of George Washington* (Houghton, Mifflin & Co., Boston).
Moody, *The Life of Dwight L. Moody* (F. H. Revell Co., Chicago).
Nicolay, *Abraham Lincoln: a Short Life* (The Century Co., New York).
Oliphant, *Savonarola* (The Macmillan Co., New York).
Paton, *John G. Paton: An Autobiography* (F. H. Revell Co., Chicago).
Pollard, *Florence Nightingale: The Wounded Soldier's Friend* (Thomas Whittaker, New York).
Sabatier, *Life of St. Francis of Assisi* (Charles Scribner's Sons, New York).
Smith, *Life of Henry Drummond* (McClure, Phillips & Co., New York).
Washington, *Up from Slavery* (Doubleday, Page & Co., New York).
Also consult any good biographical dictionary.

B. READING AND REFERENCE BOOKS FOR THE PUPIL

Brooks, *Abraham Lincoln* (G. P. Putnam's Sons, New York).
Davis, *A Maker of New Japan: the Life of Joseph Hardy Neesima* (F. H. Revell Co., Chicago).
Deane, *Wycliffe and Luther* (F. H. Revell Co., Chicago).
Douglas, *The Life Story of Mary Lyon* (Beard & Co., Minneapolis).

Drummond, *Life of Dwight L. Moody* (McClure, Phillips & Co., New York).
Gould, *Louis Agassiz* (Small, Maynard & Co., Boston).
Gracey, *Eminent Missionary Women* (Eaton & Mains, New York).
Hale, *Life of George Washington* (G. P. Putnam's Sons, New York).
Howe, *Life of Phillips Brooks* (Small, Maynard & Co., Boston).
Montefiore, *David Livingstone: His Labors and His Legacy* (F. H. Revell Co., Chicago).
Myers, *William Carey: the Shoemaker Who Became a Missionary* (F. H. Revell Co., Chicago).
Simpson, *Henry Drummond* (Charles Scribner's Sons, New York).
Stoddart, *Francis of Assisi* (E. P. Dutton & Co., New York).
Washington, *Up from Slavery* (Doubleday, Page & Co., New York).
Witts, *Life of Frances E. Willard* (Thomas Whittaker, New York).

PART IV

THE EARLY MANHOOD AND WOMANHOOD PERIOD AND THE SENIOR DEPARTMENT

CHAPTER IX

SOME CHARACTERISTICS AND NEEDS OF THE PERIOD

THE period from sixteen or seventeen to about twenty-one or twenty-two, although not marked by such distinct and sharp changes as characterize the preceding years, nevertheless is an important section of the larger period of adolescence and one which calls for specific treatment at the hands of educators, especially from those who are engaged in the difficult work of ethical and religious instruction.

Physically, growth is practically attained at nineteen or twenty years of age, and then the energy is expended upon the development of strength and agility. At this time the body should be well under the control of the mind, and development of the muscular system should be rapid and easy. All of the bodily appetites and impulses are stronger than in the preceding period, but if the individual has had a normal experience the development of the reason will have put them under better control. With a well-developed body, expressing in all of its activities an abounding physical life, guided and controlled by a keen intellect and a vigorous will, the young man, having now a more serious view of life, is ready for a larger life of service than he has heretofore entered upon.

Some characteristics of the period.— Most of the characteristics of the youth or early adolescent period continue to manifest themselves in this later period, although some of them lose their strength, while others continue their development.

Owing to the rapid and strong development of the reasoning powers there results a strengthening of the spirit of independence and a lessening of the direct influence of the teacher and companions through suggestion. The teacher at this time must depend more upon guiding the young man by an appeal to his reason than by an appeal to his affections or by an authoritative presentation of truth which is to be accepted without question.

The advance from selfishness to unselfishness is steady and strong, and during these years the altruistic emotions are likely to become dominant. Under normal conditions, *i. e.*, a normal environment and right instruction, the young man will realize the importance of identifying himself with the larger social life of which he forms a part, and will expend himself freely in the service of others.

Naturally the imitative tendency is very much weakened. The individual now sets up his own standard of life and conduct, and although open to advice and suggestion, and to the presentation of the elements of an ethically perfect life, he will only accept and act upon such presentations as appeal to his own reason. Individuality is now so strongly marked that the teacher must treat each case separately; mass teaching or class teaching must give place to more individual teaching. Not that the young men and women are not to be taught in fairly large classes, but that in such classes more attention must be paid to individual differences, appeal must be made to individual interests, individual difficulties and doubts must be met and overcome, and in every way the individuality of the members of the class must be recognized and methods adopted which will not antagonize a free and independent expression of self.

The activity, both physical and mental, which was one of the most marked characteristics of the preceding period continues in this and becomes more intense. An astonishingly large amount of the world's work has been done by adolescents.

> To recount what has been done by young men before the age of thirty would be to rewrite a large part of the world's history. Alexander and Napoleon among soldiers, Hamilton and Fox among statesmen, and Bryant, Shelley, and Byron among poets, are only the most familiar examples. Even when the work has not actually been done at this period, the inspiration and the stimulus came then.[1]

[1] BURNHAM, *Pedagogical Seminary,* Vol. I, p. 191.

One form of this mental activity, that of doubt, with its acompanying emotional agitation, is quite common, and few escape a period of doubt with reference to philosophy and religion, more especially the latter. Professor Burnham, in his study of doubt as an adolescent phenomenon, says:[2]

> In the majority of cases the beginning of the doubt concerned matters of religion. In a few cases it was more strictly intellectual. In one case it was very short and violent; in more it was prolonged, in some covering many years. A cause frequently assigned was narrow religious training. Many deemed such an experience normal. In some cases, however, it was clearly abnormal, not to say distinctly pathological. It is noteworthy that in half the cases there was considerable emotional excitement. In a few cases the emotional stress was extreme. In many cases the solvent of the doubt was found in reason leading to new hypotheses or proving the old. Among the remedies suggested by different writers were more rational religious education, action, growth, absorption in secular pursuits, the reading of Christian apologists and biographies of men who had passed through a period of storm and stress, an active interest in the moral improvement of others, historical instruction. Among the results of this doubt-experience mentioned by different writers are a better understanding of literature, an increased insight into the character of men, greater love for humanity, more toleration, greater desire for further knowledge, "a stimulus to tolerant intellectual development," a more vital faith, a readiness to leave "many questions still open and unsettled."

Such doubts are due to the increasing dominance

[2] *Ibid.*, p. 183.

of the reasoning powers, along with the development of a genuine interest in philosophic studies. Again quoting Professor Burnham in this connection, he says:[3]

> It is tolerably clear that the incentive to philosophic thought generally comes at adolescence. Not a few philosophers have written some of their best work during this period. At twenty-two Leibnitz had written several works, among them two philosophical essays. Berkeley published his *Essay on the Theory of Vision* when he was twenty-five, and *The Principles of Human Knowledge* the next year.

He gives other examples concerning the philosophic writings of Hume, Fichte, Schelling, Schopenhauer, Herbart, Beneke, Lotze, Hartmann, and Jonathan Edwards, all tending to show the great interest in philosophic thought at this period, from eighteen on to twenty-five or thirty. The importance of recognizing this philosophic interest and the state of doubt which accompanies it, or perhaps results from it, at least in part, needs only to be mentioned to be appreciated. This is especially true in the matter of religious education, for unless the religious doubts which come up during this period can be met and settled, there is great danger that the young men will give up their convictions and beliefs of the past, and, with nothing to take their place, will drift into agnosticism or infidelity. This should be a time of recon-

[3] *Ibid.*, Vol. I, pp. 191, 192.

struction, when "the world and life and eternity must all be clothed in new ethical, æsthetic, and intellectual forms." As Professor Coe says, what the adolescent at this time "most wants, after all, is room "[4] — room to turn round mentally, to see things from all view-points; room for the many new thoughts which come crowding in at this time; room for the play of new feelings and desires; room, in a word, for that intellectual and emotional expansion which should characterize this latter part of the adolescent period. Such a period of doubt, intellectual activity, and psychical reconstruction is of great value, for the

youth's mental aspirations are the very sap of the tree of knowledge. It is of the utmost value to the whole cause of truth that the mind, before attaining the relative fixity of maturity, should for a time assume an utterly free and questioning attitude toward everything. Without this, religious thought would speedily petrify.[5]

Professor Coe's answer to the question, What, then, can be done for the doubting youth? is worth quoting in full. He says:[6]

We can correct the plain misapprehensions under which he is laboring as to what Christians actually believe; we can replace foolish questions with wiser ones; we can guide his reading in the treasuries of the world's thought; we can frankly admit our inability to answer all his questions, and

[4] *The Spiritual Life*, p. 63.
[5] COE, *ibid.*, pp. 63, 64.
[6] *Ibid.*, pp. 64, 65.

we can tell him that we ourselves have passed through similar difficulties. And we can add to this intellectual food something not less needful; for the trouble of his mind is not merely that he does not know this or that, but rather that he fancies that his uncertainty involves some disloyalty, or other fault of heart or of will. He must therefore learn, in a practical way, that knowing Christian doctrine is not the same as being grounded in the Christian life. He should by all means be induced to be active in those forms of religious living that still appeal to him at all. There is, in fact, a fallacy in his reasoning. He fancies that the practical religious life stands or falls according as we accept or reject certain explanations of and reasons for it. But, as before remarked, just the reverse of this is true; the life comes first because it answers to our inarticulate needs, and the fact that it does so answer is sufficient practical justification for its continuance. Hence, religious activity and religious comforts may abide at the same time that the intellect is uncertain of how all this fits into any logical structure. Thus it comes to pass that the greatest thing we can do for the doubting youth is to induce him to give free exercise to the religious instinct. Let him not say what he does not actually believe; let him not compromise himself in any way; but it is always certain that he still believes, feels, and aspires enough to give him a place among religious people.

And Dr. Starbuck, speaking of the value of doubt, says:[7]

Doubt is a process of mental clarification; it is a step in the process of self-mastery; it is an indication that all the latent powers are beginning to be realized. . . . . Instead of trying to crush doubt, it would be wiser to in-

[7] *Psychology of Religion*, pp. 242, 243.

spire earnestness and sincerity of purpose in the use of it for the discovery of truth. If doubts are evil, it is because there is a wicked nature behind them. Doubt is a means of calling up and utilizing the latent possibilities of one's nature. If there is a boundless substratum of healthy life on which to draw, and if there is a high degree of earnestness in the desire to know truth in order to use it, doubts are rather to be met and mastered than to be shunned.

There should be, then, in the Bible school, a department for young men and women where they may make a serious study of the Christian religion in its several aspects, and where they may freely present and discuss their many difficulties and doubts, that as a result of such study and discussion they may lay a sure and reasonable foundation for the faith that has been held by them during the early years of their lives. President G. Stanley Hall, in a very suggestive and stimulating article on "Some Fundamental Principles of Sunday-School and Bible Teaching," says with reference to this need:[8]

> The complete and ideal Sunday school should make provision for maturer and cultivated young men and women according to principles not yet recognized. The Pauline writings are to some extent suited to this, but certainly not to earlier periods. This is true also but to less extent for the prophecies, which however pedagogically precede. Here too there should be some study of patristics, and the burden of church history belongs here. It would be ideal also to have a little comparative study here of the great ethnic

[8] *Pedagogical Seminary*, Vol. VIII, p. 462.

religions with a taste of the philosophy of religion, and almost any condensed germinal matter in ethics and psychology would not be out of place. A dominant aim should be to expose to the mind the results of the highest culture in all these faiths, but in a way to warm and not to chill the heart; to break down the inveterate feeling that there can be opposition between science or philosophy and religion. I have known a successful study of the higher evolution represented by Drummond's *Ascent of Man,* and of what is now often called the higher pantheism. In this new and higher story for which I plead there should be neither field nor faith for any conventional orthodoxies of creed. The type of mind once associated with the very name deacon, so far as this implies a pervervid defender of things as they are and involves an atmosphere of repression for any sincere doubt or outré opinion, should be carefully excluded. The atmosphere here should invite growth and expansion in all directions, and the period of circumnutation before the young mind selects and clasps its support should be prolonged. This should be essentially the stage of inquiry, where ingenuous youth brings its inmost burning questions and ideals.

The interests of the period.— The interests of the period are varied and strong. The scope of these interests includes the physical, intellectual, and moral fields. President Hall says: "If there is no enthusiasm, deep and strong interests in intellectual and moral fields, passion is stronger. The two are physiological or kinetic equivalents." The healthy, normal young man must do something.

Athletic, scientific, literary, or artistic interests, or plenty of hard work, is a necessity to keep the physical and mental life pure, healthy and growing. .... The enthusiasms of college life develop the college student and make him superior to one who has had no enthusiastic interests during his adolescence. .... The aim of education at this time should be, therefore, to make the most of these interests which are harmless in themselves and not likely to become permanent, to prepare the way for a greater interest in the higher religious and moral sphere and the intellectual interests which are to become permanent.[9]

Toward the close of the period, an habitual form of activity along some line which is the resultant of heredity, environment, and individual choice, becomes dominant. Some one of the multitudinous interests of adolescence persists and becomes the support of future action.[10]

The mental powers during the period.— All of the intellectual powers are strong and comparatively mature by the middle of the period. This is especially true of the creative imagination and the reason. The young man now takes a more serious view of life, and seeks to understand life's problems. The strongly developing reason makes him intellectually restless, and he is constantly using his powers to satisfy his cravings for absolute knowledge of things. The strength of the creative imagination makes this a time for planning for the future. By the close of the period,

[9] LANCASTER, *ibid.*, Vol. V, pp. 126, 127.
[10] CLOUSTON, quoted by BURNHAM, *ibid.*, Vol. I, p. 182.

about twenty-one or twenty-two years of age, most thoughtful young men have pretty definitely settled what their future career is to be. Memory is also active and strong, becoming not simply a fact or a verbal memory, but a memory for principles, classifications, and the more abstract elements of thought.

Some conclusions with reference to a course of study for the young men and women from seventeen to twenty-one years of age.— From the foregoing consideration of the characteristics, interests, and powers of the early manhood and womanhood period, this seems to be the time for a fairly thorough and systematic study of the Christian religion in its several aspects. Such a study would engage the comparatively mature intellectual powers of the young men and women, would appeal to their interest in philosophic thought, and would help to lay a deep and permanent foundation for a rational Christian faith. It would give scope to the fullest expression of difficulties and doubts, and while it would not be possible to overcome all difficulties and remove all doubts, still such a course would enable a teacher to satisfy, to a reasonable extent, the intellectual questionings which are sure to arise in the minds of the thoughtful. An historical study of the Christian religion from apostolic times to the present is one of the best means for settling any doubts as to the claims of Christianity to be the world-religion, and of awakening or strengthening a faith in such as the only religion which will completely satisfy all needs. This, followed by a study of the authoritative records of this religion, the canonical books of the Bible, and of its fundamental truths as revealed therein, both studied and interpreted in a liberal spirit, with the one desire to know the truth, and with a willingness to let all else go, would remove many difficulties of the students, broaden their mental horizon, enlarge their sympathies, and conserve their interest in the things most vital to their welfare. And lastly it would then seem profitable to make an outline study of the great religions of the world, comparing such in origin, teaching, and results with Christianity, that, by contrast, the positive beauty of our religion may be seen with greater clearness, and that its vitalizing, transforming power may be more impressively set forth.

An outline of a suggested course of study for the four years spent in the Senior Department of the Bible school is given in the next chapter. In Grade A the history of the Christian religion from the time of the apostles to the present is studied. In Grade B some of the more general evidences for the belief in Christianity as the final religion for man are considered, followed by an outline study of the books of the Old and New

Testaments. In Grade C the fundamental religious truths relating to God, to man, and to society form the subject of study. In Grade D the more important of the world's religions are studied and compared with the Christian religion.

The young men and women, pursuing such a course of study for four years under competent teachers, ought to have many of their difficulties and doubts removed, their convictions deepened, their character strengthened, and their love for and allegiance to the religion of Jesus the Christ placed beyond the possibility of change.

CHAPTER X

A COURSE OF STUDY FOR THE SENIOR DEPARTMENT

GENERAL SUBJECT: THE CHRISTIAN RELIGION IN ITS SEVERAL ASPECTS — REVEALING ITS DIVINE AUTHORITY

§ 1. OUTLINE OF THE COURSE FOR GRADE A

GRADE SUBJECT: THE CHRISTIAN RELIGION: ITS HISTORIC DEVELOPMENT

Part 1 — Christianity in the apostolic period.

    A. *Beginnings of Christianity in Jerusalem*

1. The foundations of Christianity.
2. The beginnings of Christianity.
3. Primitive church life.
4. Early struggles against persecution.
5. Stephen the first martyr.
6. *Review.*

    B. *Early expansion of Christianity*

7. The work of Philip.
8. The conversion of Cornelius.
9. The conversion of Saul.
10. Christianity in Syrian Antioch.
11. The spread of Christianity in Asia Minor.
12. The Council at Jerusalem.
13. *Review.*

  C. *Further expansion of Christianity during the apostolic period*

14. The entrance of Christianity into Europe.
15. The growth of Christianity in Europe.
16. The closing years of Paul.

Senior Department Course

17. Christianity to the close of the apostolic period.
18. The Christian life and beliefs of the period.
19. *Review.*

Part 2 — Christianity from the apostolic period to the reformation.

20. The Heroic Age of Christianity.
21. Christianity's triumph in the Roman empire.
22. Christianity among the Germanic nations.
23. The growth of the papacy.
24. The full power of the papacy.
25. The beginnings of reform.
26. *Review.*

Part 3 — Christianity from the reformation to the present.

27. The early reformers.
28. Luther and the Reformation in Germany.
29. Zwingli and the Swiss Reformation.
30. The Reformation in the north and east.
31. Calvin and the Reformation in Geneva.
32. The Reformation in France.
33. *Review.*
34. The Reformation in England and Scotland.
35. The Reformation in Italy and Spain.
36. Christianity in the early American settlements.
37. Church organization during the period.
38. Doctrinal changes during the period.
39. *Review.*
40. Christian missions in India.
41. Christian missions in China.
42. Christian missions in Japan.
43. Christian missions in Africa.
44. Christian missions in Western Asia.
45. Christian missions in papal lands.
46. Christian missions in the Isles of the Sea.

47. *Review.*
48. Denominational church history.
    a) History.
49. *b)* Government.
50. *c)* Essential beliefs.

Special Lessons.
51. Christmas lesson.
52. Easter lesson.

§ 2. SUGGESTIVE LESSON PLANS FOR GRADE A
Lessons 2 to 5
Lesson 2
THE BEGINNINGS OF CHRISTIANITY

Lesson Material.
   Acts 2: 1-42; 3: 1-26.

Teacher's Study Material.
   1 Cor. 14: 1-40; Acts 10: 46; 19: 6; Purves, *The Apostolic Age,* pp. 26-34, 43-46; Schaff, *History of the Christian Church,* Vol. I, pp. 227-41; Farrar, *Life of St. Paul,* chap. v; McGiffert, *The Apostolic Age,* pp. 36-64; Trumbull, *Studies in Oriental Social Life,* pp. 295-318; Hastings, *Bible Dictionary,* art. "Pentecost;" a good critical commentary.

Organization of Material.
   1. Christ's promise fulfilled.
      a) The waiting disciples.
      b) The Spirit's manifestation.
      c) Effect upon the disciples.
      d) Effect upon the people.

2. The first sermon.
   a) The occasion.
   b) The theme — Jesus the Messiah.
   c) The effect upon the hearers.
3. The first miracle.
   a) The miracle itself.
   b) The effect upon the people.
   c) An occasion for again preaching Christ Jesus.

Presentation of Material.
Develop by questions the various sections as outlined under the heading "Organization of Material." Call to mind the events immediately succeeding the ascension: (1) the return to Jerusalem — why? (2) the meetings for prayer and conference, and (3) the choosing of a new apostle. In this connection have the class read Luke 24: 48, 49. What was the meaning of Pentecost, and what were the observances of the day? Question as to the Spirit's manifestations. How explain? What was the effect upon the disciples? Refer the class to other occasions when the gift of tongues is mentioned. (See 1 Cor., chap. 14, and Acts 10: 46; 19: 6.) Note the similarities and differences in these accounts. Question as to the different effects upon the hearers. Note how Peter grasps the opportunity to explain the seeming mystery, and to preach Jesus Christ. The conditions are favorable, the people being intensely interested in the wonderful event which they seek to explain. Peter interprets the event in the light of prophecy and then in the light of recent events. Trace carefully the development of his theme, drawing as much as possible from the class by questions.. Note in this connection, (1) God's approval of the work of Jesus shown in the signs and wonders which they had seen, (2) their guilt in his death, (3) Jesus' resurrection through the power of God (this

was a fulfilment of prophecy), (4) their witness to the fact of the resurrection, and (5) Jesus' exaltation and the resulting gift of the Holy Spirit. Lead up to the thought that this Jesus whom they crucified is both Lord and Christ. Explain meaning of the word Christ. Question as to the effect of the sermon. Note how Peter answers the appeal of the hearers; he demands (1) repentance, and (2) the acknowledgment of Jesus Christ through baptism. He also promises to them the gift of the Holy Spirit, for this power of the Spirit for service was for all believers, although the manifestation was different in different individuals. Connect the effects of Peter's sermon with the promise of power for service given to the disciples. Read John 14: 12 and Luke 24: 49, and compare with Acts 2: 33. Question concerning the miracle, noting the place where it was performed, the condition of the lame man (*cf.* Acts 4: 22), the manner of performing the miracle, and the effect upon the man and the people. Again Peter turns the thoughts of the people away from himself to Jesus Christ, the source of the wonderful power manifested, speaking to the people concerning (1) their guilt in his death, (2) his resurrection of which the disciples are witnesses, and (3) the wonderful results which come through faith in his name. Then he again preaches repentance, promising forgiveness as the result of believing in this new "prophet" foretold by Moses and the prophets of old and warning all that destruction will be the part of those who refuse to hear this prophet. Note the skilful ending of the address — the promise of blessing through this Jesus. Review the whole lesson, uniting the various sections into a connected story of the beginnings of Christianity, showing the Spirit as its life and motive power, the disciples as its heralds, and the miracles as its divine attestation.

Points to Emphasize.
1. The trustful waiting of the disciples for the promised power for their work.
2. The significance of the gift of the Holy Spirit — power for service.
3. The wideness of God's promise of the Spirit — "for all."

Student's Home Work.
Lesson study: Study carefully the lesson material, Acts 2: 1-42 and 3: 1-26.

Assigned search work: (For class report.)
1. The Feast of Pentecost — its meaning and observance.
2. Other instances of the "manifestation of tongues."
3. The meaning of baptism as administered by the apostles.
4. Brief description of the daily temple services.
5. What is a miracle?
6. Why may we believe in miracles?

Review questions for student's self-test:
1. For what were the disciples waiting in Jerusalem?
2. In what ways was the Spirit manifested?
3. How explain this "gift of tongues"?
4. In what way were the disciples now prepared for their missionary activity?
5. What is the central thought in Peter's sermon?
6. Of what was the outpouring of the Spirit an evidence?
7. What was the effect of Peter's sermon on his hearers?
8. What did he urge upon his hearers, and what did he promise them?
9. What special significance in the miracle of healing the lame man?

10. In Peter's last appeal, what added reason did he give for believing in Jesus as the Messiah?

Topics for further study:
1. The manifestations of the Spirit.
2. The cosmopolitan character of Jerusalem and its relation to the spread of Christianity.
3. Divine healing in New Testament times.
4. The Abrahamic covenant (Acts 3:25).

NOTE.— The teacher should supply references to standard literature upon the above topics. A five-minute paper upon the first topic may be assigned to a member for presentation to the class upon the Sunday following that of the lesson study. The blackboard may be used for the presentation of the "Outline" as it develops in class.

LESSON 3
PRIMITIVE CHURCH LIFE

Lesson Material.

Acts 2:42-47; 4:32-37; 5:1-11; 6:1-7.

Teacher's Study Material.

McGiffert, *The Apostolic Age*, pp. 64-81; Fisher, *The Beginnings of Christianity*, pp. 546-57; Purves, *The Apostolic Age*, pp. 33-46; Hurst, *A Short History of the Christian Church*, pp. 20-23; Hastings, *Bible Dictionary*, art. "Church;" a good critical commentary.

Organization of Material.
1. Beginnings of community life.
    a) Meetings for prayer and instruction.
    b) Special observances — baptism and the Lord's Supper.
    c) Ministrations to needy members.

2. Distinctive characteristics.
   a) Oneness of belief.
   b) A common treasury.
   c) Missionary activity.
3. Administration.
   a) Apostolic direction of the work.
   b) Management of the funds.
   c) Work of instruction.
   d) Work of discipline.

Presentation of Material.

Develop by questions the various sections as outlined under the heading "Organization of Material." Review the preceding lesson as a background for this one. Recall the constant meetings for prayer by the disciples previous to Pentecost. Show how this custom naturally continued as the disciples were bound together even more closely. As the circle widens they meet in many small companies for prayer and for further instruction from the apostles and others competent to teach the new converts the way of life as taught by Jesus. At these meetings the "breaking of bread"—undoubtedly what afterwards became the more formal Lord's Supper—was observed. Question as to the conditions of membership in the early church, and emphasize the simple requirements, namely: (1) repentance and (2) baptism in the name of Jesus Christ (Acts 2:38). A further expression of this community life was the care bestowed upon needy members of the primitive church organization. Bring out clearly the relation of the early Christians to Judaism; they continued their attendance upon the synagogue services and fulfilled all the requirements of the Jewish ceremonial law. It was at first a new life within Judaism. The Christians were still Jews, but

Jews who had found the Messiah, and who were bound together by this belief. Question as to other distinctive features. Show that the community of possessions was a spontaneous expression of unity and not obligatory, as is shown by Peter's words to Ananias (Acts 5:4). Question as to the danger in such a plan as evidenced in the story of Ananias and Sapphira. Why did Ananias and Sapphira bring part of their possessions, when such an action was not compulsory? Note the apparently harsh measures taken by the leaders, and explain why such severe measures were necessary at this time. Question as to the extent and duration of this plan. In this connection compare Acts 12:12, which shows that Mary the mother of Mark owned her house. Note the earnest missionary spirit of all. The apostles took every opportunity to preach Christ and did so with great power. The other disciples were free to give much of their time to this work, and all seem to have been engaged in it. The result of this was constant additions to their number. Point out the causes for this rapid growth: (1) deep conviction of the truth of what they taught, (2) personal testimony of what they knew, (3) divine manifestations supporting their teachings, and (4) earnest, unselfish activity for others, shown in ministering to their needs, physical as well as spiritual. With the increase in numbers there is a corresponding increase in the work, and there comes a demand for a division of functions. Note four lines of activity and responsibility: (1) general direction of the work. Recall different incidents which show who had this general direction and care. Read Acts 2:14; 3:6; 4:8; 4:1-3; 5:3, 4. That the apostles were recognized as the official administrative heads is seen in the record of the complaint of the Grecian Jews, where it is the Twelve who call the multitude together and suggest the division of functions there mentioned (Acts 6:2); (2) care of the funds. Compare Acts 4:35. This seems to indicate that the apostles were the responsible distributors; (3) ministry of instruction. The apostles were especially called to this work of teaching, they being witnesses to the life and resurrection of Jesus; (4) discipline of members. Note the case of Ananias and Sapphira in Acts 5:1-10. In closing review the entire lesson, uniting the sections, and seek to leave a clear picture of primitive church life, emphasizing the simplicity of the various services, of the conditions of membership, and of the administration.

Points to Emphasize.

1. The clear consciousness of the power and presence of God in his church at this time.
2. The unity of belief and action of the disciples.
3. The union of human effort and divine guidance in organizing the church.
4. The missionary activity of the church at its very beginning.

Student's Home Work.

Lesson Study: Study carefully the lesson material, Acts 2:42-47; 4:32-37; 5:1-11; 6:1-7.

Assigned search work: (For class report.)
1. Of what value were the early "wonders and signs" done by the apostles?
2. What dangers in having "all things common"?
3. Other Bible instances of divine retribution.
4. Reasons for the rapid growth of the church.
5. Why did the early Christians still continue as members of the Jewish church?

Review questions for student's self-test:
1. In what way did church life begin?
2. What were the conditions of membership in the early church?
3. What was probably the subject-matter of instruction in the early meetings of the church?
4. In what were the Jews and the Christians alike and unlike?
5. What were some of the distinctive features of the early church?
6. In what were Ananias and Sapphira guilty?
7. Why were such stern disciplinary measures used?
8. What was the special work of the apostles?
9. What was the work of the deacons?
10. What are some of the chief reasons for the rapid growth of the church?

Topics for further study:
1. The relation of Christianity to Judaism.
2. The Lord's Supper in the early church.
3. Community life in the early church.

NOTE.— The teacher should supply references to standard literature upon the above topics. A five-minute paper upon the first topic may be assigned to a member for presentation to the class upon the Sunday following that of the lesson study. The blackboard may be used for the presentation of the " Outline " as it develops in class.

LESSON 4

EARLY STRUGGLES AGAINST PERSECUTION

Lesson Material.

Acts 4: 1–31; 5: 12–42.

Teacher's Study Material.

Purves, *The Apostolic Age,* pp. 47–50; McGiffert, *The Apostolic Age,* pp. 81–84; " Expositor's Bible," *The Acts* of the *Apostles*, pp. 173-92, 229-45; Taylor, *Peter the Apostle*, chap. xiv; Hastings, *Bible Dictionary*, art. "Sanhedrin;" a good critical commentary.

Organization of Material.

1. The first arrest of the apostles.
    a) The imprisonment.
    b) The examination before the council.
    c) The private conference of the council.
    d) The release of the prisoners.
    e) The apostles' report to the disciples.
2. The second arrest of the apostles.
    a) The imprisonment and miraculous release.
    b) The defense before the council.
    c) Gamaliel's warning words to the council.
    d) The punishment and final release of the prisoners.

Presentation of Material.

Develop by questions the various sections as outlined under the heading "Organization of Material." Before taking up the immediate events of the lesson bring out by questions the following significant facts: (1) the great interest awakened by the events of the day of Pentecost, and by the healing of the lame man; (2) the enthusiasm and activity of the believers; (3) the public preaching and teaching of the apostles; (4) the central thought in the teaching — Jesus, whom they crucified, the Savior of Israel; (5) the constant increase in numbers of the believers. Show how naturally opposition would arise from the priests and other leaders because of the growing influence of the apostles and the disbelief of the Sadducees in the resurrection. As it was not lawful to have a trial before the Sanhedrin in the evening, the apostles were placed in ward for the night. When brought before the council for what are they examined? Bring out the main elements in Peter's defense, showing his earnest witnessing to Jesus as (1) the Messiah, (2) the fulfilment of prophecy, and (3) the only savior of men. Question as to some of the proofs that Peter's testimony was true: (1) his boldness, indicating some great change in him, (2) his power as a witness, although unlearned and ignorant, and (3) the presence of the lame man who was healed. Note the clear conviction of duty shown in the response by the apostles. To whom do they go after their release? In that interview note (1) the confidence of the disciples in God's over-ruling power, (2) their self-forgetfulness in trial, and (3) their earnest desire for boldness in proclaiming the gospel. Note the growth in numbers of the believers (Acts 5:14). Question on the miracles of healing and the influence of these on the public. Connect with this the jealousy of the Sadducees and the second arrest of the apostles. Question on the events following, including the release from prison, the meeting of the council, the discovery of the escape, the report to the council and the consequent perplexity. Note how the alarm is increased by the news that the apostles are teaching in the temple. The second arrest then follows. At the time of the first arrest they are simply questioned; in this they are accused. Bring out by questions the points in the accusation: (1) disobedience to the Sanhedrin, and (2) sedition. In what sense was this last true? What is the meaning of "to bring this man's blood upon us"? In view of this double charge note (1) the boldness of the apostles' answer, "We ought to obey God rather than men," which implies a refusal to obey them; (2) the reference to the resurrection, to which some of the council were opposed; (3) the open accusation concerning the Jews' guilt in the death of Jesus; (4) the exaltation of Jesus to whom they were all bitterly opposed; and (5) the apostles' belief in the testimony of the Holy Spirit to their teaching. The force and intensity of the words are evidenced by their effect upon the council. Question as to Gamaliel's part in the trial. His argument a plea for non-interference with the disciples. What force was there to this argument? Was it wise? What was the effect of the argument on the council? Note the injustice of the punishment and the foolishness of the charge preceding the release. Emphasize the effect of the trial upon the disciples. How did they regard their sufferings? Note their special blessings: (1) the divine power and protection in their work, (2) large results from their labors, and (3) joy in the consciousness of duty performed in the face of difficulties and suffering. Make plain the possibility of such joy when one has this consciousness. In closing, review the entire lesson, uniting the sections, and impressing the thought that righteousness is to prevail in this world in spite of persecution and suffering.

Points to Emphasize.
1. The self-forgetfulness and boldness of the apostles in their work.
2. The joy of service, even though it brings suffering.
3. The clear conviction of one's duty — to obey God rather than men.

Student's Home Work.
Lesson study: Study carefully the lesson material, Acts 4: 1–31; 5: 12–42.
Assigned search work: (For class report.)
1. Why did the Sadducees especially oppose the work of the apostles?
2. In what respects was the first recorded miracle of the apostles a notable one?

3. How interpret the release by the "angel of the Lord"?
4. With what were the apostles charged before the council, and upon what grounds?
5. Upon what did Gamaliel base his warning words?

Review questions for student's self-test:
1. What was the cause of the arrest of the apostles?
2. What caused the alarm of the priests and Sadducees?
3. In regard to what were the apostles examined?
4. Why were they finally released?
5. What was the cause of the second arrest of the apostles?
6. What indications at this time of increased opposition to the disciples?
7. Of what were the apostles accused and upon what grounds?
8. In the apostles' defense what facts in Christ's life did they emphasize?
9. In what ways did the Holy Spirit witness to the apostles' teaching?
10. What was the final action of the council, and why was such action taken?

Topics for further study:
1. The characteristic beliefs of the Pharisees and the Sadducees.
2. The membership and functions of the Sanhedrin.
3. The policy advocated by Gamaliel and the wisdom of it.

NOTE.— The teacher should supply references to standard literature upon the above topics. A five-minute paper upon the first topic may be assigned to a member for presentation to the class upon the Sunday following that of the lesson study. The blackboard may be used for the presentation of the "Outline" as it develops in class.

LESSON 5
STEPHEN THE FIRST MARTYR

Lesson Material.
Acts 6: 8–15; 7: 1–60; 8: 2.

Teacher's Study Material.
Purves, *The Apostolic Age*, pp. 51–55; McGiffert, *The Apostolic Age*, pp. 83–93; Gilbert, *The Student's Life of Paul*, pp. 21–24; Conybeare and Howson, *Life and Epistles of St. Paul*, Vol. I, pp. 63–75; "Expositor's Bible" series, *The Acts of the Apostles*, pp. 298–305; Hastings, *Bible Dictionary*, art. "Stephen;" a good critical commentary.

Organization of Material.
1. Stephen the man of faith.
   a) Teaches the people with wonderful success.
   b) Is opposed by the foreign Jews.
   c) Is arrested and brought before the council.
2. Stephen before the council.
   a) The false accusation.
   b) The theme of Stephen's address: "The Progressive Witness of Israel's God."
   c) Historical development of this theme.
      (1) God's witness to Abram.
      (2) God's witness to his people in Egypt.
      (3) God's witness through the prophet Moses and the "living oracles."
      (4) God's witness through the tabernacle and the temple.

d) Abrupt break in the argument and the rebuke of the rulers.
  e) His vision of Jesus.
3. Stephen's martyrdom.
  a) The stoning of Stephen.
  b) His prayer of forgiveness.

Presentation of Material.

Develop by questions the various sections as outlined under the heading "Organization of Material." Seek first to gain a definite idea of Stephen as a man. In the statement about him note (1) the phrase "full of grace and power," (2) his ability to work miracles, and (3) his power as a speaker. The first signs of opposition come in the disagreement of the foreign Jews with him, resulting in open persecution as his power is felt. Question as to who were these Jews, why they opposed him, and by what means. What were the specific charges made before the council? What were the grounds for the charges? Note possible grounds for such charges in the teachings of Jesus as set forth by Stephen. In this connection *cf.* John 4: 21–24. The former persecutions had been led by the Sadducees, but the preaching of Stephen roused the ritualistic party, the Pharisees. Why? Develop by questions Stephen's address of defense. It is not a direct defense of himself, but only indirectly of his position. He traces the witness of Jehovah to his people, beginning with the revelation to Abram. In the subsequent history God's revelation and promises were not connected with any lands or buildings or permanent place. Stephen is accused of blasphemy against Moses and the law. On the contrary he recognizes Moses as a prophet, refers to the law as "living oracles," recognizes its divine character, and its obligations. This same Moses had pointed to the coming witness of a later prophet.

Stephen had been charged with blasphemy against the temple. In answer he traces Jewish history before the time of the temple, showing how God had revealed himself to Abram in one place (vs. 2), to Joseph in another (vss. 9, 10), to Moses in the burning bush (vss. 30-33), to Israel in the church in the wilderness (vs. 38), and finally when the temple was built God declared that it could not confine him within its walls. He shows that the idea of a spiritual worship, not necessarily connected with the temple, is not a new idea, but one distinctly taught by the prophets (vss. 48-50). Seemingly he would have further shown God's witness of himself through the later prophet to whom Moses pointed — Jesus the Christ — if it had not been for some interruption indicated by the sudden break at the close of vs. 50. Perhaps their displeasure was so manifest at this point that he abruptly closes with a rebuke to the leaders. Of what did he accuse the members of the council? Note these three distinct accusations: (1) resistance to the Holy Spirit, (2) murder of the Righteous One of whom the prophets spake, and (3) disobedience to the divine law. Thus he condemns them as the real criminals and offenders. Note the effect of this charge upon his hearers. Question as to the vision of Stephen, noting the elements in it which would arouse the anger of the council, especially the phrase "the Son of Man standing on the right hand of God." Here is the ground for their final charge of blasphemy. Question as to the legal and illegal points in the trial and execution. Contrast in closing the violence of the people, who in spite of great privilege were in spiritual darkness, and the spirit of Stephen, who, like the Master, prayed for his enemies. In closing briefly review the whole outline, seeking to leave a clear idea of the event and its bearing upon the development of Christianity, showing the struggle of Christianity against the opposition of those in high places, and the consequent growth through the devotion of the disciples who willingly laid down their lives for the sake of the gospel.

Points to Emphasize.
1. The power of a faith-filled life.
2. The danger of resisting divine revelation.
3. Stephen's exemplification of the Christ spirit.

Student's Home Work.

Lesson study: Study carefully the lesson material, Acts 6:8-15; 7:1-60; 8:2.

Assigned search work: (For class report.)
1. What was the source of the opposition to Stephen?
2. What were the charges brought against Stephen, and upon what grounds were they brought?
3. What were the legal and illegal aspects of the trial and execution?
4. In what respects was Stephen in advance of his times?
5. What does this lesson show is to be the fixed attitude of the rulers toward Christianity?

Review questions for student's self-test:
1. By whom was Stephen opposed in his work?
2. What were the charges brought against him?
3. What were the grounds for these charges?
4. In what respects was the teaching of Stephen considered dangerous to Judaism?
5. What method did Stephen pursue in meeting the charges?
6. In what respects did the historical address of Stephen vindicate his teaching?

SENIOR DEPARTMENT COURSE 337

7. What was the probable cause of the abrupt breaking off of the argument?
8. With what does Stephen suddenly charge his hearers?
9. Why did Stephen's words describing his vision so enrage his hearers?
10. What justification did the council have for its final action?

Topics for further study:
1. The views of Jesus concerning the temple and its services.
2. The effect of the death of Stephen upon the development of Christianity.
3. The relation of the work of the apostles and Stephen upon the career of Paul.

NOTE.— The teacher should supply references to standard literature upon the above topics. A five-minute paper upon the first topic may be assigned to a member for presentation to the class upon the Sunday following that of the lesson study. The blackboard may be used for the presentation of the "Outline" as it develops in class.

§ 3. BOOKS RELATING TO THE WORK OF GRADE A

A. REFERENCE READING FOR THE TEACHER

Christianity and the Christian Church

Fisher, *The Beginnings of Christianity* (Charles Scribner's Sons, New York).
Hurst, *A Short History of the Christian Church* (Harper and Brothers, New York).
McGiffert, *The Apostolic Age* (Charles Scribner's Sons, New York).
Ramsay, *Paul the Traveler and Roman Citizen* and *The Church in the Roman Empire* (G. P. Putnam's Sons, New York).

Riggs, *A History of the Jewish People during the Maccabean and Roman Periods* (Charles Scribner's Sons, New York).

"Ten Epochs of Church History:" series edited by Dr. John Fulton (Charles Scribner's Sons, New York): (1) *The Apostolic Age*, by Bartlet; (2) *The Post-Apostolic Age*, by Waterman; (3) *The Ecumenical Councils*, by DuBose; (4) *The Age of Charlemagne*, by Wells; (5) *The Age of Hildebrand*, by Vincent; (6) *The Age of the Crusades*, by Ludlow; (7) *The Age of the Renaissance*, by van Dyke; (8) *The Age of the Great Western Schism*, by Locke; (9) *The Protestant Reformation*, by Walker; (10) *The Anglican Reformation*, by Clark.

Christian Missions

Beach, *A Geography and Atlas of Protestant Missions* (Student Volunteer Movement, New York).

Beach and others, *Protestant Missions in South America* (Student Volunteer Movement, New York).

Bliss, *Encyclopædia of Missions*, 2 vols. (Funk and Wagnalls, New York).

Dennis, *Christian Missions and Social Progress*, 3 vols. (F. H. Revell Co., Chicago).

Dennis, *Centennial Survey of Foreign Missions* (F. H. Revell Co., Chicago).

Hamlin, *My Life and Times* (F. H. Revell Co., Chicago).

Lawrence, *Modern Missions in the East* (F. H. Revell Co., Chicago).

Noble, *The Redemption of Africa*, 2 vols. (F. H. Revell Co., Chicago).

Warneck, *Outline of a History of Protestant Missions* (F. H. Revell Co., Chicago).

Williams, *The Middle Kingdom*, 2 vols. (Charles Scribner's Sons, New York).

Williams, *Missionary Enterprises in the South-Sea Islands* (Presbyterian Board of Publication, Philadelphia).

Zwemer, *Arabia the Cradle of Islam* (F. H. Revell Co., Chicago).

Senior Department Course

B. READING AND REFERENCE BOOKS FOR THE PUPIL

Christianity and the Christian Church

Lindsay, *The Reformation* (Charles Scribner's Sons, New York).

Moncrief, *A Short History of the Christian Church* (F. H. Revell Co., Chicago).

Thatcher, *Sketch of the History of the Apostolic Church* (Houghton, Mifflin & Co., Boston).

Summers, *The Rise and Spread of Christianity in Europe* (F. H. Revell Co., Chicago).

Christian Missions

Cary, *Japan and Its Regeneration* (Student Volunteer Movement, New York).

Carey, *Adventures in Tibet* (United Society of Christian Endeavor, Boston).

Griffis, *Honda, the Samurai* (Pilgrim Press, Boston).

Hodder, *Conquests of the Cross,* 3 vols. (Cassell & Co., New York).

Holcomb, *Men of Might in Indian Missions* (F. H. Revell Co., Chicago).

Lhamon, *Heroes of Modern Missions* (F. H. Revell Co., Chicago).

Paton, *John G. Paton: An Autobiography,* 3 vols. (F. H. Revell Co., Chicago).

Thornton, *Africa Waiting* (Student Volunteer Movement, New York).

Wheeler, *Missions in Eden* (F. H. Revell Co., Chicago).

---

§ 4. OUTLINE OF THE COURSE FOR GRADE B

GRADE SUBJECT: THE CHRISTIAN RELIGION: ITS EVIDENCES AND SACRED BOOKS

Part 1 — Its evidences.

1. The evidence from prophecy.
2. The evidence from miracles.
3. The evidence from its adaptiveness to all.

4. The evidence from its transforming effects.
5. The evidence from the character of the system.
6. The evidence from the character of Jesus.
7. The evidence from its contrast with other religions.
8. *Review.*

Part 2—Its sacred books.

A. *The Canon*

9. Formation of the Old Testament canon.
10. Formation of the New Testament canon.
11. Authenticity and genuineness of the Old Testament writings.
12. Authenticity and genuineness of the New Testament writings.
13. Inspiration and the canon.
14. History of our English Bible.
15. History of our English Bible.
16. *Review.*

B. *The Old Testament Books*

§ 1. The Hexateuch

17. Genesis, Exodus.
18. Leviticus, Numbers.
19. Deuteronomy, Joshua.

§ 2. The Historical Books

20. Judges, Ruth.
21. 1 and 2 Samuel.
22. *Review.*
23. Kings and Chronicles.
24. Ezra, Nehemiah, Esther.

§ 3. The Poetical Books

25. Job.
26. Psalms.

27. Proverbs, Ecclesiastes, Song of Songs.
28. *Review.*

§ 4. The Earlier Prophets

29. Amos.
30. Hosea.
31. Isaiah.
32. Micah, Nahum, Zephaniah.
33. Jeremiah.
34. Lamentations, Habakkuk.

§ 5. The Later Prophets

35. Ezekiel.
36. Obadiah, Haggai, Zechariah.
37. Malachi, Joel, Jonah.
38. *Review.*

C. *The New Testament Books*

39. Matthew, Mark.
40. Luke, John.
41. Acts, 1 and 2 Thessalonians.
42. 1 and 2 Corinthians.
43. Galatians, Romans.
44. *Review.*
45. The imprisonment epistles.
46. The pastoral epistles.
47. Hebrews, James.
48. Peter, John.
49. Jude, Revelation.
50. *Review.*

Special Lessons.

51. Christmas lesson.
52. Easter lesson.

§ 5. SUGGESTIVE LESSON PLANS FOR GRADE B
LESSONS 29 AND 30
LESSON 29
THE BOOK OF AMOS

Lesson Material.

The book of Amos.

Teacher's Study Material.

Driver, *Introduction to the Literature of the Old Testament,* pp. 313-18; Cornill, *The Prophets of Israel,* pp. 37-46; Kirkpatrick, *The Doctrine of the Prophets,* pp. 83-108; Driver, " The Book of Amos," in the *Cambridge Bible for Schools and Colleges;* Smith (G. A.), *The Book of the Twelve Prophets,* in " Expositor's Bible " series, Vol. I, pp. 61-207; Smith (W. R.), *The Prophets of Israel,* pp. 90-143; Sanders and Kent, *The Messages of the Earlier Prophets,* pp. 23-44; Moulton, *Daniel and the Minor Prophets,* in the " Modern Reader's Bible " series.

Analysis and Organization of Material.

I. Historical setting of the book.
  1. Political situation.
     a) A period of external peace and internal prosperity under Jeroboam II.
     b) A corrupt aristocracy tyrannized over the people.
  2. Social conditions.
     a) Two classes only — the rich and the poor.
     b) Oppression, cruelty, injustice and all forms of vice prevailed.
     c) The people indifferent, intolerant, without fear of judgment.

Senior Department Course 343

   3. Religious life.
      a) Ceremonies of worship zealously observed.
      b) Offerings, feasts, and sacrifices in abundance.
      c) People's sins canceled by a money equivalent.
      d) Priests allied with the corrupt court aristocracy.

II. The writer of the book.
   1. Personal history.
      a) Home in Tekoa of Judah.
      b) By occupation a shepherd and dresser of sycamore trees.
      c) Possessed of knowledge of nature and life in the open.
      d) No special training for the prophetic office.
   2. Character.
      a) Simple, straightforward, and earnest.
      b) Fearless in right-doing.
      c) With a developed sense of justice.
   3. Qualifications for the work.
      a) His knowledge of the laws and history of Israel.
      b) His knowledge of the social and political life of the times.
      c) His simple, rather austere, life in Judah.

III. The Book.
   1. The message delivered at Bethel, in the north kingdom.
   2. Probably written at Tekoa about 755–750 B. C.
   3. Purpose.
      a) To proclaim a God of justice and righteousness.

b) To denounce the sins and vices of the people.
c) To demand justice and righteousness between man and man.
d) To emphasize the moral requirements of Jehovah.

4. Style of the book.
    a) Language pure, sentences clear.
    b) Discourses connected.
    c) Much nature-imagery employed.
5. Contents of the book.
    a) The prologue — chaps. i, ii.
        (1) The judgments upon the six nations (1:3 — 2:3).
        (2) The judgment upon Israel (2:6-16).
    b) The three addresses — chaps. iii-vi.
        (1) Israel's crimes will not be pardoned.
        (2) Ritual cannot save them.
        (3) Israel's punishment certain; the instrument indicated.
    c) The five visions of judgment — chap. 7-9:6.
        (1) The vision of the locust plague (7:1-3).
        (2) The vision of the drought (7:4-6)).
        (3) The vision of the plumbline (7:7-9).
        (4) The vision of the basket of ripe summer fruit (8:1-14).
        (5) The vision of the destruction of the temple (9:1-6).
    d) The epilogue — 9:7-15.
        (1) Sinners to be destroyed: a remnant to escape (9:8-10).
        (2) The house of David to be restored (9:11-15).

IV. The message of the book.
  1. Justice between man and man demanded by God.
  2. Elaborate worship without righteous living an abomination to God.
  3. The privileges enjoyed determine the measure of punishment to those who sin.

Presentation Suggestions.
Develop the outline as much as possible by questions. Briefly describe the political situation during the time of Amos. Jeroboam II. proved a strong, aggressive king, and while Assyria and Syria were engaged in their struggle, he was enabled to bring his kingdom to a condition which approached Solomon's time in glory and extent. The effect of war, however, was to eliminate the middle class and to leave only two classes — the rich and the poor. The rich aristocrats, allied with the corrupt court, tyrannized over the people. To show the social conditions in the kingdom have members of the class read Amos 2:6-7; 3:10; 4:1; 5:7, 12; 8:4-6. Concerning the attitude of the people see Amos 6:6; 5:10; 6:1, 13. Concerning the religious life see Amos 2:7, 8; 4:4, 5; 5:21-24. Also read Smith, *The Prophets of Israel*, pp. 98, 99. The people believed that God was with them; that they were his people and he would not desert them. Their prosperity was an evidence of this. If they continued to offer an abundance of sacrifices the Lord would never turn against them. It was against this view that Amos had to contend. Question the class about the personal history of Amos, having read such passages as Amos 7:14; 2:13; 3:4, 5, 12; 5:19; 8:1, etc. That he was a keen observer of the social and political life of his times is shown in the prophecies concerning the nations round about Israel, and in his indication of the in-

strument of Israel's punishment. It was this knowledge together with his knowledge of Israel's laws and history that qualified him for his prophetic work. See Cheyne's "Introduction" to the *Book of Amos*. The character elements suggested are inferred from the somewhat meager notices we have of his personal history. For an account of the coming of Amos to Bethel to deliver his message, see Cornill, *The Prophets of Israel*, pp. 39, 40. After delivering his message, Amos returned to his home in Tekoa and wrote out his prophecies. Emphasize the purpose of Amos, reading such sections of his work as will most clearly show the fourfold purpose indicated in the outline. The keynote of the book might be given as *righteousness*. For a discussion of the style of Amos see Cheyne's "Introduction" to *The Book of Amos*, § 5. In discussing the contents of the book, note the form in which the matter of the prologue is arranged: an opening formula, only varied by the names of the doomed nations; then recitative prose expressing actual offenses; then the formula expressing the doom; and lastly recitative prose giving the details of punishment. See in this connection Moulton, *Daniel and the Minor Prophets*, pp. 94 ff. Then note the nations upon which judgment is pronounced and the reasons for such judgments. Then comes the indictment against Israel. The next section, the three addresses, cannot be taken up in detail on account of the shortness of the time; simply read such parts as will best indicate the general thought of the discourses (see "Outline"). In discussing the visions of judgment note that the first two plagues are averted in answer to Amos's prayer. But the visions of the plumbline and the basket of ripe summer fruit indicate that the last hope is gone — the end is near. The final destruction of the national life is pictured in the last vision, the destruction of the temple.

SENIOR DEPARTMENT COURSE 347

The epilogue was probably added by a later hand. In discussing the great message of the book read Kirkpatrick, *The Doctrine of the Prophets,* p. 106.

Student's Home Work.

Lesson study: A careful reading of the book of Amos.
Assigned search work: (For class report.)
1. The political situation during Amos's prophetic activity.
2. The social conditions of the times.
3. The religious life of the period.
4. Amos's conception of God.
5. The personal history of Amos.

Review questions for student's self-test:
1. What was the political situation in the northern kingdom in the time of Amos?
2. What were the social conditions of the period?
3. Against what religious views did Amos have to contend?
4. Describe the life and probable training of Amos.
5. What qualifications did he have for the prophetic work?
6. To whom was his message delivered and at what place?
7. About what date was the book written?
8. What is the style of Amos's writing?
9. What are the principal contents of the book?
10. What is the great message of the book?

Topics for further study:
1. Amos's acquaintance with the laws and history of his nation.
2. His figures of speech drawn from natural phenomena.
3. Comparison of the character and work of Elijah and Amos.

Lesson 30
THE BOOK OF HOSEA

Lesson Material.

The book of Hosea.

Teacher's Study Material.

Sanders and Kent, *The Messages of the Earlier Prophets,* pp. 47-76; Smith (W. R.), *The Prophets of Israel,* pp. 144-90; Smith (G. A.), *The Book of the Twelve Prophets* in "Expositor's Bible" series, Vol. I, pp. 211-354; Kirkpatrick, *The Doctrine of the Prophets,* pp. 109-142; Cornill, *The Prophets of Israel,* pp. 47-55; Driver, *Introduction to the Literature of the Old Testament,* pp. 300-307; Cheyne, "The Book of Hosea" in the *Cambridge Bible for Schools and Colleges;* Moulton, *Daniel and the Minor Prophets* in the "Modern Reader's Bible" series.

Analysis and Organization of Material.

I. Historical setting of the book.
  1. Political situation.
     a) In Jeroboam's reign, external success and internal prosperity.
     b) The following reigns a period of anarchy.
  2. Social conditions.
     a) The first period one of luxury, and of oppression of the poor.
     b) The last period one of general lawlessness.
  3. Religious life.
     a) Priesthood corrupt.
     b) Worship a mere form.
     c) People idolatrous and immoral.

II. The writer of the book.
  1. Personal history.
     a) Son of Beeri. Home in Israel, probably in Galilee.
     b) Passed through a sad domestic experience.
     c) Possessed a thorough knowledge of the internal and external affairs of the kingdom.
  2. Character.
     a) Longsuffering, forgiving nature.
     b) Deeply religious.
     c) Poetic and intensely patriotic.
  3. Qualifications for the work.
     a) Knowledge of conditions in the kingdom.
     b) His religious nature.
     c) His domestic experience — this his call and education.
III. The book.
  1. The sermons addressed to northern Israel.
  2. The date, about 738-735 B. C.
  3. Purpose.
     a) To proclaim a God of forgiving love.
     b) To expose the sin of the people.
     c) To urge a return with a promise of restoration.
  4. Style of the sermons.
     a) Impassioned and disconnected.
     b) Figurative and poetic.
  5. Contents of the book.
     a) Hosea's domestic life — chaps. i–iii.
        (1) The narrative of his domestic experience (1:1—2:1).
        (2) The interpretation of the narrative (2:2–23).
        (3) Symbolism of Hosea's disciplinary measures (chap. iii).

b) Hosea's prophecies — chaps. iv–xiv.
   (1) Israel's guilt exposed (4:1—8:14).
   (2) Israel's punishment pronounced (9:1—11:11).
   (3) Israel's repentance urged and restoration promised (11:12—14:9).
IV. The message of the book.
   1. God's nature one of forgiving love.
   2. Punishment for sin is certain.
   2. Repentance brings restoration through discipline.

Presentation Suggestions.

Develop the outline as much as possible by questions. Briefly bring to view a picture of the times in which Hosea lived and worked, that the prophet's message may be more thoroughly understood. Driver, in his *Introduction to the Literature of the Old Testament,* pp. 301, 302, gives a clear and concise account of the political situation. For an account of the social and moral conditions see Sanders and Kent's *Messages of the Earlier Prophets,* pp. 47–50. To summarize, the nation was in a state of almost complete moral and religious collapse. The end suggested by Amos's picture of the basket of ripe summer fruit (Amos 8:1, 2) is now at hand. Hosea presents a similar picture, but one even more appalling (Hosea 4:1, 2). Have members of the class read passages from Hosea which show the conditions mentioned in the outline under the first heading. Next question the class concerning what is known from the book itself of Hosea's personal history. Dwell briefly upon his marriage with Gomer, her faithlessness, the children and their significant names, the wife's desertion of her home, the recovery by Hosea, the time of discipline, and the final restoration to all the rights and privileges of wifehood.

In this connection read Dean Plumptre's poem "Gomer" in the collection *Lazarus and Other Poems*. Note the character of the prophet, and have the class read passages which indicate the character-elements suggested in the outline. Then show his qualification for the special work to which he was called, noting that the prophet's peculiar domestic experience constituted both the *call* to the prophetic office and the *education* for the prophetic work (see Smith, *The Prophets of Israel*, pp. 181 ff.). In dealing with the next section of the outline, the book itself, try to have the members of the class discover as much as possible for themselves, helping them with questions. For a discussion of the style of the utterances see Cornill, *The Prophets of Israel*, pp. 51, 52, and Cheyne, *The Book of Hosea*, chap. v of the Introduction. Question the class so as to bring out the analysis of the contents as suggested in the outline. The last section, chaps. xi–xiv, pictures the yearning of God toward Israel and his desire to bring Israel to repentance that forgiveness may follow. For a beautiful rendering of these chapters see Moulton's *Daniel and the Minor Prophets*, pp. 68–74. Lastly indicate the great message of love and yearning which the book brings, comparing such with the stern message of the prophet Amos.

Student's Home Work.

Lesson study: A careful reading of the book of Hosea.
Assigned search work: (For class report.)
1. The political situation during Hosea's prophetic activity.
2. The social and religious conditions of the period.
3. Relation of Hosea's domestic experience to his prophetic work.
4. The character of Hosea.
5. Hosea's conception of God.

Review questions for student's self-test:
1. What was the difference in the political situation during the earlier and the later periods of Hosea's prophetic activity?
2. Against what social and religious obstacles did he have to contend?
3. What peculiar domestic experience was he called upon to pass through?
4. What does this experience reveal to us of the character of Hosea?
5. What effect did this experience have upon his prophetic work?
6. What is the probable date of the book of Hosea?
7. To whom were the sermons and exhortations addressed?
8. What is the style of Hosea's writings?
9. What are the principal contents of the book?
10. What is the great message of the book?

Topics for further study.
1. Comparison of the religious conceptions and work of the prophets Amos and Hosea.
2. The prophet's use of the symbolism of marriage.
3. The figurative language of the prophet.

NOTE.— The teacher should supply references to standard literature upon these study topics. A five-minute paper upon the first topic may be assigned to a member for presentation to the class upon the Sunday following that of the lesson study. The blackboard may be used for the presentation of the "Outline" as it develops in class.

§ 6. BOOKS RELATING TO THE WORK OF GRADE B

A. REFERENCE READING FOR THE TEACHER

Clarke, *What Shall We Think of Christianity?* and *Can I Believe in God the Father?* (Charles Scribner's Sons, New York).

Senior Department Course 353

MacKenzie, *Christianity and the Progress of Man* (F. H. Revell Co., Chicago).

Stewart, *A Handbook of Christian Evidences* (A. D. F. Randolph & Co., New York).

Storrs, *The Divine Origin of Christianity Indicated by Its Historical Effects* (A. D. F. Randolph & Co., New York).

Bennett and Adeney, *A Biblical Introduction* (Thomas Whittaker, New York).

Cambridge Bible for Schools and Colleges, 26 vols. on the Old Testament; the New Testament complete in 19 vols. (edited by J. J. S. Perowne and A. F. Kirkpatrick; the Macmillan Co., New York).

Driver, *Introduction to the Literature of the Old Testament* (Charles Scribner's Sons, New York).

Gladden, *Who Wrote the Bible?* (Houghton, Mifflin & Co., Boston).

Kirkpatrick, *The Doctrine of the Prophets* (The Macmillan Co., New York).

McFadyen, *Old Testament Criticism and the Christian Church* (Charles Scribner's Sons, New York).

Ryle, *The Canon of the Old Testament* (The Macmillan Co., New York).

Salmon, *An Historical Introduction to the Study of the Books of the New Testament* (John Murray, London).

Smith (G. A.), *The Book of the Twelve Prophets*; 2 vols; in the "Expositor's Bible" series (A. C. Armstrong & Son, New York).

Smith (W. R.), *The Prophets of Israel* (A. & C. Black, London).

Stanton, "The New Testament Canon," in Hastings's *Bible Dictionary*.

Westcott, *History of the Canon of the New Testament* (The Macmillan Co., New York).

Westcott, *History of the English Bible* (The Macmillan Co., New York).

Woods, "The Old Testament Canon," in Hastings's *Bible Dictionary*.

"The Messages of the Bible;" 12 vols; series edited by Professors F. K. Sanders and Charles F. Kent (Charles Scribner's Sons, New York): (1) *Messages of the Earlier Prophets*, by Sanders and Kent; (2) *Messages of the Later Prophets*, by Sanders and Kent; (3) *Messages of Israel's Lawgivers*, by Kent; (4) *Messages of the Prophetical and Priestly Historians*, by McFadyen; (5) *Messages of the Psalmists*, by Moxom; (6) *Messages of the Sages*, by F. K. Sanders; (7) *Messages of the Poets*, by Schmidt; (8) *Messages of the Apocalyptic Writers*, by Porter; (9) *Messages of Jesus according to the Synoptists*, by Hall; (10) *Messages of Jesus according to John*, by J. S. Riggs; (11) *Messages of Paul*, by Stevens; (12) *Messages of the Apostles*, by Stevens.

B. READING AND REFERENCE BOOKS FOR THE PUPIL

Fisher, *A Manual of Christian Evidences* (Chautauqua Press, Meadville, Pa.).

Ladd, *What is the Bible* (Charles Scribner's Sons, New York).

Lovett, *The Printed English Bible* (F. H. Revell Co., Chicago).

McClymont, *The New Testament and Its Writers* (A. D. F. Randolph & Co., New York).

Martin, *Origin and History of the New Testament* (Hodder and Stoughton, London).

Moulton and others, *The Bible as Literature* (Thomas Y. Crowell & Co., New York).

Robertson, *The Old Testament and Its Contents* (A. D. F. Randolph & Co., New York).

Smyth, *How We Got Our Bible* (James Pott & Co., New York).

Willett and Campbell, *The Teachings of the Books* (F. H. Revell Co., Chicago).

§ 7. OUTLINE OF THE COURSE FOR GRADE C

GRADE SUBJECT: THE CHRISTIAN RELIGION: ITS FUNDAMENTAL TRUTHS

Part 1 — Truths relating to God.

A. *God the Father*

1. God's nature and character.
2. God's attributes.
3. God's relations to the universe.
4. God's threefold manifestation — Father, Son, Spirit.
5. God's purpose — the establishment of his kingdom.
6. *Review.*

B. *Jesus the Son*

7. Jesus in relation to prophecy — the Messiah.
8. Jesus in relation to prophecy — the Messiah.
9. Jesus in relation to history — the Ideal Character.
10. Jesus in relation to history — the Ideal Character.
11. Jesus in relation to history — the Ideal Character.
12. Jesus in relation to God — the Full Revelation.
13. Jesus in relation to God — the Full Revelation.
14. *Review.*
15. Jesus in relation to the world — the Redeemer.
16. Jesus in relation to the world — the Redeemer.
17. Jesus in relation to man — the Personal Savior.
18. Jesus in relation to man — the Personal Savior.
19. Jesus in relation to the future life — the Risen Lord.
20. *Review.*

C. *The Holy Spirit*

21. The Holy Spirit and the world.
22. The Holy Spirit and the revelation of truth.
23. The Holy Spirit and the beginnings of divine life.
24. The Holy Spirit and the progress of the divine life.
25. The Holy Spirit and the progress of the divine life.
26. *Review.*

Part 2 — Truths relating to the individual.
A. *Man*
27. Man's nature — body and soul.
28. Man a moral being.
29. Man a moral being.
30. Man and eternal life.

B. *Evil and Sin*
31. Nature of evil and sin.
32. Nature of evil and sin.
33. Reality and universality of sin.
34. Penalty of sin.
35. Freedom from sin.
36. *Review.*

Part 3 — Truths relating to society.
37. Christianity and the family.
38. Christianity and the family.
39. Christianity and the state.
40. Christianity and the state.
41. Christianity and business.
42. Christianity and business.
43. *Review.*
44. Christianity and the problem of wealth.
45. Christianity and the problem of wealth.
46. Christianity and the Sabbath question.
47. Christianity and the temperance question.
48. Christianity and the problem of the world's evangelization.
49. Christianity and the problem of the world's evangelization.
50. *Review.*

Special Lessons.
51. Christmas lesson.
52. Easter lesson.

§ 8. SUGGESTIVE LESSON PLANS FOR GRADE C
FULL PLANS FOR LESSONS 21 AND 27
ANALYTIC OUTLINES FOR LESSONS 22 TO 25 AND 28 TO 35
LESSON 21
THE HOLY SPIRIT AND THE WORLD

Lesson Material.

Gen. 1: 1–31; 8: 20—9: 17; Ps. 104: 1–35; Job 38: 1—39: 30; Rom. 8: 28; John 3: 1–8; 6: 63; 16: 7–11, 13–15; 1 Cor. 2: 14–16; Eph. 3: 14–19; Heb. 3: 12–15; 1 Pet. 4: 6; 1 John 3: 1–8.

Literature.

Clarke, *An Outline of Christian Theology*, pp. 369–81; Hyde, *God's Education of Man*, pp. 31–35; Fiske, *Through Nature to God*, pp. 127–30, 147–51; Fiske, *The Idea of God*, pp. 158–67; Hastings, *Bible Dictionary*, art. " Holy Spirit; " Tyler, *The Whence and the Whither of Man*, chap. i; a good critical commentary.

Analytical Outline.

THE HOLY SPIRIT AND THE WORLD

1. In the world of nature.
   a) Creates life.
   b) Sustains life.
   c) Controls and correlates life.
2. In the world of humanity.
   a) Awakens and brings to consciousness the divine life in man.
   b) Convinces of sin.
   c) Reveals righteousness.
   d) Clarifies spiritual judgment.
   e) Inspires to spiritual activity.

Suggestions for Developing the Outline.

Develop the outline so far as possible by questions. Note first the story of creation as told in Genesis. The general statement is made that "In the beginning God created the heavens and the earth." Then follows the account of one creative event upon another, apparently in rapid succession. Note that the agency which seems to bring order and life out of chaos and death is the brooding Spirit of God, or the *operating power of God* in the world. (This conception of the Spirit of God as the operating power of God is used in all the lessons of this section.) Higher and more perfect forms are gradually developed until finally there appears as the crowning work of creation, man, a being created in God's very image, *i. e.,* with godlike powers. Although the Bible is not a book from which to teach science, and there is no need of any attempt at "harmonizing of science and the Bible," still it might be well to show that the biblical account of creation parallels in a very general way the scientific account, *i. e.,* the lower forms of life come first, and then successively higher and higher forms, until we have the crowning work — the creation of man. Explain the term "brooding" as of a bird upon her nest, "vitalizing the germs which the Divine Word is about to call forth." This vitalizing energy is continuous. Note how the Old Testament speaks of the Spirit as the sustainer of life (Ps. 104: 1–35). It is through the providence of God that life is supported. In Gen. 8: 20 to 9: 17 we have the promise that so long as the earth remains there shall be seed time and harvest; and the token of this covenant is the rainbow. This constant dependence upon the Spirit of God is expressed in Ps. 104: 30. Another phase of this power working in nature is noted in Job 38: 1–41, which speaks of God's control of all the processes of Nature. Dwell briefly on the verses illustrating this. Bring out clearly the thought that back of all manifestations there is a divine power that makes for righteousness, and a purpose or goal toward which the Spirit is working. Read to the class from Fiske's *Through Nature to God,* chap. xii. Parallel to the work in the realm of nature there is a special work of the Spirit in the life of man. The germ of divine life is present in every individual, and it is the work of the Spirit to awaken this life and bring it to the consciousness of man. "We cannot tell just what part of the better action of mankind is due to powers that God implanted in the soul of man and what to the present action of the Spirit working in and with these powers," but of the fact of the Spirit's activity we are sure. Have the class read John 6:63a and Eph. 3:14-19. Note the figure by which this awakening is described in John 3:1-8. Make plain that it is not a gift of new faculties, but by the quickening of the divine life to which the will of man consciously responds, that a new character is gradually wrought out. Emphasize the thought that while we do not at present understand the mysterious mode of action of the Spirit of God on the spirit of man the consequences are apparent and prove the fact. (In this connection see James's *The Varieties of Religious Experience,* pp. 511-15.) Turn to Christ's promise in John 16:8-11, and show the significance of the three lines of the Spirit's activity there indicated: (1) He convinces of sin, by showing man his failures, his own sin, and in a broader sense reveals what sin is; (2) He reveals righteousness. Righteousness is the opposite of sin; it is the ideal of God. By bringing to man the true standard as revealed in Christ, it is made plain to him what righteousness is; (3) He clarifies spiritual judgment. "Between sin and righteousness there is a true and unerring judgment of God, upon which the action of God is founded and the destiny of man depends. This judgment the Spirit reveals to the conscience of man. He is the great teacher of humanity concerning right and wrong, good and evil, and the relation between the two." The presence of the Spirit in the life of man leads to a spiritual activity and is evidenced by it. Review the points already discussed with this thought in view. The extent to which the will of man responds to the divine guidance is made evident in character — the first field for spiritual activity. The clearness with which sin is seen and righteousness apprehended, and the extent to which the judgment is clarified are shown in the life. "By their fruits ye shall know them." See 1 Peter 4:6 and 1 John 3:1-8. The Spirit stirs to activity the inner life of man, which shows itself outwardly in deeds. In conclusion emphasize the thought that God is actively at work in the world today through his Spirit, and that as man responds to the impulse and guidance of this Spirit he hastens the time when the purpose of God shall be realized in all its fulness.

Applicatory Summary.
1. The Spirit of God is an immanent power in the world today, creating, sustaining and controlling all life.
2. The Spirit is working to realize the moral purpose of God.
3. One function of the Spirit in the world of humanity is to awaken the divine life in every man. This awakening conditions the higher life.
4. Another function of the Spirit in the world of humanity is to convince man of sin, progressively reveal to him the ideal life, and to clarify his spiritual judgment, that he may discern clearly between good and evil. These conditions progress in the higher life.

Senior Department Course

5. A final function of the Spirit is to inspire man to activity in the spiritual sphere, that thus may be realized God's great creative purpose — a perfect manhood.

Student's Home Work.

A. Assigned search work on the lesson:
   1. The biblical account of creation.
   2. Biblical evidence for the immanence of God.
   3. Man's spiritual (religious) nature — inherent at birth or implanted later?
   4. The need and function of an ideal.
   5. Conditions governing the realization of the ideal.

B. Review questions for self-test:
   1. What are the activities of the Spirit in the world of nature?
   2. What is the order of creation?
   3. To what are all of the Spirit's activities tending?
   4. When does man acquire a spiritual nature?
   5. What is the work of the Spirit with reference to this spiritual nature?
   6. What is the work of the Spirit with reference to sin?
   7. What with reference to righteousness?
   8. What with reference to man's spiritual judgment.
   9. What conditions the realization of God's creative purpose?
   10. What is the relation of the Spirit to this realization?

C. Topics for further study.
   1. The testimony of history to the presence in the the world of a "power that makes for righteousness."

2. The method of the Spirit in his manifold activities.
3. The connection between the spirit of man and the Spirit of God.

Note.— The teacher should supply references to standard literature upon the above topics. Reports of the results of this study may be presented to the class from time to time.

Lesson 27
MAN'S NATURE — BODY AND SOUL

Lesson Material.
Eccl. 12:7; Matt. 10:28; 1 Thess. 5:23; Clarke, *An Outline of Christian Theology*, pp. 182–92; Bain, *Mind and Body*, pp. 6–16; James, *Talks to Teachers*, pp. 155–68, 64–78; Sully, *Teacher's Handbook of Psychology*, pp. 34–44.

Literature.
James, *Psychology*, Vol. I, pp. 104–27; Tyler, *The Whence and the Whither of Man*, pp. 210–40; Baldwin, *The Story of the Mind;* Radestock, *Habit in Education;* Halleck, *The Education of the Central Nervous System*, pp. 61–93.

Analytical Outline.

MAN'S NATURE — BODY AND SOUL

1. The body.
   a) In its material, organization and functions, is animal.
   b) In relationship with the higher thought powers, is man.
2. The soul (mind).
   a) Its activities.
      (1) Feelings — motives to action.
      (2) Intellect — guide to action.
      (3) Will — power for action.

b) Its unity.
      (1) This unity is personality.
      (2) This entire unity affected by its separate activities.
      (3) This unity in activity determines character.
3. The relation of body and soul.
   a) The body and impressions.
      (1) Impressions come through the senses.
      (2) The activity of mind receives and elaborates these impressions.
      (3) This mental activity is conditioned by brain activity.
   b) The body and expression.
      (1) Soul (mind) expresses itself through the body.
      (2) All thought tends to express itself in action.
      (3) The resultant of action is character.

Suggestions for Developing the Outline.
Develop the outline so far as possible by questions. The twofold division of man into body and soul has been recognized from early times. This division the Bible also recognizes. Have the class read Eccl. 12:7 and Matt. 10:28. Man is connected on the one hand with the physical universe, on the other he is allied to God. Note in regard to the body that (1) it is composed of "the dust of the earth," *i. e.*, of substances similar to those which compose the earth's crust, and hence is controlled by the laws of physical and chemical action; and (2) in organization it resembles the bodies of animals in general and is classified with them. We find in the two the same sense organs, the same general functions of muscle, nerve, and brain, and find life sustained by the same means and governed by the same natural laws. But this body, animal in its material, organization, and functions, is, through its relation with higher thought

powers, more than animal — it is Man. This relationship brings to man the upright position, articulate speech and other characteristics by which he is raised to the highest plane although still akin to the animal world. Show here the dignity and true place of the body, See 1 Cor. 6: 19. Seek to impress upon the class this thought of Paul's. In 1 Thess. 5: 23 we have a threefold division made — body, soul, spirit. Perhaps the best interpretation of this is that soul and spirit refer to the same element in man viewed in different relations. See Clarke, *An Outline of Christian Theology*, p. 183. While we cannot analyze the soul (mind) by the same means we apply to the body, we are each one conscious of possessing three forms of mental activity: (1) the feelings which serve as strong motives to action; (2) the powers of intellect (we perceive, remember, reason, etc.) which serve as guides to action; and (3) the powers of will which enable us to choose a line of action and execute our choice. These activities, seemingly separate, in reality never act alone, but form a unity which we call personality. While no personality is complete without these three elements, they are not always present in the same manner and proportion, and this difference produces individuality. Although we speak of the mind's separate activities we must remember that the mind (soul) is an organic unity and that every activity affects the entire organism. When we think we also feel and will; when we feel we also think and will, etc. When training any one of these so-called faculties we must consider its relation to the others in order to develop the most complete character. The soul like the body grows and develops as exercised, and when the various powers are exercised in the right proportion we have the well-balanced personality. What we are to become will be determined by the way this unity acts; if

Senior Department Course 365

it acts vigorously and in the right proportion, our character, as already suggested, will be a well-balanced one; if vigorously and in the right direction, the resulting character will be a noble one, and if less vigorously and in the wrong direction, a weak and evil one. Note next the relation of body and soul. The exact nature of the connection between the body and mind cannot be explained, but note some of the facts which show that it is an intimate one. See Bain, *Mind and Body*. Question briefly as to how impressions are received through the senses. See Sully, *Teacher's Handbook of Psychology*, pp. 22-25. Show importance of healthy sense-organs. Just how the activity of the mind receives these we cannot explain, but the new impression coming into the mind is met by old ideas, related to and interpreted by them. In the light of the old the new impression is understood, and by the new impression our knowledge is increased. See James's *Talks to Teachers*, pp. 155-68. This activity in receiving and elaborating these impressions is conditioned by the activity of the brain centers. Mental activity at any time depends largely upon the amount of available brain activity, and this latter depends upon (1) nutrition, (2) oxygen, (3) rest, and (4) general health. "A sound mind in a sound body" is the ideal. The body is not only the servant of the mind in gaining impressions, but also in giving expression to thought. Explain briefly the physical basis of this. See Sully, *Teacher's Handbook of Psychology*, pp. 22-25. Every thought of the mind tends to express itself in action through the body. Where they are allowed to express themselves without hindrance, we speak of the person as impulsive; where the action follows only after a lapse of time or is entirely stopped, we speak of the person as reflective or deliberate. The resultant of actions which involve the moral element is character. Show the importance of habit in this connection. See James's *Talks to Teachers*, pp. 64–78. In conclusion emphasize the thought that it is the purpose of education to make these actions numerous and perfect.

Applicatory Summary.
1. Man is more than animal through the possession of the higher thought powers.
2. Each of the soul's threefold activities must be developed that we may act vigorously and wisely.
3. Every activity affects the entire self and the resultant of the various activities determines character.
4. The soul depends upon the body for its impressions, and in its receiving and elaborating activity is conditioned by the activity of the brain. Hence the necessity for a sound body.
5. All of the soul's activities tend to express themselves in movement, in action. We have the power to check or to allow such. What we finally choose to do determines our moral character.

Student's Home Work.
  A. Assigned search work on the lesson:
     1. The evolution of the body (very briefly).
     2. The inter-relations of the soul's activities.
     3. The value of the senses to man.
     4. Conditions necessary to the highest brain activity.
     5. Relation of action to character.
  B. Review questions for self-test:
     1. In what respects is man related to the animal world?
     2. In what respects is man distinguished from animals?

3. What are the distinctive functions of the three activities of the soul or mind?
4. What conditions the development of a well-balanced character?
5. Give some evidence for the close relationship of mind and body?
6. What is the relation of the senses to mental growth?
7. Explain briefly the physical basis of mental life.
8. What conditions vigorous mental activity?
9. What is the relation of thought to action?
10. What is the relation of action to character?

C. Topics for further study:
1. The relation of the soul's unity to religious education.
2. Environment as a factor in character formation.
3. The importance of expression for development.

NOTE.— The teacher should supply references to standard literature upon the above topics. Reports of the results of this study may be presented to the class from time to time.

LESSON 22

Analytical Outline.

THE HOLY SPIRIT AND THE REVELATION OF TRUTH

1. Revealing truth to the world in general.
    a) Through nature.
    b) Through human experience.
    c) Through direct impression upon the human mind.
    d) Conditioned by man's attitude.
2. Revealing truth to God's chosen messengers.
    a) To the prophets — his message to Israel.
    b) To the apostles and first disciples — his message to the Gentiles.

c) To preachers and teachers — his message to the world.
d) Conditioned by the messengers' natures.
3. Revealing truth to the Christian.
    a) Progressively reveals the glory of Christ.
    b) Brings to remembrance Christ's teachings.
    c) Guides the believer into all truth.
    d) Conditioned by the believer's spirit and opportunities.

Lesson 23

Analytical Outline.

THE HOLY SPIRIT AND THE BEGINNINGS OF THE DIVINE LIFE

1. The divine life in man.
    a) One aspect of man's life at birth.
    b) Should develop with other parts of his nature.
    c) This development dependent upon conditions.
2. The work of the Spirit.
    a) To nurture this life from the beginning.
    b) To awaken this life when its development has been neglected.
    c) To begin the actualization of possibilities.
        (1) By presenting truth.
        (2) By inspiring to an active living of the truth.
3. The work of man.
    a) To turn from wrong-doing.
    b) To seek the truth.
    c) To trust in the Divine Character as revealed.

Lesson 24

Analytical Outline.

THE HOLY SPIRIT AND THE PROGRESS OF THE DIVINE LIFE

1. Implications of progress.
    a) A spiritual ideal.
    b) A struggle toward this ideal.
    c) A gradual realization of the ideal in life.

SENIOR DEPARTMENT COURSE

2. Conditions of progress.
    a) Fulfilled by man.
        (1) Right attitude — openness to truth.
        (2) Right desire — hunger and thirst after righteousness.
        (3) Right action — action according to light.
    b) Fulfilled by the Spirit.
        (1) Reveals truth to the open mind.
        (2) Inspires right desires.
        (3) Gives power for right action.

Lesson 25

Analytical Outline.

THE HOLY SPIRIT AND THE PROGRESS OF THE DIVINE LIFE
(CONCLUSION)

1. Implications of progress. } Review Lesson 24.
2. Conditions of progress.
3. Aids to progress.
    a) Prayer.
    b) Worship.
    c) Study and meditation.
    d) Service.
4. Inspiration to progress.
    a) Increase of knowledge.
    b) Development of power.
    c) Widening of the field of service.
    d) Possibility of a character like unto Christ's.

Lesson 28

Analytical Outline.

MAN A MORAL BEING

1. Implications of moral being.
    a) Power to form ethical ideals.
    b) Power of choice in view of such ideals.

      c) A moral sense, *i. e.*, a sense of obligation, of "oughtness" with reference to the right.
  2. Elements of moral action.
     a) Ethical knowledge.
     b) Right motive.
     c) Freedom of choice.

Lesson 29

MAN A MORAL BEING (CONCLUSION)

Analytical Outline.

  1. Implications of moral being. ⎫
  2. Elements of moral action.   ⎬ Review Lesson 28.
  3. Man's moral nature.
     a) Potential, not actual, at birth.
     b) Developed through service.
     c) This development dependent upon instruction and example.
  4. Man's moral responsibility.
     a) Elements of responsibility.
        (1) Responsible for use of intellect which determines truth.
        (2) Responsible for control of feelings which impel to action.
        (3) Responsible for activity of will which makes choices.
     b) Factors limiting responsibility.
        (1) An abnormal nature.
        (2) A degrading environment.
        (3) A lack of education.

Lesson 30
Analytical Outline.
MAN AND ETERNAL LIFE
1. Meaning of eternal life.
    a) Continuous existence — immortality.
    b) Continuous development.
    c) Condition of happiness.
2. Conditions necessary to eternal life.
    a) An eternal being — God.
    b) A being with capacity for such life — man.
    c) A vital relation between these two — God and man.
3. Biblical basis for belief in eternal life.
    a) With reference to immortality.
    b) With reference to development.
    c) With reference to happiness.
4. Scientific basis for belief in eternal life.
    a) With reference to immortality.
    b) With reference to development.
    c) With reference to happiness.

Lesson 31
Analytical Outline.
NATURE OF EVIL AND SIN
1. Evil — its nature and relation to life.
    a) Definition: Any choice or action which interferes with the highest development of our nature, physical, mental, or spiritual.
    b) Is relative, not absolute; determined by individual conditions.
    c) Is learned first by experience.
    d) Persisted in, tends to loss and finally death.

2. Evil — its relation to law.
   a) Known evil determines individual and national customs.
   b) National customs are crystallized into laws.
   c) Laws are substituted for experience as guides.

Lesson 32

Analytical Outline.

NATURE OF EVIL AND SIN (CONCLUSION)

1. Evil — its nature and relation to life. ⎫ Review
2. Evil — its relation to law. ⎬ Lesson 31.
3. Sin — its relation to law.
   a) Law furnishes a standard of conduct.
   b) Failure to attain this known standard is sin.
   c) The guilt of sin depends upon knowledge of the standard and the power to resist.
4. Sin — its several aspects.
   a) In relation to its own character — the condemnable.
   b) In relation to the nature of man — the abnormal.
   c) In relation to the standard of duty — any departure from such.
   d) In relation to its motive — the selfish.
   e) In relation to God's moral government — any opposition to such.

Lesson 33

Analytical Outline.

REALITY AND UNIVERSALITY OF SIN

1. The testimony of revelation.
   a) The Old Testament revelation.
      (1) The earlier prophets and national sin.
      (2) The later prophets and individual responsibility.

b) The New Testament revelation.
    (1) The experience and teaching of Jesus.
    (2) The experience and teaching of the apostles.
2. The testimony of man.
    a) Each one condemned by his own conscience.
    b) All pronounced sinful by the general moral judgment of man.
3. The testimony of facts.
    a) The witness of personal experience.
    b) The witness of observed experiences of others.

Lesson 34

Analytical Outline.

PENALTY OF SIN

1. The nature of penalties.
    a) As related to physical law (a true penalty).
        (1) A fixed amount of suffering.
        (2) Operative upon all alike.
        (3) Retributive in character.
    b) As related to moral law (a true punishment).
        (1) Suffering determined in amount by guilt.
        (2) Individual in application, conditioned by circumstances.
        (3) Educative in character.
2. The purposes of penalties.
    a) To increase respect for law.
    b) To warn the evil-minded.
    c) To guide the right-minded.
    d) To reclaim the law-breaker.
3. The character of the penalty for sin.
    a) Conditioned by guilt.
    b) Certain in operation.
    c) Final outcome spiritual death.

Lesson 35

Analytical Outline.

FREEDOM FROM SIN

1. Through forgiveness of the past.
    - *a*) Nature of forgiveness.
        - (1) Removes the cause of offense.
        - (2) Checks the moral consequences of sin.
        - (3) Restores to fellowship the sinner.
    - *b*) Conditions of forgiveness.
        - (1) Turning from the old life.
        - (2) Acceptance of a new ideal of life.
        - (3) Willingness to make amends for past misdeeds.
        - (4) Readiness to forgive others.
    - *c*) The plan of forgiveness.
        - (1) Universal in scope.
        - (2) Fulfilment of conditions required of all.
        - (3) Revealed and exemplified by Jesus.
2. Through bestowal of power for the present.
    - *a*) The work of the Spirit.
    - *b*) Sufficient for every need.

---

§ 9. BOOKS RELATING TO THE WORK OF GRADE C

A. REFERENCE READING FOR THE TEACHER

Bridgman, *The Master Idea* (The Pilgrim Press, Boston).

Caird, *Fundamental Ideas of Christianity* (The Macmillan Co., New York).

Clarke, *An Outline of Christian Theology* (Charles Scribner's Sons, New York).

Fiske, *The Idea of God,* and *Life Everlasting* (Houghton, Mifflin & Co., Boston).

Gladden, *Tools and the Man* (Houghton, Mifflin & Co., Boston).

Senior Department Course

Goodspeed, *Israel's Messianic Hope to the Time of Jesus* (The Macmillan Co., New York).

Gordon, *The Witness to Immortality in Literature, Philosophy, and Life*, and *Ultimate Conceptions of Faith* (Houghton, Mifflin & Co., Boston).

Heuver, *The Teaching of Jesus concerning Wealth* (F. H. Revell Co., Chicago).

Hyde, *God's Education of Man*, and *Jesus' Way* (Houghton, Mifflin & Co., Boston).

Mathews, *The Social Teaching of Jesus* (The Macmillan Co., New York).

Palmer, *The Field of Ethics* (Houghton, Mifflin & Co., Boston).

Peabody, *Jesus Christ and the Social Question* (The Macmillan Co., New York).

Salmond, *The Christian Doctrine of Immortality* (Charles Scribner's Sons, New York).

Van Dyke, *The Gospel for an Age of Doubt*, and *The Gospel for a World of Sin* (The Macmillan Co., New York).

B. READING AND REFERENCE BOOKS FOR THE PUPIL

Coe, *The Religion of a Mature Mind* (F. H. Revell Co., Chicago).

Gilbert, *A Primer of the Christian Religion* (The Macmillan Co., New York).

Gladden, *The Church and the Kingdom* (F. H. Revell Co., Chicago).

Jefferson, *Things Fundamental* (Thomas Y. Crowell & Co., New York).

Palmer, *The Nature of Goodness* (Houghton, Mifflin & Co., Boston).

Peabody, *The Religion of an Educated Man* (The Macmillan Co., New York).

Speer, *The Principles of Jesus* (F. H. Revell Co., Chicago).

Willett, *Basic Truths of the Christian Faith* (The Christian Century Co., Chicago).

§ 10. OUTLINE OF THE COURSE FOR GRADE D

GRADE SUBJECT: THE CHRISTIAN RELIGION: ITS SUPREME WORTH, AS COMPARED WITH OTHER GREAT WORLD RELIGIONS

Part 1 — Judaism.
1. The Hebrew people.
2. Primitive Judaism.
3. Judaism in the national period.
    a) In the period of the united kingdom.
4. *b)* In the period of the divided kingdom.
5. Its development in the exile period.
6. Its essential elements in the time of Christ.
7. The fruits of Judaism.
8. Judaism and Christianity.
9. *Review.*

Part 2 — Zoroastrianism.
10. Persia and its people.
11. Zoroaster and the origin of Zoroastrianism.
12. Its sacred books.
13. An outline of its teachings.
14. An outline of its teachings.
15. Its forms of worship.
16. The fruits of Zoroastrianism.
17. Zoroastrianism and Christianity.
18. *Review.*

Part 3 — Confucianism.
19. China and its people.
20. The life of Confucius.
21. Its sacred books.
22. An outline of its teachings.
23. An outline of its teachings.
24. Its form of worship.

Senior Department Course

25. The fruits of Confucianism.
26. Confucianism and Christianity.
27. *Review.*

Part 4 — Mohammedanism.

28. The Moslem lands and peoples.
29. The life of Mohammed.
30. Its sacred books.
31. An outline of its teachings.
32. An outline of its teachings.
33. An outline of its teachings.
34. Its forms of worship.
35. The fruits of Mohammedanism.
36. Mohammedanism and Christianity.
37. *Review.*

Part 5 — The religions of India.

38. The land and people of India.
39. Origin and development of the various religions.
40. The sacred books.
41. The sacred books.
42. An outline of their teachings.
43. An outline of their teachings.
44. *Review.*
45. An outline of their teachings.
46. An outline of their teachings.
47. The various forms of worship.
48. The fruits of the Indian religions.
49. The Indian religions and Christianity.
50. *Review.*

Special Lessons.

51. Christmas lesson.
52. Easter lesson.

§ 11. SUGGESTIVE LESSON PLANS FOR GRADE D

LESSONS 19 TO 23

LESSON 19

CHINA AND ITS PEOPLE

Analytical Outline.

1. The country.
   a) Geographical features.
   b) Influence upon the people.
2. The history.
   a) Mythical period (before 2850 B. C.) — achievements of godlike heroes.
   b) Legendary period (2850–1122 B. C.) — beginnings of inventions, commerce, literary, and political culture.
   c) Historic period (1122 B. C.–1840 A. D.) — development of institutions.
   d) Modern historic period (1840–   ) — contact with Western nations, missionary work, and effects.
3. The people.
   a) Characteristics.
      (1) As individuals — filial piety, industry, temperance, immorality.
      (2) As a nation — clannishness, respect for authority, conservatism.
   b) Life of the people.
      (1) Social — rather unsocial, strict ceremonial observed.
      (2) Intellectual — elementary education universal.
      (3) Religious — superstitious and materialistic.

4. The main religions.
    a) Confucianism — a code of ethics based upon authority.
    b) Taoism — metaphysical and retributive.
    c) Buddhism — aims at annihilation.

LESSON 20
THE LIFE OF CONFUCIUS

Analytical Outline.

1. The times.
    a) Feudal system in force.
    b) A period of anarchy and discord.
2. Birth and ancestry of Confucius.
3. His education and early life.
4. Important periods in his life.
    a) Life as an officer, to fifty-sixth year.
    b) Twelve years of wandering.
    c) Five years of teaching.
5. Work accomplishel.
    a) Founded a new system of morals, characterized by:
        (1) Subordination to superiors.
        (2) Upright dealings with fellow-men.
        (3) Prudential virtue.
        (4) Unity of family and national life.
    b) Modified and universalized the educational system.
6. Traits of character.
    a) Unpretentious simplicity.
    b) Frank practicalness.
    c) Prudence.
    d) Confidence.

7. Estimate of character and work.
    a) "K'ung, the ancient teacher, the perfect sage." — From the Chinese.
    b) "A transmitter and not a maker, believing in and loving the ancients." — Confucius (of himself).
    c) "He taught ethics, letters, devotion of soul, and truthfulness." — From the Analects.

Lesson 21
THE SACRED BOOKS OF CHINA

Analytical Outline.
1. Names and contents.
    a) The Five Classics.
        (1) *Yi-King* or *Book of Changes* — A kind of nature system.
        (2) *Shû-King* or *Book of History* — Historical documents.
        (3) *Shih-King* or *Book of Odes* — National airs, lesser eulogies, greater eulogies and the Song of Homage.
        (4) *Li King* or *Book of Rites* — Ceremonies for officers and scholars.
        (5) *Chun-Tsew* or *Spring and Autumn Annals* — A record of events by Confucius.
    b) The Four Books.
        (1) *Ta-Heo* or *The Great Learning* — Duties of political government.
        (2) *Chung-Yung* or *The Doctrine of the Mean* — An expository treatise.
        (3) *Lun-Yu* or *The Analects of Confucius* — Sayings of the Master.
        (4) *Mang-Tsze* or *Works of Mencius* — By a pupil.

SENIOR DEPARTMENT COURSE

2. Characteristics of style.
    a) Purity.
    b) Didactic maxims.
    c) Laconic expressions.
3. Characteristic teachings.
    a) Prudential virtue the highest ideal of the moral system.
    b) Filial duty emphasized.
    c) Details of etiquette and conduct shown.
    d) A united and peaceful empire the ideal.
    e) Example is all but omnipotent.
    f) The Law of Retaliation regarded.
    g) Learning is necessary to every pursuit and virtue.
    h) Man is by nature originally good.

LESSON 22
AN OUTLINE OF CONFUCIAN TEACHINGS

Lesson Material.

Grant, *The Religions of the World*, pp. 44–54.

Literature.

Douglas, *Confucianism*, pp. 65–170; Legge, *Life and Teachings of Confucius*, pp. 100–115; Legge, *Religions of China*, pp. 1–58, 67–149; Loomis, *Confucius and the Chinese Classics*, pp. 56–62; Edkins, *Religion in China*, pp. 18–38.

Analytic Outline.

AN OUTLINE OF CONFUCIAN TEACHINGS

1. The conception of deity.
    a) Vague concept of an intelligent First Cause.
    b) Characteristics of this First Cause.
        (1) Creating and ruling all.
        (2) Not actively concerned with man.

2. The conception of spirits.
   a) Belief in their existence universal.
   b) The two classes.
      (1) Nature spirits (rivers, mountains, sun, wheat, etc.).
      (2) Ancestral spirits.
3. The conception of worship.
   a) Emperor alone can worship Heaven, the First Cause.
   b) The Emperor and the educated classes can worship nature spirits.
   c) Everyone worships ancestral spirits.

Suggestions for Developing the Outline.

Develop the outline so far as possible by questions. At the proper time have the papers prepared upon the topics suggested under "Assigned search-work on the lesson" read to the class. Encourage a free discussion of the good and bad points of the Confucian beliefs and teachings. At the close of the hour briefly review the developed outline, and summarize the points made by the class in the discussion.

Student's Home Work.

A. Assigned search-work on the lesson:
   1. The belief in a Creative Principle.
   2. The relation of the First Cause to man.
   3. Development of the belief in nature-spirits.
   4. Development of the belief in ancestral-spirits.
   5. The idea of worship.
B. Review questions for self-test:
   1. What is the oldest Chinese idea of deity?
   2. What is the present idea?
   3. What is the relation of the First Cause to man?
   4. What are the causes of the belief in spirits?

5. What classes of spirits are believed in?
6. Characterize both.
7. How does this belief affect their domestic and social life?
8. What are the objects of worship for the different classes of people?
9. What are some of the good points in the ideas presented in the outline?
10. What are some of the objections to these ideas?

C. Topics for further study:
1. Primitive nature-worship in China.
2. Origin and development of ancestor-worship.
3. The worship of "Heaven."

NOTE.— The teacher should supply references to standard literature upon the above topics. Reports of the results of this study may be presented to the class from time to time.

LESSON 23
AN OUTLINE OF CONFUCIAN TEACHINGS (CONCLUSION)

Lesson Material.
See preceding lesson.

Literature.
See preceding lesson.

Analytic Outline.

AN OUTLINE OF CONFUCIAN TEACHINGS (CONCLUSION)

1. The conception of deity.
2. The conception of spirits. } Review Lesson 22.
3. The conception of worship.
4. The conception of man.
   a) His nature.
      (1) Intelligent and essentially good.
      (2) Development results in sin or the preservation of original purity.

  b) Classes of men.
    (1) Sage — the equal of heaven.
    (2) Superior man — attainable by all who will.
    (3) Ordinary man — on a low plane, without hope.
  c) The ideal the superior man.
    (1) Definition: one who carefully perfects the original goodness of his nature.
    (2) Steps in attainment.
      Learning.
      Sincerity.
      Heart set on virtue.
      Cultivation of person, family, state.
      Valor, benevolence, loyalty, etc.
    (3) This attainment dependent upon the individual's own power.
 5. The conception of the ideal state.
  a) The ultimate aim of both education and religion.
  b) Essential elements.
    (1) An ideal ruler — the Great Father.
    (2) An implicitly obedient people — the reverent children.
  c) Citizenship means salvation.

Suggestions for Developing the Outline.

Develop the outline so far as possible by questions. At the proper time have the papers prepared upon the topics suggested under "Assigned search work on the lesson" read to the class. Encourage a free discussion of the good and bad points of the Confucian beliefs and teachings. At the close of the hour briefly review the developed outline, and summarize the points made by the class in the discussion.

Student's Home Work.

A. Assigned search work on the lesson:
   1. The nature of man.
   2. The results of the development of this nature.
   3. A description of the classes of men.
   4. Ideal manhood and its attainment.
   5. The essential elements in the ideal state.

B. Review questions for self-test:
   1. What is the Chinese idea of man's nature?
   2. What is the Confucian idea of sin and righteousness?
   3. What are the three classes of men?
   4. What are the characteristics of the highest class?
   5. What are the characteristics of the second?
   6. What are the steps in attaining the latter ideal?
   7. By what power is this ideal attained?
   8. What becomes of the men who do not attain this ideal?
   9. What is the Confucian conception of an ideal state?
   10. What are some of the objections to these teachings?

C. Topics for further study.
   1. The character of a sage.
   2. The "superior" man as an ideal.
   3. The effects of the vagueness of the belief in immortality of the soul.
   4. The motives to higher living found in Confucianism.

NOTE.— The teacher should supply references to standard literature upon the above topics. Reports of the results of this study may be presented to the class from time to time.

§ 12. BOOKS RELATING TO THE WORK OF GRADE D

A. REFERENCE READING FOR THE TEACHER

Bettany, *The World's Religions* (Charles Scribner's Sons, New York).

Clarke, *Ten Great Religions*, 2 vols. (Houghton, Mifflin & Co., Boston).

Fairbairn, *The Philosophy of the Christian Religion* (The Macmillan Co., New York).

Giles and others, *Great Religions of the World* (Harper and Brothers, New York).

Hopkins, *Religions of India* (Ginn & Co., Boston).

Legge, *Religions of China* (Charles Scribner's Sons, New York).

Menzies, *History of Religion* (Charles Scribner's Sons, New York).

Moffat, *Comparative History of Religions* (Dodd, Mead & Co., New York).

Smith, *Mohammed and Mohammedanism* (Harper and Brothers, New York).

Tisdall, *Religion of the Crescent* (Thomas Nelson & Son, New York).

Toy, *Judaism and Christianity* (Little, Brown & Co., Boston).

B. READING AND REFERENCE BOOKS FOR THE PUPIL

Burrell, *The Religions of the World* (Presbyterian Board of Publication, Philadelphia).

Farrar and others, *Non-Biblical Systems of Religion* (Eaton & Mains, New York).

Grant, *Religions of the World* (A. D. F. Randolph & Co., New York).

Hardwick, *Christ and Other Masters* (The Macmillan Co., New York).

PART V
THE MANHOOD AND WOMANHOOD PERIOD AND THE ADULT DEPARTMENT

CHAPTER XI

SUGGESTED COURSES OF STUDY WITH SELECTED REFERENCE BOOKS

IN the Adult Department all work should be elective, the required graded courses ending with the Senior Department. In the classes in this department, some subjects which have been studied in outline and in a more or less elementary way in other departments of the school, may now be studied more comprehensively and thoroughly. In addition to these subjects there are many others which are not only suitable for the advanced classes forming this department, but which will prove both interesting and profitable if presented by competent teachers. A number of such courses of study are suggested in the two sections following, with lists of text and reference books.

§ 1. COURSES OFFERED BY THE AMERICAN INSTITUTE OF SACRED LITERATURE

Address: Hyde Park, Chicago

(The lists of books for these courses have been prepared by Professor Clyde W. Votaw, Ph.D., of The University of Chicago.)

I. THE LIFE OF CHRIST

Text Books:
Nine (monthly) bulletins for study of The Life of Christ; prepared by the American Institute of Sacred Literature.

Burton and Mathews, *Constructive Studies in the Life of Christ* (University of Chicago Press, Chicago).

Reference Books:

Rhees, *Life of Jesus of Nazareth* (Charles Scribner's Sons, New York).

Sanday, art. "Jesus Christ" in Hastings's *Dictionary of the Bible*, Vol. II (Charles Scribner's Sons, New York).

Edersheim, *The Life and Times of Jesus the Messiah*, 2 vols. (A. D. F. Randolph & Co., New York).

Andrews, *The Life of Our Lord* (Charles Scribner's Sons, New York).

Weiss, *The Life of Christ*, 3 vols. (Charles Scribner's Sons, New York).

Seeley, *Ecce Homo* (Little, Brown & Co., Boston).

Stevens and Burton, *A Harmony of the Gospels* (Silver, Burdett & Co., Boston).

II. THE FORESHADOWINGS OF THE CHRIST

Text Books:

Nine (monthly) bulletins for study of The Foreshadowings of the Christ; prepared by the American Institute of Sacred Literature.

Harper, *Constructive Studies in the Prophetic Element in the Old Testament* (The University of Chicago Press, Chicago).

Reference Books:

Goodspeed, *Israel's Messianic Hope* (The Macmillan Co., New York).

Kirkpatrick, *The Doctrine of the Prophets* (The Macmillan Co., New York).

Smith (W. R.), *The Prophets of Israel* (The Macmillan Co., New York).

Davidson, *Old Testament Prophecy* (Charles Scribner's Sons, New York).

Driver, *The Life and Times of Isaiah* (A. D. F. Randolph & Co., New York).

Cheyne, *The Life and Times of Jeremiah* (A. D. F. Randolph & Co., New York).

Smith (G. A.), *The Book of the Twelve Phophets*, 2 vols. (A. C. Armstrong & Son, New York).

Riehm, *Messianic Prophecy* (Charles Scribner's Sons, New York).

Briggs, *Messianic Prophecy* (Charles Scribner's Sons, New York).

III. THE FOUNDING OF THE CHRISTIAN CHURCH

Text Books:

Nine (monthly) bulletins for study of The Founding of the Christian Church; prepared by the American Institute of Sacred Literature.

Burton and Mathews, *Constructive Studies in the Apostolic Age* (The University of Chicago Press, Chicago).

Reference Books:

Purves, *The Apostolic Age* (Charles Scribner's Sons, New York).

Rackham, *Commentary on the Acts of the Apostles* (E. S. Gorham, New York).

McGiffert, *The Apostolic Age* (Charles Scribner's Sons, New York).

Weizsäcker, *The Apostolic Age of the Christian Church*, 2 vols. (G. P. Putnam's Sons, New York).

Bartlet, *The Apostolic Age* (Charles Scribner's Sons, New York).

Ramsay, *St. Paul the Traveller and Roman Citizen* (G. P. Putnam's Sons, New York).

Chase, *The Credibility of the Acts of the Apostles* (The Macmillan Co., New York).

IV. THE WORK OF THE OLD TESTAMENT SAGES

Text Books:

Nine (monthly) bulletins for study of The Work of the Old Testament Sages; prepared by the American Institute of Sacred Literature.

Kent, *Wise Men of Ancient Israel* (Silver, Burdett & Co., Boston).

Reference Books:

Davison, *The Wisdom Literature of the Old Testament* (C. H. Kelly, London).

Davidson, *Commentary on Job* (The Macmillan Co., New York).

Cheyne, *Job and Solomon* (The Macmillan Co., New York).

Plumptre, *Commentary on Ecclesiastes* (The Macmillan Co., New York).

Toy, *Commentary on the Book of Proverbs* (Charles Scribner's Sons, New York).

Horton, *The Book of Proverbs* (A. C. Armstrong & Son, New York).

V. THE WORK OF THE OLD TESTAMENT PRIESTS

Text Books:

Nine (monthly) bulletins for study of The Work of the Old Testament Priests; prepared by the American Institute of Sacred Literature.

Harper, *Constructive Studies in the Priestly Element in the Old Testament* (The University of Chicago Press, Chicago).

Reference Books:

Smith (W. R.), *The Religion of the Semites* (The Macmillan Co., New York).

Wellhausen, *Prolegomena to the History of Israel* (The Macmillan Co., New York).

Budde, *The Religion of Israel to the Exile* (G. P. Putnam's Sons, New York).

Cheyne, *Jewish Religious Life after the Exile* (G. P. Putnam's Sons, New York).

Montefiore, *The Religion of the Ancient Hebrews* (Williams and Norgate, London).

Schultz, *Old Testament Theology*, 2 vols. (Charles Scribner's Sons, New York).

Murray, *Origin and Growth of the Psalter* (Charles Scribner's Sons, New York).

Kirkpatrick, *Commentary on the Psalms* (The Macmillan Co., New York).
Cheyne, *Origin and Religious Contents of the Psalter* (Kegan Paul, Trench, Trübner- & Co., London).

VI. SOCIAL AND ETHICAL TEACHING OF JESUS

Text Books:
Nine (monthly) bulletins for study of The Social and Ethical Teaching of Jesus; prepared by the American Institute of Sacred Literature.
Stevens, *The Teaching of Jesus* (The Macmillan Co., New York).

Reference Books:
Bruce, *The Kingdom of God* (Charles Scribner's Sons, New York).
Wendt, *The Teaching of Jesus*, 2 vols. (Charles Scribner's Sons, New York).
Mathews, *The Social Teaching of Jesus* (The Macmillan Co., New York).
Peabody, *Jesus Christ and the Social Question* (The Macmillan Co., New York).
Cone, *Rich and Poor in the New Testament* (The Macmillan Co., New York).
Watson, *The Mind of the Master* (Dodd, Mead & Co., New York).
Harnack, *What is Christianity?* (G. P. Putnam's Sons, New York).

§ 2. OTHER COURSES SUGGESTED FOR THIS DEPARTMENT

For the following courses the text-books suggested, with one or two exceptions, are not ones which have been prepared for class purposes, for there are few such, but those which will be found helpful to the teacher as general guides in the presentation of the various subjects. The lists of reference books are arranged alphabetically by authors, as it was not possible to arrange them in any order of general usefulness, for what would prove most useful to one teacher might not prove so useful to another. I am further indebted to Professor Votaw for a number of titles in these lists.

VII. THE HISTORY OF THE HEBREW PEOPLE

Text Books:

Kent, *A History of the Hebrew People*, 2 vols. (Charles Scribner's Sons, New York).

Moss, *From Malachi to Matthew.*

Reference Books:

Cornill, *History of the People of Israel* (The Open Court Publishing Co., Chicago).

Kent, *A History of the Jewish People: Babylonian, Persian, and Greek Periods* (Charles Scribner's Sons, New York).

Kittel, *History of the Hebrews*, 2 vols. (Williams and Norgate, London).

McCurdy, *History, Prophecy, and the Monuments*, 3 vols. (The Macmillan Co., New York).

Riggs, *A History of the Jewish People: Maccabean and Roman Periods* (Charles Scribner's Sons, New York).

Schürer, *The Jewish People in the Time of Jesus Christ*, 5 vols. (Charles Scribner's Sons, New York).

Smith (G. A.), *The Historical Geography of the Holy Land* (A. C. Armstrong & Son, New York).

Smith (H. P.), *Old Testament History* (Charles Scribner's Sons, New York).

VIII. DEVELOPMENT OF THE HEBREW RELIGION

Text Book:

Montefiore, *The Origin and Growth of Religion as Illustrated by the Religion of the Ancient Hebrews* (Williams and Norgate, London).

Reference Books:

Budde, *Religion of Israel to the Exile* (G. P. Putnam's Sons, New York).

SUGGESTED COURSES OF STUDY 395

Cheyne, *Jewish Religious Life after the Exile* (G. P. Putnam's Sons, New York).

Kirkpatrick, *The Doctrine of the Prophets* (The Macmillan Co., New York).

Kuenen, *The Religion of Israel*, 3 vols. (Williams and Norgate, London).

Robertson, *The Early Religion of Israel*, 2 vols. (Thomas Whittaker, New York).

Schultz, *Old Testament Theology*, 2 vols. (Charles Scribner's Sons, New York).

Smith (W. R.), *The Religion of the Semites* (A. & C. Black, London).

Toy, *Judaism and Christianity* (Little, Brown & Co., Boston).

IX. THE BIBLE AS LITERATURE

Text Book:

Moulton, *The Literary Study of the Bible* (D. C. Heath & Co., Boston).

Reference Books:

Genung, *The Epic of the Inner Life* (Houghton, Mifflin & Co., Boston).

Moulton and others, *The Bible as Literature* (Thomas Y. Crowell & Co., New York).

Moulton, *The Modern Reader's Bible:* the Bible in modern literary form, 22 vols. (The Macmillan Co., New York).

Palmer, *The Drama of the Apocalypse* (The Macmillan Co., New York).

X. THE BIBLE AND ARCHÆOLOGY

Text Book:

Price, *The Monuments and the Old Testament* (The Christian Culture Press, Chicago).

Reference Books:

Ball, *Light from the East* (Thomas Nelson & Sons, New York).

Harper, *The Bible and Modern Discoveries* (A. P. Watt & Son, London).

Hilprecht, *Recent Research in Bible Lands* (The Sunday School Times Co., Philadelphia).

Hogarth, Driver, and others, *Authority and Archæology, Sacred and Profane* (Charles Scribner's Sons, New York).

Hommel, *Ancient Hebrew Tradition as Illustrated by the Monuments* (Thomas Nelson & Sons, New York).

McCurdy, *History, Prophecy, and the Monuments*, 3 vols. (The Macmillan Co., New York).

Sayce, *Fresh Light from Ancient Monuments* (F. H. Revell Co., Chicago).

Sayce, *The Higher Criticism and the Monuments* (Society for Promotion of Christian Knowledge, London).

XI. RELIGION AND SCIENCE

Text Book:

Le Conte, *Religion and Science* (D. Appleton & Co., New York).

Reference Books:

Abbott, *The Theology of an Evolutionist* (Houghton, Mifflin & Co., Boston).

Bascom, *Evolution and Religion* (G. P. Putnam's Sons, New York).

Drummond, *Natural Law in the Spiritual World* and *The Ascent of Man* (James Pott & Co., New York).

Fiske, *Through Nature to God, The Destiny of Man,* and *The Idea of God* (Houghton, Mifflin & Co., Boston).

Le Conte, *Evolution and Its Relation to Religious Thought* (D. Appleton & Co., New York).

Shaler, *The Interpretation of Nature* and *The Individual* (Houghton, Mifflin & Co., Boston).

Smyth, *Through Science to Faith* and *The Place of Death in Evolution* (Charles Scribner's Sons, New York).

Tyler, *The Whence and the Whither of Man* (Charles Scribner's Sons, New York).

XII. ORIGIN AND DEVELOPMENT OF RELIGION

Text Book:
   Menzies, *History of Religion* (Charles Scribner's Sons, New York).

Reference Books:
   Adeney, *A Century's Progress in Religious Life and Thought* (Thomas Whittaker, New York).
   Bascom, *The Philosophy of Religion* (G. P. Putnam's Sons, New York).
   Caird, *The Evolution of Religion* (The Macmillan Co., New York).
   Gould, *Origin and Development of Religious Belief*, 2 vols. (Longmans, Green & Co., New York).
   Jevons, *Introduction to History of Religion* (The Macmillan Co., New York).
   Lang, *The Making of Religion* (Longmans, Green & Co., New York).
   Tiele, *Outlines of History of Religion* (Charles Scribner's Sons, New York).

XIII. HISTORY OF THE CHRISTIAN CHURCH

Text Book:
   Moncrief, *A Short History of the Christian Church* (F. H. Revell Co., Chicago).

Reference Books:
   Fisher, *History of the Christian Church* (Charles Scribner's Sons, New York).
   Hurst, *A Short History of the Christian Church* (Harper and Brothers, New York).
   Moeller, *History of the Christian Church*, 2 vols. (The Macmillan Co., New York).
   Schaff, *History of the Christian Church*, 7 vols. (Charles Scribner's Sons, New York).
   Sohm, *Outlines of Church History* (The Macmillan Co., New York).
   Ten Epochs of Church History; 10 vols.; series edited by Dr. John Fulton (Charles Scribner's Sons, New York).

XIV. HISTORY OF MODERN MISSIONS

Text Book:

Warneck, *Outline of a History of Protestant Missions* (F. H. Revell Co., Chicago).

Reference Books:

Beach, *A Geography and Atlas of Protestant Missions*, 2 vols. (Student Volunteer Movement, New York).

Beach and others, *Protestant Missions in South America* (Student Volunteer Movement, New York).

Bliss, *Encyclopedia of Missions*, 2 vols. (Funk & Wagnalls, New York).

Dennis, *Christian Missions and Social Progress*, 3 vols. (F. H. Revell Co., Chicago).

Dennis, *Centennial Survey of Foreign Missions* (F. H. Revell Co., Chicago).

Hodder, *Conquests of the Cross*, 3 vols. (Cassell & Co., New York).

Lawrence, *Modern Missions in the East* (F. H. Revell Co., Chicago).

Noble, *The Redemption of Africa*, 2 vols. (F. H. Revell Co., Chicago).

Williams, *The Middle Kingdom*, 2 vols. (Charles Scribner's Sons, New York).

SUMMARY AND CONCLUSION

CHAPTER XII
A GENERAL SUMMARY OF THE COURSE

IN the following pages a summary of the course is presented, that the reader may get a more connected idea of the course as a whole. The general topics only are presented; for the subdivisions of these topics the reader is referred to the grade outlines. In each grade provision is made for a Christmas and an Easter lesson, but these are not mentioned in this summary.

PRIMARY DEPARTMENT
GRADES A, B

Course: *Topical.*
Source of material: *Nature.*
Guiding thought for the teacher: *God the Workman.*
Grade A — Subject of the year's work: *God the Creator providing all things for all of his creatures.*

Topics presented:
1. God creating all things.
2. God providing food for all.
3. God providing drink for all.
4. God providing clothing for all.
5. God providing shelter for all.
6. God providing rest for all.
7. God providing pleasure for all.

Grade B — Subject of the year's work: *All nature working together with God the Creator.*
   Topics presented:
      1. The work of the sun.
      2. The work of the rain.
      3. The work of the wind.
      4. The work of the seasons.
      5. The work of the insects.
      6. The work of the birds.
      7. The work of the animals.
      8. The work of man.

GRADES C, D, AND E

Course: *Topical.*
Source of material: *The Bible.*
Guiding thought for the teacher: *God the loving Father and his children.*

Grade C — Subject of the year's work: *God the loving Father providing for his children's needs.*
   Topics presented:
      1. God the Father providing care.
      2. God the Father providing help.
      3. God the Father providing protection.
      4. God the Father providing a home.
      5. God the Father providing a guide-book.
      6. God the Father providing a helper.

Grade D — Subject of the year's work: *God the loving Father providing wise laws for his children.*
   Topics presented:

      PART I. THE CHILD AND HIMSELF
      1. The law of the body: "Glorify God in your body."
      2. The law of the mind: "Whatsoever things are true .... pure .... think on these things."

General Summary of the Course

3. The law of the life: "Be ye doers of the word and not hearers only."

PART II. THE CHILD AND OTHERS

4. The law of the home: "Honor thy father and thy mother."
5. A second law of the home: "Be ye kind one to another."
6. The law of helpfulness: "By love serve one another."
7. The law of truthfulness: "Speak ye every man the truth to his neighbor."
8. The law of unselfishness: "Thou shalt love thy neighbor as thyself."
9. The law of kindness: "Be kindly affectioned one to another, with brotherly love."

PART III. THE CHILD AND GOD

10. The law of trust: "Trust in him at all times."
11. The law of obedience: "Thou shalt obey the voice of the Lord thy God."
12. The law of God's day: "Remember the sabbath day to keep it holy."
13. The law of God's house: "Enter into his gates with thanksgiving and into his courts with praise."
14. The law of God's name: "Thou shalt not take the name of the Lord thy God in vain."
15. The law of prayer: "Watch and pray that ye enter not into temptation."

Grade E — Subject of the year's work: *God the loving Father providing guidance and help through Jesus the Friend.*

Topics presented:
1. The coming of the Friend.
2. The Friend preparing for his work.

3. The Friend and the children.
4. The Friend in the home.
5. The Friend helping the needy everywhere.
6. The Friend teaching about many things.
7. The Friend teaching about happiness.
8. The Friend returning to his heavenly Father.

JUNIOR DEPARTMENT

Course: *Historical* (narratives).
Sources of material: *Bible and missionary literature.*
Guiding thought for the teacher: *God the law-giver and ruler seeking to bless the world.*
Grade A — Subject of the year's work: *The story of God's people — the Hebrews.*
   Topics presented:
      Chap. 1. The beginnings.
      Chap. 2. Seeking a new home.
      Chap. 3. Settlement in their new home.
      Chap. 4. The united kingdom.
      Chap. 5. The divided kingdom.
      Chap. 6. The people in exile.
      Chap. 7. The return from exile.
Grade B — Subject of the year's work: *The story of God's Son — Jesus Christ.*
   Topics presented:
      Chap. 1. The coming of Jesus.
      Chap. 2. The boyhood of Jesus.
      Chap. 3. Jesus begins his work.
      Chap. 4. Jesus and the people.
      Chap. 5. Jesus and his disciples.
      Chap. 6. Jesus completes his work.
      Chap. 7. Jesus returns to his Father.

Grade C — Subject of the year's work: *The story of God's early messengers.*
  Topics presented:
    Chap. 1. The messengers at work in Jerusalem.
    Chap. 2. The messengers at work in Judea and Samaria.
    Chap. 3. The messengers at work in Syria.
    Chap. 4. The messengers at work in Asia Minor.
    Chap. 5. The messengers at work in Europe.
    Chap. 6. The messengers finishing their work in Asia Minor.
    Chap. 7. The messengers' closing days.
Grade D — Subject of the year's work: *The story of God's later messengers.*
  Topics presented:
    Chap. 1. The messengers at work in India.
    Chap. 2. The messengers at work in China.
    Chap. 3. The messengers at work in Japan.
    Chap. 4. The messengers at work in Africa.
    Chap. 5. The messengers at work in the Isles of the Sea.
    Chap. 6. The messengers at work in Mohammedan lands.
    Chap. 7. The messengers at work in America.

INTERMEDIATE DEPARTMENT

Course: *Biographical.*
Sources of material: *Bible and biographical literature.*
Guiding thought for the teacher: *God as a character-former, revealed in the lives of great men and women.*
Grade A — Subject of the year's work: *Great characters in the Old Testament.*

Characters studied:

PART I. DURING THE PERIOD OF THE MIGRATIONS
1. Abram the pioneer.
2. Jacob the prince.
3. Joseph the prime minister.
4. Moses the liberator.
5. Miriam the prophetess.

PART II. DURING THE PERIOD OF THE SETTLEMENT
6. Joshua the soldier.
7. Deborah the woman-judge.
8. Gideon the warrior-judge.
9. Ruth the model daughter.
10. Hannah the model mother.
11. Samuel the prophet-judge.

PART III. DURING THE PERIOD OF THE KINGDOM
12. Saul the wilful king.
13. David the godly king.
14. Jonathan the friend.
15. Solomon the magnificent king.
16. Elijah the prophet of fire.
17. Elisha the prophet of peace.
18. Joash the boy-king.
19. Amos the prophet of righteousness.
20. Hosea the prophet of love.
21. Isaiah the statesman-prophet.
22. Josiah the reformer-king.
23. Jeremiah the prophet of tears.

PART IV. DURING THE PERIOD OF THE PROVINCE
24. Ezekiel the prophet of visions.
25. Daniel the captive prince.
26. Zerubbabel the leader of the return.
27. Ezra the scribe.
28. Nehemiah the governor.

GENERAL SUMMARY OF THE COURSE 407

Grade B — Subject of the year's work: *The life of Jesus the Ideal Man.*
  Topics presented:
  1. Jesus and his ministry.
  2. Jesus' ministry to the religious leaders.
  3. Jesus' ministry to the common people.
  4. Jesus' special ministry to the apostles.
  5. Jesus' ministry drawing to a close.
  6. The triumphant close of Jesus' ministry.
  7. The disciples commissioned to continue Jesus' ministry.

Grade C — Subject of the year's work: *Other great characters in the New Testament.*
  Characters studied:
  1. John the Baptist.
  2. The apostolic band.
  3. John the beloved.
  4. Peter the apostle.
  5. Paul the missionary.

Grade D — Subject of the year's work: *Great characters in post-apostolic times.*
  Characters studied:
  PART I. GREAT CHARACTERS IN THE EARLY CHURCH
  1. St. Francis of Assisi.
  2. Savonarola.
  3. Martin Luther.
  PART II. GREAT CHARACTERS IN MODERN MISSIONS
  4. Zinzendorf.
  5. John Elliott.
  6. William Carey.
  7. David Livingstone.
  8. John G. Paton.

9. Joseph Neesima.
10. John Kenneth Mackenzie.
11. Fidelia Fiske.

PART III. GREAT CHARACTERS IN THE WORLD'S SERVICE

12. Queen Louise of Prussia
13. George Washington.
14. Mary Lyon.
15. Abraham Lincoln.
16. Louis Agassiz.
17. George Peabody.
18. Florence Nightingale.
19. Frances Willard.
20. Henry Drummond.
21. Bishop Brooks.
22. Queen Victoria.
23. Dwight L. Moody.
24. Booker T. Washington.

SENIOR DEPARTMENT

Course: *Philosophical* (a study of the Christian religion).
Sources of material: *Bible and special literature.*
Guiding thought for the teacher: *God the source of truth, revealed in a study of the Christian religion in its several aspects.*

Grade A — Subject of the year's work: *The Christian religion: its historical development.*

Topics presented:

PART I. CHRISTIANITY IN THE APOSTOLIC PERIOD

1. Beginnings of Christianity in Jerusalem.
2. Early expansion of Christianity.
3. Further expansion of Christianity during the period.

GENERAL SUMMARY OF THE COURSE 409

PART II. CHRISTIANITY FROM THE APOSTOLIC PERIOD TO THE REFORMATION

4. The Heroic Age of Christianity.
5. Christianity's triumph in the Roman empire.
6. Christianity among the Germanic nations.
7. The papacy.
8. The beginnings of reform.

PART III. CHRISTIANITY FROM THE REFORMATION TO THE PRESENT TIME

9. The early reformers.
10. Luther and the Reformation in Germany.
11. Zwingli and the Swiss Reformation.
12. The Reformation in the north and east.
13. Calvin and the Reformation in Geneva.
14. The Reformation in France, England, Scotland, Italy, and Spain.
15. Christianity in the early American settlements.
16. Church organization during the period.
17. Doctrinal changes during the period.
18. A short history of Christian missions.
19. Denominational church history.

Grade B — Subject of the year's work: *The Christian religion: its evidences and sacred books.*

Topics presented:

PART I. ITS EVIDENCES

1. Evidence from the system itself.
2. Evidence from its historical effects.

PART II. ITS SACRED BOOKS

3. The canon.
4. The Old Testament books.
5. The New Testament books.

Grade C — Subject of the year's work: *The Christian religion: its fundamental truths.*

Topics presented:

PART I. TRUTHS RELATING TO GOD

1. God the Father.
2. Jesus the Son.
3. The Holy Spirit.

PART II. TRUTHS RELATING TO THE INDIVIDUAL

4. The nature of man.
5. The problem of evil and sin.

PART III. TRUTHS RELATING TO SOCIETY

6. Christianity and the family.
7. Christianity and the state.
8. Christianity and business.
9. Christianity and the problem of wealth.
10. Christianity and the sabbath question.
11. Christianity and the temperance question.
12. Christianity and the problem of the world's evangelization.

Grade D — Subject of the year's work: *The Christian religion: its supreme worth as compared with other great religions.*

Religions studied and compared with Christianity:

1. Judaism.
2. Zoroastrianism.
3. Confucianism.
4. Mohammedanism.
5. The religions of India.

CHAPTER XIII

CONCLUSION

IN the curriculum presented in the foregoing chapters an attempt is made to outline for a graded school a course of study in harmony with the generally accepted principles of religious education, and one which shall be workable by the superintendent of the school in co-operation with his department supervisors. Theory must precede practice and present working plans; practice must follow theory and correct or modify it as the results seem to demand. A working plan for a seventeen-years' course of graded study is here presented, with sufficient helps to enable a superintendent to make a fair trial of the course or any part of it, that through a practical test of the plan its elements of strength and weakness may be discovered. Thus in every grade there is given the topics for the year's study — fifty topics, excluding the Christmas and Easter lessons — several lessons worked out in full, sometimes a complete topic thus worked out, and a selected list of reference books for the teacher, from which material may be gathered for the remaining lessons of the grade. It is hoped that this plan will appeal to the superintendents of schools and supervisors of departments, and induce them to make a practical trial of the course.

Attention is also called to the constructive work suggested for each grade, such being indicated in the lesson plans under the heading "Scholar's Home Work." Such constructive work not only tends to fix in mind the lessons taught in class, but greatly increases the interest of the pupils in their work. To some this constructive work may appear too simple and slight. To these we reply that one must not expect too much from the average Bible-school pupil in the way of work outside the class; to ask of him a little which he may be reasonably expected to do is better than to ask of him so much that he will not attempt anything. To others some of the suggested constructive work may appear to be too difficult, calling for more time and thought than the pupil will be willing to give. To these the reply is that a practical test of this feature of the curriculum has been made in a number of schools, and this required work has not only been willingly done, but has created an enthusiastic interest in the course of study pursued.

An objection may be made to any such course of study as is here proposed, that it is not adapted to the smaller schools in towns and villages, schools with a membership of one hundred or less, and only partly graded, and that the great majority of our schools belong to this class. While this may be freely admitted, the answer is that the problem of a rational Bible-school curriculum is to be solved by the larger city schools which have facilities for making thorough practical tests of any system of lessons which may be proposed. When an approved course of study is finally evolved, then its adaptation to the smaller schools will be comparatively easy.

One other point requires a word of explanation. In the grade outlines and suggestive lesson plans no attempt has been made to differentiate the various literary elements in the material used — myth, legend, tradition, history. The stories selected from the earlier books of the Old Testament should be told simply as *stories* which set forth some great ethical or religious truth. But when the child begins to question the historicity of such stories, asking, Are they true? then explanations, within the comprehension of the child, should be given by the teacher. In this connection I cannot do better than to quote the words of a recent writer in discussing the question of teaching the Old Testament to children:[1]

> The stories of the Old Testament do not need to be labeled as parables. But many Christian teachers have yet to learn their full use in imparting divine truth. To attempt to explain the first chapters of Genesis in accordance with

[1] Editorial note in the *Congregationalist*, December 5, 1903.

scientific facts of comparatively recent discovery, of which the child learns in school, is to confuse his ideas of religion and weaken his confidence in the Bible as interpreting the voice of conscience. To present to him these chapters as the sublime poem of creation is to open to him the mysteries of the being of God in his world. It will not increase the child's reverence for the Bible to tell him that its trustworthiness depends on evidence that Jonah in the belly of a sea-monster wrote a song, which is mainly a mosaic of sentences from the Psalms, some of which were written centuries after Jonah's time. But let the story-teller have his place, tell the child that Jonah stands for God's people fleeing from duty to which they were faithless, and that the monster is Babylon, which swallowed them and let them go forth again, and he will understand the wonderful meaning and message of the ancient story. He will not be deeply impressed by your knowledge or your ability if you tell him he must believe that Job in the agonies of disease sat around with his friends on a heap of refuse and extemporized the magnificent poems ascribed to them. But let the story-teller have his way, and the child will be prepared to understand by and by how a soul which trusts in God meets the deepest problems of experience and grows noble through suffering. The Bible is a literature as well adapted to the child mind as any of the great classics, ancient or modern, and it surpasses them all, though they are all works of the imagination. But to treat it as a text book on history, geology, astronomy, and other sciences, miraculously prepared many centuries in advance of the time when it could be understood, is to do violence to it and to any tenable theory of inspiration. The Bible is a library revealing the mind of God through prophets who had divine insight and used all forms of literature to make known what they saw. It should be taught to children as prophets spoke and wrote it.

Conclusion

Such a revelation of the Bible as a great literature will preserve the child's respect for the sacred book as he grows in years, which otherwise might be impaired or completely lost. Let us not put doubts or questions into the child's mind, but when such doubts or questions arise, we should not refuse to answer such with frank statements of what we believe to be true.

CHAPTER XIV
A SHORT LIST OF HELPFUL BOOKS FOR THE BIBLE-SCHOOL TEACHER

THE MORAL AND RELIGIOUS LIFE AND TRAINING

Adler, *The Moral Instruction of Children* (D. Appleton & Co., New York).
Coe, *The Spiritual Life* (Eaton & Mains, New York).
Coe, *The Religion of a Mature Mind* (F. H. Revell Co., Chicago).
Du Bois, *Beckonings from Little Hands* (Dodd, Mead & Co., New York).
Du Bois, *The Natural Way in Moral Training* (F. H. Revell Co., Chicago).
Forbush, *The Boy Problem* (The Pilgrim Press, Boston).
Starbuck, *The Psychology of Religion* (Charles Scribner's Sons, New York).

GENERAL EDUCATIONAL PRINCIPLES

Butler, *The Meaning of Education* (The Macmillan Co., New York).
Butler, Doane and others, *Principles of Religious Education* (Longmans, Green & Co., New York).
Dutton, *Social Phases of Education* (The Macmillan Co., New York).
Fitch, *Educational Aims and Methods* (The Macmillan Co., New York).
Froebel, *The Education of Man*. Hailmann translation (D. Appleton & Co., New York).
Hughes, *Frœbel's Educational Laws* (D. Appleton & Co., New York).
Lange and De Garmo, *Herbart's Outlines of Educational Doctrine* (The Macmillan Co., New York).
MacCunn, *The Making of Character* (The Macmillan Co., New York).
MacVicar, *Principles of Education* (Ginn & Co., Boston).

List of Helpful Books 417

Ostermann, *Interest in Its Relation to Pedagogy* (E. L. Kellogg & Co., New York).

Spalding, *Education and the Higher Life* (A. C. McClurg & Co., Chicago).

PSYCHOLOGY AND CHILD STUDY

Baldwin, *The Story of the Mind* (D. Appleton & Co., New York).

Harrison, *A Study of Child Nature* (Chicago Kindergarten College).

James, *Psychology*. Briefer course (Henry Holt & Co., New York).

James, *Talks to Teachers on Psychology* (Henry Holt & Co., New York).

Kirkpatrick, *Fundamentals of Child-Study* (The Macmillan Co., New York).

Radestock, *Habit in Education* (D. C. Heath & Co., Boston).

Royce, *Outlines of Psychology* (The Macmillan Co., New York).

Sully, *Studies of Childhood* and *Teacher's Handbook of Psychology* (D. Appleton & Co., New York).

Taylor, *The Study of the Child* (D. Appleton & Co., New York).

Warner, *The Study of Children* and *Mental Faculty* (The Macmillan Co., New York).

PRINCIPLES AND METHODS OF TEACHING

De Garmo, *The Essentials of Method* (D. C. Heath & Co., Boston).

Hervey, *Picture Work* (F. H. Revell Co., Chicago).

Hinsdale, *Jesus as a Teacher* (Christian Publishing Co., St. Louis).

Landon, *Principles and Practice of Teaching and Class Management* (The Macmillan Co., New York).

Lukens, *Dorpfeld's Thought and Memory* (D. C. Heath & Co., Boston).

Mark, *The Teacher and the Child* (F. H. Revell Co., Chicago).

McMurry, *General Method* and *The Method of the Recitation* (The Macmillan Co., New York).

Vincent, *Christ as a Teacher* (A. D. F. Randolph & Co., New York).

THE BIBLE SCHOOL

Burton and Mathews, *Principles and Ideals for the Sunday School* (The University of Chicago Press, Chicago).

Haslett, *The Pedagogical Bible School* (F. H. Revell Co., Chicago).

Mead, *Modern Methods in Sunday-School Work* (Dodd, Mead & Co., New York).

Sheldon, *An Ethical Sunday School* (The Macmillan Co., New York).

Trumbull, *Yale Lectures on the Sunday School* (Charles Scribner's Sons, New York).

Vincent, *The Modern Sunday School* (Eaton & Mains, New York).